TRADE & PEACE
WITH OLD SPAIN

TRADE AND PEACE WITH OLD SPAIN
1667–1750

*A study of the influence of
commerce on Anglo-Spanish Diplomacy
in the first half of the
eighteenth century*

BY

JEAN O. McLACHLAN, M.A., Ph.D.
Formerly Research Fellow of Girton College

WITH A FOREWORD BY THE LATE
PROFESSOR HAROLD TEMPERLEY

OCTAGON BOOKS

A DIVISION OF FARRAR, STRAUS AND GIROUX

New York   1974

First published 1940

Reprinted 1974
by permission of Cambridge University Press

OCTAGON BOOKS
A DIVISION OF FARRAR, STRAUS & GIROUX, INC.
19 Union Square West
New York, N. Y. 10003

Library of Congress Cataloging in Publication Data

McLachlan, Jean Olivia.
    Trade and peace with old Spain, 1667-1750.

    Reprint of the 1940 ed. published at the University Press, Cambridge.

    Bibliography: p.
    1. Great Britain—Commerce—Spain. 2. Spain—Commerce—Great Britain. 3. Great Britain—Foreign relations—Spain. 4. Spain—Foreign relations—Great Britain. I. Title.

HF3508.S7M3   1974   382'.0942'046   74-9611
ISBN 0-374-95520-4

382.0942
M161

Manufactured by Braun-Brumfield, Inc.
Ann Arbor, Michigan

Printed in the United States of America

To

M. M.

J. D. M.   M. G. J.

H. W. V. T.

for without any one of them this book
could never have been written

CONTENTS

FOREWORD

This work of Miss McLachlan illustrates, even more dramatically than usual, the truth that both diplomacy and politics rest on a solid commercial foundation. In the eighteenth century, indeed, commerce really was the steel framework of the political machine. The work is also valuable in that it compares, in each case from the archives, the Spanish with the British version of events. This double check on inaccuracy at once yields results. The old ideas about the New World and Spanish American trade with this country, are shown to be as erroneous as were the old ideas as to the relation between Britain and her North American colonies.

In the *Expansion of England* Seeley showed himself the prince among generalisers. Like Balboa he gazed at Spanish America from a high mountain, but did not make a scientific survey of it. He took a broad sweep of history and applied simple generalisations to complex facts. His influence and his maxims convinced us for a generation, until a new age learned that these generalisations were not supported by the facts of research. Modern historians find that most of the old generalisations have the brilliance, but also the fragility, of bubbles.

The newer school produces less startling but surer generalisations. For instance, it is instructive to learn that Spaniards knew that the British trade was draining their bullion supplies. But they approved of its doing so, for they knew that trade was a necessity, and trade with England happened to be the least of several evils. All nations were ready to drain Spain of bullion, but England took more of her commodities than anyone else could do. Spanish trade in fact ranked fourth with England, inferior only to the British imperial, the German and the Dutch trades. Here we touch the most important of Miss McLachlan's conclusions, namely that the trade of Old Spain and the Mediterranean was, at the dawn of the eighteenth century, always more important to England than the trade of New Spain and of the West Indies. Hence we must revise our ideas of the reason why British merchants supported William III and Anne in the War of the Spanish Succession. It was not, as Seeley says, because France was shutting us out of New Spain and the Caribbean, but because France was shutting us out of Old Spain and the Mediterranean. In that inland sea merchants were to find more real and precious products than in the fabled riches of the Golden Spanish Main.

The treaty of Utrecht did not reveal Bolingbroke as an economist and, while gaining possessions and influence in different parts of the earth, England did not regain her old Spanish trade in the Mediterranean. It was not till the workaday Bubb superseded the brilliant Bolingbroke in the business of commercial negotiation that things began to improve. Bubb's commercial treaty of 1715 was at first more important politically and in theory than economically and in practice, but as political relations improved most of the old Mediterranean trade of England with Spain was revived. Thus Bubb succeeded where Bolingbroke failed.

The year 1739, which witnessed Walpole wringing his hands over the outbreak of the Spanish war, is now seen in a new light from Spanish records. We find that Walpole himself suggested the offer of a lump sum of payment to Spain, and that the Convention of the Pardo, a masterpiece of wise and conciliatory statesmanship, was wrecked by the unholy alliance between the ambitious South Sea Company and the factious opposition, which Armstrong called the "Public house Protestants". The interested and jealous South Sea Company is revealed as interfering in every kind of politics, British or Spanish. It frightens Newcastle, it pays the Spanish king's bills and even his ambassadors' salaries. It fails to make a profit out of the Asiento, or to avert the war, or even to recover its £68,000 from the King of Spain. All the old legends suffer, even that of the great annual ship, which was refilled in the dark. It was not a great source of profit even when refilled. There was indeed plenty of smuggling apart from the annual ship altogether, but this abundance benefited individuals and not the Company. The latter really made its money out of negroes, and by getting negro sloops past the British and Spanish authorities. No one is now likely to think that the South Sea Company had clean hands or a clear conscience or an efficient management. On the other hand we must remember, as Miss McLachlan tells us in an Appendix rich with detail, that Patiño was the ablest and most successful of

Spanish national administrators, that his regime had only just ended, and that its effects still irritated and excited British traders.

The last conclusion, which may be called a generalisation, is that the year 1750, and the new commercial treaty which it witnessed, formed an epoch in Anglo-Spanish relations. The result was due in the main to Carvajal, whose "great and noble ideas", so different from the exclusive nationalism of Patiño, aimed at a working partnership of trade and policy between the two nations. Under these circumstances the new treaty gave back to England the status of 1667 and restored to her all the trade with Old Spain which she had lost in the War of the Spanish Succession. Had statesmanship on both sides continued as wisely as it had here begun, the results on world policy would have been very different.

I might perhaps here give a hint of the fascinating details culled from Spanish archives, which may not be used again in this generation, or may actually have perished altogether. It is most interesting to know that the crews of the Spanish annual fleets, whether quick or slow, fed on English dried fish throughout their weary voyages. They called it *Bacalao*, or "poor (very poor) John". The soap, known as that of Castile, soon came mainly from France. Sack, or Sherris sack from Xeres, was superseded in quality by wine of Cadiz. At the latter place were *metidores*—an organised corps of bullion smugglers—who obliged "the merchants of all nations" with impartial injustice. Last of all, British merchants used His Majesty's packet boats to carry their silver, and prevented the Spaniards from exercising their right of search by pleading diplomatic privilege! These concrete facts, drawn from the archives of the countries, give us more of the flavour of the eighteenth century and its commerce than a hundred protocols or documents. A score of other such picturesque details may be found in these pages. They support the maxim that a correct relation, observed between concrete detail and generalisation, is the right and indeed the only method of illustrating, and laying bare, the spirit of an age.

HAROLD TEMPERLEY

INTRODUCTION

The origin of this study was Professor Temperley's article in the *Transactions of the Royal Historical Society* on "The causes of the War of Jenkins' Ear". It solved one particular problem brilliantly but there remained several other points which were not quite clear, and the attempt to clarify these ultimately led to an investigation of Anglo-Spanish relations during half a century.

Sir John Seeley's idea that the wars of the Spanish Succession and of Jenkins' Ear were part of a series in which British statesmen fought France and Spain to obtain territory in the New World provoked investigation. It was found to be completely unfounded in the case of the war of 1701–13. Instead of fighting to secure a footing in America, Englishmen were reluctantly forced into war to maintain their trade in the Mediterranean.

Another interesting problem was the significance of the crisis of 1737–9 in Anglo-Spanish relations. Was this a "colonial" war? Was the chief interest at stake the right to freedom of navigation in American waters, and were British statesmen keenly alert to protect British West Indian trade? Much has been written on the influence of colonial trade on policy; in this study an attempt has been made to assess the importance of colonial trading interests when compared with those of other merchants. In 1738–9 the British merchants trading to Old Spain wanted peace, and the responsible ministers in both countries tried desperately to avoid war. Their efforts were defeated by the political tactics of the English opposition, and the selfish policy of the Directors of the South Sea Company.

The interests of the British merchants trading to Cadiz are also studied in relation to those of the South Sea Company and the West Indian illicit traders, who tried to secure a share in the bullion of the New World by direct trade contacts instead of being content to share in it at second hand by supplying goods for the annual Spanish fleets trading to the New World from Old Spain. If this study has any value, it is because it presents a new explanation of

Anglo-Spanish diplomatic disputes, the interests of British traders to Old Spain.

Several other problems of less importance but great interest were presented by a closer study òf the depredations crisis of 1737–9. Were the depredations which began it as serious a menace to British colonial trade as was maintained at the time? What was their significance in relation to earlier and later Anglo-Spanish relations in the West Indies? It seems that for a time there had been a lull in these incidents, why did they begin again towards the end of 1737? Was this the result of deliberate Spanish policy? What was the Spanish view of them, particularly among the colonial officials in the Indies?

The position of the South Sea Company also provoked investigation. What were the reasons for the surprising obstinacy of the directors which in 1738–9 ruined the efforts of the statesmen to preserve peace? How did the Company come to owe His Catholic Majesty the conveniently large sum of £68,000? Was the Company's illicit trade responsible for the depredations that began the crisis, as Parliament thought at the time?

The position of the Spanish court also deserved some consideration. Was the crisis part of an aggressive Bourbon policy against England, or was it due to an unfortunate accident which the Spanish ministers did their best to remedy?

The investigation of these problems involved a study of British trade with Old Spain from the commercial treaty of 1667 throughout the first half of the eighteenth century to show its character, history, and the interaction between it and the political relations of the two countries. This study has been based on the commercial pamphlets of the period, together with the consular papers in the Public Record Office.

The problem of West Indian depredations deserves a book to itself, and here only the events of 1737, the policy of the Spanish court and colonial governors have been treated in detail. For this, reference has been made to the contemporary political pamphlets, the diplomatic correspondence of the British and Spanish ambassadors now in the Public Record Office and the Archivo General de Simancas, and the Spanish colonial papers now in the Archivo General de Indias in Seville.

A most illuminating study on the depredations in the earlier part of the century, based on the British colonial records, is in an unpublished thesis by F. L. Horsfall, M.A., in the Institute of Historical Research in London University. A preliminary study of the later aspects of the problem from material in the Spanish diplomatic and colonial archives has already appeared in the *English Historical Review*.

On certain aspects of the history of the South Sea Company, some most interesting monographs have been written by Miss V. L. Brown. The following study is based on further material from the same Spanish archives in Simancas, Madrid and Seville, where are the correspondence and private papers of the Spanish representative on the Company's board of directors. In addition use has been made of the Company's official minute books in the British Museum, and of the private correspondence of one of the sub-governors, photostat copies of which were deposited in the British Museum by the courtesy of Mr Adams of the W. L. Clements Library at Ann Arbor.

An investigation into the importance of the Spanish court in-volved, in this case, a study of the personalities, careers and policies of two ministers, Señor de la Quadra and Don Jose de Carvajal y Lancaster. For the one the reports of the British ambassador, Benjamin Keene, were consulted in the Public Record Office, for the other Señor Ferrendis's most illuminating monograph proved invaluable. No study of early eighteenth-century Spanish com-mercial relations could omit some reference to the reforming genius of Don Josef Patiño, and as some interesting, but not strictly relevant, material was found in a late eighteenth-century Spanish biography, an Appendix has been devoted to this most able minister.

It may seem as if some apology were necessary for the presentation of yet another lengthy study of a crisis which has been treated by Professor Temperley, Professor Michael and Professor Vaucher, to say nothing of the *Cambridge History of the British Empire*, Armstrong, Baudrillart, Lecky and a recent book of Mr R. Pares. The justifica-tion is firstly that this is an attempt to interpret the history of Anglo-Spanish relations in the first half of the eighteenth century from the point of view of the British merchants trading to Old Spain, and secondly that this work is based on hitherto unused Spanish materials, diplomatic, commercial and colonial, in Simancas, Madrid and Seville.*

That this book has ever appeared is due to the kindness and encouragement of other people rather than to the industry or skill of the author. Miss Jones originally suggested that such work should be undertaken, the Mistress and Council of Girton College generously granted a Cairnes Studentship from 1932–5, various officials in archives and libraries in England and Spain found documents and offered advice, Mr H. R. Mallett gave the Index a professional appearance, Cambridge University honoured the work by awarding it the Seeley Medal and half the Prince Consort Prize in 1938, and the Cambridge University Press made the path of publication very easy. What Professor Temperley contributed in suggestions, criticisms, encouragement, time and sympathy it is quite impossible to convey. It is only possible to record my very lively and sincere gratitude.

These eighteenth-century commercial and diplomatic problems have proved fascinating to investigate, and to try to elucidate. It is hoped that all the interest has not dried up with the ink.

* Unfortunately, owing to the political situation in Spain, it has been impossible to check some of the extracts already taken from Spanish documents. In some cases only a paraphrase or précis was made of the document, and, although in every case the greatest care was taken to maintain the sense of the original, it is not possible to guarantee the verbal accuracy of every quotation, since a final revision could not be made from the archives themselves.

CHAPTER I

"THE DARLING AND THE SILVER MINE OF ENGLAND"

A Study of the British trade with Spain, 1667–1700

A proper understanding of the nature of the British trade with Spain in the first half of the eighteenth century is of more than a purely economic or social interest. During that period, commerce exercised a considerable influence on the diplomatic relations of the two powers, and, in the eighteenth century, Anglo-Spanish diplomacy was to determine the character of the development of the whole of North America.

After the weakness and humiliation of the last years of the Hapsburgs, Spain experienced a remarkable recovery under the early Bourbons. French financiers did much to balance the Spanish budget, and the example of France suggested a successful attempt to mould Spain's many provinces into a single state. Able Spanish ministers were inspired to revive the Spanish navy and encourage Spanish trade. In the second decade of the eighteenth century Spain, under the ambitious Elizabeth Farnese, was able once more to play a vigorous role in European affairs. The attention of the new Spanish rulers was fixed on Europe, but as Spain was mistress of a colonial empire embracing half the new world, her revived political activity could not but affect the development of events on the other side of the Atlantic. In the eighteenth century the heroic struggle for colonial power between Great Britain and France dwarfed the parallel conflict between Great Britain and Spain, but this was nevertheless of importance, and it has been suggested that though Spain was far behind France as a source of real danger, she was in some respects in front of her as a source of constant irritation. Because France and Spain were ruled by branches of the same royal family, and united from time to time by treaties, nicknamed Family Compacts, it has been assumed that the two courts were usually animated by the same feelings of rivalry towards Great Britain. This, however, was not the case.

By the eighteenth century the religious differences, which had inspired the Anglo-Spanish wars of the sixteenth century, had become less violent. Sources of direct colonial dispute between the two courts were few, except for the ships seized in the West Indies and accused of illicit trade. In Europe, although the Spanish Bourbons were sometimes opposed to the traditional ally of Great Britain, the emperor, they were by no means always closely united with the Bourbons of France. When the policy of Versailles conflicted with the ambitions of Madrid the Spanish court, even under the most French of all the Spanish Bourbons, was ready to consider seeking the help of Britain.[1] In the changes of policy, considerations of trade must be added to those of dynastic ambition, colonial strength, religion and personal caprice, as one of the influences which caused the decisions of the statesmen of Hanoverian Britain and Bourbon Spain.

Much has been written of the determining factors in the policy of the time, but little has been said of the relative importance of commercial considerations in relation to the other motive forces of diplomacy. The weight of trade interests, and the particular influence exercised at different times by the trade to Old Spain as opposed to that of the Asiento trade of the South Sea Company, offers an additional clue to the problems of Anglo-Spanish relations in the period which culminated in the war of 1739–48.

§ 1

To understand the relative importance of the South Sea Company's Asiento trade and of the free general trade carried on by British merchants with Old Spain, it is necessary to realise the place these bullion trades occupied in the general commercial system of early eighteenth-century Britain and Spain. Their place in the economic life of Great Britain is of chief interest, for at this period British interests were of more weight than those of Spain. By 1700 the Spanish empire had declined so much in economic and political strength that, although the Spanish court could galvanise the kingdom into some sort of action in support of dynastic policy, in commercial affairs, which did not attract the personal interest of the first two Bourbons, the Spaniards remained passive or at most on the defensive. Any initiative with regard to commercial relations came from Spain's energetic neighbours France, Holland or Britain.

From the point of view of British merchants, economists or statesmen, the Spanish trade was valuable because it provided bullion, and the whole nature of British trade in the early eighteenth century made a regular supply of bullion essential. For at that time the mercantilist theory, which had been developed in the sixteenth century and had obtained much prestige from the successful career of the French fiscal expert Colbert, was generally accepted as the principle on which any healthy commerce must be regulated.

The object of British statesmen was to keep their country adequately and safely supplied with provisions and other necessaries, the means of defence and a sufficiency of coin. They also wished to maintain a numerous, healthy and prosperous population. To achieve these objects the statesmen concentrated their attention primarily upon the development of the internal resources of Great Britain, her agriculture, textile and metal manufactures, and fishery. It was only in so far as trade stimulated or supplemented home production that it was esteemed by mercantilists.

The colonial trade was most esteemed, for colonies were believed to be nothing but potential sources of increased security to the mother country. They could offer markets for British manufactures, supply such necessaries as timber and pig iron, and provide tropical luxuries such as sugar and tobacco which could be re-exported in exchange for the remaining necessaries which Great Britain was unable to produce either at home or in her own colonies.[2] In the old colonial empire, the most valuable colonies from the economic point of view were thought to be the West Indian islands. As late as 1763 it was still possible for Pitt to think Guadeloupe more valuable commercially than Canada.[3] The West Indies could hardly be considered as a source of naval stores necessary in war time, or of staple provisions or raw materials necessary in time of peace. Their trade balance was usually against Great Britain. But there was no danger of their competing against British manufactures, and their natural products such as dyes, spices and fruits, especially sugar and its products molasses and rum, were valuable for re-export in Europe.

That this highly valued trade of the West Indian plantations might flourish, two other branches of trade were necessary. There must be a temperate source of provisions and a tropical source of labour. The British Isles could supply part of the first, and the mainland colonies were ready to supplement the supply of corn, draught animals and timber to make casks for the sugar and rum. British merchants were jealous of their American competitors, and although the trade balance with the mainland colonies was usually favourable to Great Britain, statesmen in London always suspected that the colonists might compete with the mother country in manufactures as in agriculture, and disliked the colonies and their trade as they did not dislike the other two sides of the West Indian commercial triangle. The supply of labour in the West Indian sugar and cocoa plantations came in the form of slaves from Africa. The slaves were obtained by American or English merchants, who traded with West Indian rum and British woollens and gunpowder. The only other African export of any importance besides slaves was ivory, and on the whole the trade showed a balance favourable to Great Britain. The whole triangle of trade not only encouraged production within Great Britain and her own colonies, provided markets in Africa and the West Indies for British manufactures, and some bullion and much West Indian tropical produce for re-export, but the long voyages also encouraged shipbuilding and trained sailors.

There was, however, one disadvantage to the British colonial trade. It failed to make good a serious deficiency in naval stores, which could be supplied neither from British forests nor the steadily declining British ironworks. As mercantilism in England had as its aim the development of maritime power, this deficiency had to be made good through British trade to the north-east of Europe. From Sweden, Norway and Russia[4] came timber, iron and sail-cloth, and although British merchants could only find a market in these countries for some woollens and West Indian goods, and had to pay the balance in bullion, in the eighteenth century Great Britain could not make herself independent of this trade.

There remained the trade in luxuries which could not be produced in Great Britain or her colonies, and as this usually involved the export of bullion, it was always a source of anxiety to British statesmen and economists. The Levant[5] and East India trades,[6] although they both showed an adverse balance, were, however, tolerated by British statesmen. From Asia came such luxuries as silks, carpets, dyes, drugs, muslins and some jewels and gold. The market in Asia and the Near East for British woollens and metal manufactures was small, but the luxuries that came from the Levant and East Indies were very valuable, and the East India trade especially was a useful school for seamen, and involved the upkeep of a considerable fleet. The trade in luxuries from Europe did nothing to encourage the mercantile marine and, as it drained the country of bullion, it was strongly discouraged by British statesmen. The best example of this dangerous luxury trade was that carried on with France.[7] English consumers were eager for brandy, wines, silks, velvets, laces and lawns, but the French, being blessed with a climate as mild and a government as efficient as those of Great Britain, had been able to develop their own agriculture, manufactures and foreign trade. They had established tropical colonies and carried on their own trade to the East Indies, so they offered no market for British manufactures or colonial produce.

From the point of view of British statesmen, the German states[8] were half-way between this parity trade and the necessary but expensive trade in naval stores. Holland,[9] though she was in the same strong economic position as France, actually imported British manufactures and colonial produce because the Dutch resources were not sufficient to supply the huge re-export trade that had its centre in Holland.

Italy,[10] although a Mediterranean power, belonged economically to the same parity zone as France, for although Italy needed British woollens and fish, she could offer in return valuable manufactures such as silks and velvets, so that the trade balance was actually in favour of Italy. The typical Mediterranean trades to Spain and Portugal[11] were those where British merchants could be sure of a favourable trade balance which supplied part of the bullion needed to supplement British woollens and colonial produce to carry on the valuable trades to the Baltic, Levant and East

Indies. The Spanish trade had also the advantage of being a source of valuable raw materials necessary for British manufactures, and of cheap luxuries much appreciated by English consumers.

§ 2

The British trade with Old Spain, though it may not have deserved the extravagant praise given it by some commercial writers, who called it "the best flower in our garden", or "the Darling and the Silver Mine of England"[12] had, in fact, the characteristics of an essentially healthy trade, benefiting both countries engaged in it.

The first essential of a valuable trade, according to the eighteenth-century writer Cary, was that it should take off our products and manufactures.[13] This the trade to Old Spain certainly did. The Mediterranean countries in general offered a good market for English woollens,[14] for by the eighteenth century neither Spain nor Portugal had any considerable woollen industry, and the weavers of Italy specialised in silks and velvets. The lighter and finer cloths had an excellent sale, and even the heavy cloths were bought in great quantities to make habits for the numerous communities of friars, monks and nuns. In late seventeenth-century Spain the demand for English woollens was particularly great because of the character of the national costume. The "grave habits, cloaks of bays and says, and the rest of the Spanish garb" required large quantities of very fine quality woollen cloth.

Like the other Christian states on the shores of the Mediterranean, Spain was an excellent market for British fish. As a devoutly Roman Catholic country she had to observe many fast days,* but the Mediterranean, though it produces some delectable shell fish and octopus, does not produce many other fishes that are good, cheap, or will last long enough to be carried inland. A usual dish in Spanish families on fast days was and is *bacalao* or salt cod, and most of this fish that was eaten in Spain in the eighteenth century was supplied by British merchants and came from what Defoe, writing in 1713, called "that inexpressibly rich codbank of Newfoundland...which may be esteemed our mines of gold and silver".

---

* Special indulgences allowed Spaniards to eat meat on fast days, but even so many people did not avail themselves of this permission.

The Spaniards also bought fish caught by British fishermen in the North Sea, and salmon from the rivers of Ireland. They were also ready to buy the metal which the fish ships used as ballast, so the trade encouraged the British fishery, which politicians were always eager to protect since it stimulated shipbuilding and trained seamen.

Old Spain also offered a market for British lead, tin, silk and worsted stockings, butter, tobacco, ginger, leather and beeswax,[15] and in spite of having "great quantities of extraordinary oak and fine large pine trees suitable for masts, especially in Aragon and Catalonia",[16] it was thought by at least one commercial expert, Joshua Gee,[17] that Old Spain offered a potentially valuable market for timber from the mainland colonies. Even if the navy never recovered after 1588, and the mercantile marine was in decay, timber for wine casks was an important necessity in Spain.

An additional advantage of the Old Spanish trade, from the point of view of the British merchants and statesmen, was that it was carried on in British bottoms,[18] and this provided an opportunity for British ships to secure a considerable part of the carrying trade to Spain. "The Spaniards are a stately people little given to trade or manufactures themselves, therefore the first they carry on by such chargeable and dilatory methods, both for their ships and ways of navigation, that other trading nations such as the English, French, Dutch and Genoese, take advantage of them."[19]

In 1662 an Act of Parliament had been passed to encourage the use of moderately large and well-armed ships in the trade to Old Spain.[20] Thereafter English merchants made considerable profits by carrying a great deal of Spain's foreign trade.

Just as it was the highlands of Castile and Aragon that provided a market for English woollens and Newfoundland fish, so it was these high arid central districts which provided one of the most valuable commodities which Old Spain—apart from the riches of her colonial empire—had to offer in return. It was not unusual for eighteenth-century writers to divide the trade of Old Spain into three parts:[21] "Spain by which I mean that part from the Bay of Cadiz inclusive eastwards into the straits of Gibraltar, as far as Catalonia, Biscay by which I mean all that part under the Spanish government which lies in the bay of that name, or adjoining it, a third part of our Spanish trade is that to Flanders, whereby

I mean all those provinces that were formerly under its government but are now under the emperor's." It was from the second of these districts, the Biscayan provinces, that Great Britain obtained the most important of the commodities, so valuable, in fact, that the wool trade alone, it was asserted, would havè made the Old Spanish connection valuable even if there had been no favourable balance in England's favour.[22]

According to the economist, Cary, the second characteristic of an advantageous trade was that it should supply Great Britain with raw materials used in her manufactures. This the trade with Old Spain certainly did, for it supplied commodities essential to the most valuable of English industries, the manufacture of woollens. The Biscay trade, concentrated in the ports of San Sebastian and particularly Bilbao,[23] provided an outlet for the wool from the Castilian mountains, "A commodity which is the growth of Spain only, and is to be had from no other country."[24] Even as late as the eighteenth century there were great flocks of spindle-shanked, thin sheep migrating over the face of Spain, oppressing agriculture, and growing the best wool in Europe. The wools of Spain were divided into three classes, the finest being the Segovia wool which "is sold (neither sorted or washed but just as it comes off the sheep's back) at 70 *reals de vellon* the *arroba*".[25] The *arroba* was 25 lb., and the mid-eighteenth-century value of the *real de vellon* was about $2\frac{3}{4}d$. The second quality wool was called Soria from the small town near the source of the river Duero, that was, like Segovia, high in the mountains of Castile. The Andalusian wools were the worst and coarsest, and the difference between these wools and those of Castile was so great that an *arroba* of Andalusian wool fetched only 20 *reals de vellon*. In Spain itself, only the inferior wools were used in manufacture, large quantities of the better quality wools being exported. In the second half of the seventeenth century it was calculated that the total export of wool from Old Spain amounted to between 36,000 and 40,000 bags, with eight *arroba* of wool in each bag. Of these about 27,000 bags were of Segovia or Soria wools. From Bilbao alone 20,000 bags of all sorts of wool were exported each year, and it was estimated that the countries which were the chief customers for this wool trade were Holland and Hamburg who took off about 22,000 bags, England who took between 2000 and 7000 bags, France who took between 6000 and 7000, Venice and the other ports of Italy bought 3000, and Africa 1000. By the middle of the eighteenth century it was estimated that Great Britain imported about 6000 bags of Spanish wool each year, which "commodity employs a pretty large body of manufacturers in the West of England...as Spanish cloth is a manufacture worn and coveted by all degrees of people who are able to purchase it".

At the time of the outbreak of the war in 1739 an anonymous pamphleteer, calling himself "a Sussex farmer", suggested that the Spanish wool ought to be prohibited during the war, since it provided the material for only one seventy-seventh of the British woollen manufactures, and might be replaced by sorting out the finest locks of English wool. The same pamphleteer also suggested that the prohibition of Spanish wool might encourage the bringing of wool from Ireland, and so prevent owling, or smuggling, of Irish wool to France or Holland. However, in normal times wool continued to be one of the chief English exports from Biscay until, in the nineteenth century, the Australian wool trade developed.

Other valuable raw materials needed in the woollen industry came from the Mediterranean coast of Spain. Castile soap is still famous, though much of what goes by that name is made in France. In the eighteenth-century southern and south-eastern Spain and the Canary Islands provided much of the soap and olive oil which were needed in the processes for cleaning wool. Before the discoveries of Chevreul and Leblanc in the nineteenth century revolutionised soap-making, olive oil was one of the chief fats used in the manufacture of soap. The anonymous British pamphleteer, "Sussex Farmer", when writing to advocate the prohibition of Spanish goods in war time, pointed out that equally good oil could be got from Portugal, Leghorn or Gallipoli; and that even English rape oil could be used in working wool, since the inconvenience and the disagreeable fetid smell is soon overcome by use and time. He suggested that English tallow could replace Spanish olive oil in the London soap industry, and that soap "as proper for all branches of our manufactures as any imported from Alicante, commonly known by the name of Castile soap" might be got ready made from Leghorn, which exported both Italian and French soap,

or even from Joppa. However, in peace time, British merchants
continued to buy Castile soap and Andalusian *barilla*. This was
an impure alkali made from burning a saltwort plant common in
the south of Spain, and was highly esteemed as an ingredient in
making soap.

Yet another raw material of vital importance to the English
woollen manufacturers were dyes, and of these a very considerable
supply came from Cadiz. Most of these came from the Spanish
colonies in the New World, but they belong rather to the valuable
raw materials which Spain could export, than to the bullionist
attraction exercised over foreign merchants by the Spanish colonial
trade. British manufacturers could get dyes grown in His Britannic
Majesty's West Indian colonies, or from Asia by way of the East
India Company, and some dyes were also obtained from the Levant
and from France, but Spanish indigo and cochineal, not to mention
logwood, anata and other less known dyes, were so generally
used by English manufacturers, that any threat of war alarmed
the dyers exceedingly, and even such an opponent of the Spanish
trade as the pamphleteer, "Sussex Farmer", advocated the continuation of the trade in dyes even in time of war.[26]

Other Spanish exports were of less importance to Great Britain.
One valuable raw material exported from the Biscay ports was
iron.[27] This was of high quality and used in England for the
manufacture of ordnance. But at the beginning of the eighteenth
century the English output of iron was declining, and what was
most urgently needed was fuel to replace the exhausted timber
supply from the Surrey Weald, rather than more raw iron ore.
Until as late as about 1770, Sweden was the chief source of the
raw iron needed in Great Britain. The Spanish supply could have
been surpassed by the British colonies in North America, if their
pig-iron industry had been encouraged, and although the Biscayan
ore was of high quality, it alone would never have made the trade
to Old Spain so highly esteemed by British merchants.

The most obvious of the Spanish exports, fruits and wines, so
far from being regarded as valuable by British writers, were looked
upon as undesirable luxuries which could only be tolerated in view
of the other characteristics of the Spanish trade. The fact which
most modified British opinion in favour of the Spanish trade was

that, although Old Spain as a Mediterranean country was a valuable trade connection, it was far more advantageous to do business with Spain, the queen of a great colonial empire rich in gold and silver.

Since Old Spain was unable to supply the needs of the huge Spanish empire in central and southern America, and yet the colonists were forbidden to produce the manufactured goods they needed or to trade direct with more industrial countries, the Spanish trade was admirably suited to give vent to British products and manufactures. The Spaniards had failed to make the best advantage economically of the rich new world which Columbus, Cortez and Pizarro had acquired for His Catholic Majesty. The new colonies were so rich in the precious metals and easily produced tropical luxuries that, as M. Mounier has pointed out, they only led to the degeneration of Spanish trade.[28]

Under Ferdinand and Isabella a misguided fiscal policy was begun which, under the Hapsburgs, choked Spanish industry and trade with multifarious taxes. Religious fanaticism began under Philip II, and led under Philip III to the expulsion of the most able financiers, merchants and agriculturists. Any fundamental fiscal reform was made impossible, for during the later sixteenth and early seventeenth centuries Spain's championship of the ideals of the Counter-Reformation, and her dynastic connection with the rulers of the Holy Roman Empire, involved her in a never-ending series of expensive and disastrous wars, which destroyed the Spanish navy and crushed Spanish trade with taxation. The acquisition and development of a colonial empire did nothing to counteract the evil economic conditions at home. The sudden need of developing such a vast empire led to the concentration of population in the coastal provinces, and encouraged maritime trade at the expense of internal communications. By the late seventeenth century Spain had become "essentially an agricultural country which failed to produce sufficient manufactured products to supply the needs of the Peninsula, yet called upon to furnish a huge dependent empire with that very class of supplies".[29]

The Spanish colonists were strictly forbidden to manufacture goods for their own use, so all kinds of merchandise in very considerable quantities had to be sent to America from Old Spain, but of this trade the Spaniards retained the control of very little. Spain's foreign trade had gradually decayed, until, in Cary's view, "only their trade to their West Indies hath, on strict penalties, been reserved to themselves, but having no manufactures of their own the profit thereof comes very much to be reaped by those that furnish them". This was written in 1745, but it would have been even more applicable to the period of Spanish decadence at the end of the seventeenth century. In the mid-seventeenth century a memorial had been submitted to Colbert which showed that the shares of the Dutch, German, English and French in the colonial trade of Spain was considerable. The Spanish economist Zabala, writing early in the eighteenth century, reckoned that the total value of foreign goods exported yearly from Seville to the Indies was between 15,000,000 and 20,000,000 Spanish dollars. (The Spanish dollar, or piece of eight, was in the mid-eighteenth century worth about 4s. 2d.) By about 1741, in spite of the Bourbon reforms, it was estimated that, out of 38,000,000 dollars imported to Spain from the Indies each year, 5,000,000 went to the Dutch, 4,500,000 to the British, 3,000,000 to the French and 2,000,000 to other nations, apart from the amount that had to be paid by Spanish merchants because of the adverse trade balance. It was asserted that Spain's share in a trade that was theoretically her own monopoly was limited to supplying wine, oil, olives "and some sort of sweetmeats that are liked in the Indies".[30] The official Spanish figures[31] for the register ships sent out from 1748 to 1753, when an experiment was tried of supplying the Spanish empire by these ships rather than by the annual merchant fleets, though they do not altogether bear out this gloomy view of the decadence of Spanish colonial trade, certainly show that even after the reforms of such a vigorous and far-sighted minister as Don Josef Patiño, and during the administration of the Marquis de la Ensenada who was particularly interested in the problems of colonial trade, there was still a large market in Spain for foreign goods to be re-exported to the Indies.

The goods which were wanted in the Spanish colonies included at least two which England was well suited to supply. Woollens[32] were long in great demand, partly because of the cold climate in the mountainous regions of Chile, the Andes, and even parts of what is now the Argentine Republic; partly because even in tropical heat the Spanish colonists continued to wear the same style of costume as had been usual in Spain. Besides such woollen goods as bays and flannels, the British merchants supplied hats of all sorts, stockings of silk and worsted, rich silks, copper, brass and iron ware, toys, clocks and watches, and salt provisions from Ireland. Dried fish was another commodity for which the Spanish colonial empire offered a great market. *Bacalao*—or, as it was sometimes called, Poor John—was used to feed the crews of the annual fleets, register ships and the *azogues*, or quicksilver ships, used in the colonial trade. It was also the staple food of the negro slaves in the new world. Thus the Spanish colonial empire gave direct stimulus to two of the most valued branches of British commerce.

The Spanish colonial trade would, however, have been cherished even if it had not encouraged British fisheries and woollen manufactures. Valued for its great bulk, it was not of so much importance what commodities were sold to Cadiz merchants for re-export to the New World. What was appreciated was that, because of the size of the Spanish empire and the decadence of the industries of Old Spain, so much merchandise had to be sold to the Seville, and later to the Cadiz, merchants that it was impossible for the Spanish merchants to sell wool, oil, dyes, fruits or wines to an equal amount, and a substantial balance always remained to be paid in bullion.

This bullion was the essential attraction of the trade with Old Spain. British merchants needed bullion in order to buy naval stores from the Baltic, exotic luxuries from Asia and more familiar luxuries from France. A supply of the bullion, needed because of the character of the general trade of Great Britain, could be obtained steadily by the trade to Old Spain.

The colonial trade[33] was the focus of foreign trade to Spain; Seville, and later Cadiz, were the chief centres of trade, because there the annual fleets took in their cargoes and there the fleets returned to unload cochineal, indigo, logwood, quinine, hides, tobacco, sugar, and, most important of all, precious stones and bullion. In the eighteenth century all the foreign merchants of any standing had their agents, correspondents or factors at Cadiz.[34]

There the foreign merchandise was sold to the Spanish merchants either for bullion or for tropical products brought home by the silver fleets. Foreign merchants even managed to secure a direct share in the trade, although this was strictly prohibited. The prohibition was evaded by the foreigners taking the names of Spanish merchants, and thus "the very probity of the Spanish merchants is destructive of their country, for, as they are never known to betray their trust, consequently the foreigners who made use of their names to cover their commerce in the Indies, reap the entire advantage of the high price at which their goods sell".[35] Great profits could be made by trading in the silver fleets and galleons, and the reality of profits as great as 100 per cent are borne out by official Spanish sources.[36]

Most of these profits on the colonial trade were paid in bullion, and, although the export of gold and silver from Spain was illegal, long practice had made the foreign merchants proficient in this kind of smuggling. At Cadiz there was an organised corps of bullion smugglers, *metidores*, "who are made use of by merchants of all nations in carrying off their money for exportation, as also sometimes in the running and introducing that which comes to them from the Spanish West Indies out of register".[37] British merchants were so adept at using His Majesty's packet boats to carry their silver, that the British consul at Corunna spoke of it as "the usual exportation", and strongly resented a Spanish claim to search the packets in the same way as the Customs officials already inspected ordinary merchant vessels.[38] British merchants had also the advantage that several clauses in the commercial treaty of 1667 gave indirect protection to the export of bullion. By article 15 of this treaty the export of bullion had been explicitly prohibited, but several loopholes had been obtained to allow the practice to continue. By article 5, ships being laden and customs paid, the goods were not to be detained in port under any pretext whatever, nor were factors, who had bought and loaded goods, to be questioned after the ships had set sail. By a *cedula* of 1645, incorporated in the treaty, merchants' houses were not to be searched, nor under article 31 might their books be demanded in courts of law.[39] The profits made by the foreign merchants on the Spanish colonial trade were well protected.

There were, however, some considerable disadvantages under

which foreign merchants laboured, who were interested in the trade of the silver fleets and galleons. These were most clearly expressed by the French author on commercial problems, Savary.[40]

The chief drawback to the Cadiz trade was that it was uncertain and slow. Any merchant who engaged in it needed a great deal of capital or very sound credit, for a year at least had to pass before any payment could be expected. Expenses, on the contrary, had to be met at once in cash, and the duties on import and export and the charges on commission were notoriously heavy in Spain. The profit on luxuries might be tempting but the only safe course was to deal in necessaries, and even so, it was vitally important to insure the goods. A failure to do so had caused many bankruptcies in Paris between 1720 and 1742. Because of the long delays it was both difficult and dangerous to trade with borrowed capital, and in Savary's experience the Spanish merchants had lost their old faith and honour, and could no longer be trusted to shelter foreign merchants. In addition to these minor inconveniences it was never certain that the silver fleet or galleons would trade at a profit. Sometimes the goods were actually sold at a loss. For whether the Mexican or Peruvian merchants had large or small supplies of bullion, the cargoes of the silver fleets or galleons were sold in exchange, irrespective of their value, so that the profit of a venture depended on the yield of the silver mines during that particular year.

It was no wonder that British merchants chafed at the numerous obstacles in the Cadiz trade, and since the discovery of the New World, both merchants and statesmen had tried to get into direct contact with the Spanish colonies to secure a share in the bullion unrestricted by the petty regulations, uncertainties and anxieties of the Cadiz trade. Until 1713, however, the only way in which the British had been able to enter into direct trade with the Spanish colonies had been by way of contraband carried on from the British West Indies. This had been as uncertain as the trade through Cadiz, and had been of little use to the London merchants, so, as the trade to Old Spain had continued very profitable, the British merchants had concentrated on this flourishing trade, and been content to share in the bullion of the Indies in payment of the balance on their trade to Old Spain.

It may seem curious that the Spanish merchants did not object to a trade which drained them of the bullion they so highly esteemed, but, in fact, Spanish statesmen and economists approved of the English trade because it was the least of several possible evils. Spain had to obtain manufactured goods for her colonial and her home market, as well as provisions for her fleets, and although all the trading nations of Europe were eager to supply her in return for gold and silver, most of them wished to take as few as possible of the commodities that Spain could offer as part payment for their manufactures. An English pamphleteer, writing to urge the prohibition of the Spanish trade in time of war, estimated that "the English nation consumes near two thirds of the produce of Spain, which is exported. Therefore, the greatest part of their trade for their own produce depends upon a friendly intercourse between the two nations. The French are too fruitful, the Northern nations too poor, and the Dutch too frugal to dabble much in the luxury Spain produces. 'Tis therefore to Great Britain they are beholden for the consumption of the produce of Old Spain, and the greatest part of their trade."[41] The truth of his comment on the Dutch trade may be questioned, for a more impartial author, Joshua Gee, writing thirteen years earlier, gave Holland as Spain's second most valuable customer, but he too placed Great Britain first, saying, "if it were not for the great consumption of Spanish wines, fruits and oils in England, their sales of these commodities would amount but to a trifle".[42] Such a well-informed and generally unprejudiced observer as Horace Walpole the elder was of the opinion that "As to the subjects of Old Spain, they must be sensible that the commerce of England is more beneficial to them than that of any other nation whatsoever, and they would gladly see a perpetual peace and friendship between the two nations, according to their own proverb peace with England although in war with all the world besides."[43]* The figures of Spanish exports and imports at the end of the eighteenth century given by the commercial expert, Canga Arguelles, support this view that English trade was most valued as it took off most Spanish products. At that time Spain's three important customers were Great Britain,

* Walpole's Memoir, which was prepared to inform the Secretary of State for the Southern Department, is of much higher value than the various pamphlets written by merchant journalists.

France and the Empire, which included Flanders. The Empire sold most commodities to Spain, but Great Britain sold nearly as many and bought considerably more.[44]

In England strict mercantilists might frown on the import of wines and fruits since these commodities were unproductive, but since the public demanded sherries and Canary wine, grapes, almonds and oranges, Cary asserted that "since we must drink wines, 'tis better to have them from the Spaniard than from the French"; of all the produce which the Spanish sold in return for English goods "the wine is the principal which is so much esteemed all over Europe, for its richness and excellent flavour".[45] During the eighteenth century Mediterranean wines were in great demand in England. The malmsey which had been generally drunk in the later middle ages could no longer be obtained after the capture of Crete by the Turks in the seventeenth century, and Madeira wine, which was of the same quality and eventually became very popular, only began to be developed after 1745, when an Englishman interested himself in the trade. Italian wines, which had been imported by the Genoese in the seventeenth century in place of malmsey, never hit the public fancy, partly because of their high price, and partly because they would not keep. German vineyards had suffered badly during the Thirty Years' War, and Great Britain does not seem to have bought any considerable amount of wine from the Empire. The French wines which had been the usual drink in England during that period of the middle ages when England and Gascony were intimately connected and the wine was cheap, had become less popular after the loss of the English king's possessions in France had raised the price, and fell entirely out of use after the prohibitions and heavy taxation of William III. There remained port, sherry and the other sorts of sack and red wines produced in the Iberian Peninsula and the Canary Islands. Sherry had become popular in England in the sixteenth century. As early as 1517 English merchants had received special licence to trade to Jerez, Port St Mary and Seville for wine. This wine was natural and, though not very bitter, was so different from the familiar sweet malmsey that it was called sack, from the Spanish *secco*. It became so popular that similar wines were imported to England from other parts of Spain, from

Madeira and from the Canaries. To distinguish the original wine it was called jerez or sherris-sack, and finally sherry. Even when Queen Elizabeth was forced to make war on Spain the supply of sack was maintained, and for three centuries sherry never suffered from the vagaries of fashion in England. It is curious that in the eighteenth-century literature dealing with the trade to Old Spain, though there are several references to Spanish wine, there is hardly any mention of the best and most famous of these. Malaga sold sack,[46] but the other kinds of wine mentioned seem to have been red, as was that exported from Alicante, while the best wine in Spain was reported to come from Cadiz. But whether the wine bought by British merchants was sherry, or the white Spanish wines, or Spanish claret, it found a good market in Great Britain, and the trade was popular with Spaniards. Other Spanish products which found a ready sale among British merchants were oranges, lemons, almonds, raisins and other fruits. For this reason the Spanish economic theorists liked the English trade, but their appreciation was very mild when compared with the lavish praise given to the trade by British writers on commerce.

Since the trade to Old Spain provided a supply of vitally necessary bullion, a market for the staple English products, a source both of valuable raw materials and of cheap popular luxuries, and, moreover, was not monopolised by any company, it is not surprising that it was sometimes given such extravagant a title as "the Darling and the Silver Mine of England", or spoken of as "our most valuable commerce".[47] It is noticeable, however, that the trade was most praised when it was thought to be in danger. When in 1713 merchants were remembering past advantages, and complaining of the present decline in the trade, the authors of *The British Merchant* spoke of the trade to Spain as having formerly produced the most favourable trade balance of all.[48] When the trade was threatened by war either at the time of the Spanish Succession or of Jenkins' Ear, it was praised as the most profitable of all English trades.[49] The actual figures of the Customs returns,[50] though they certainly show that the trade to Old Spain was among the most valuable branches of English commerce, do not support the claim that it was "the Darling and the Silver Mine of England".

It would seem that, in the eighteenth century, the Spanish trade was among the first four most important British connections. The most valuable, apart from the trades to the British colonies and to Ireland, was the trade to Holland and, till the middle of the century, the trade to Germany. The Portuguese trade, which, in 1712, Godolphin had asserted "brought to England in times of war double the wealth of the trade of Spain in time of peace",[51] certainly did show a greater balance in favour of Great Britain, but this was only because, although the total values of goods exported to Spain and Portugal were roughly the same, the value of those imported from Spain was nearly double that of the goods imported by British merchants from Portugal. As a rule the Spanish trade was among the four foreign trades most valuable to Great Britain, and it was always among the first half-dozen.

The trade to Old Spain might be less valuable than some of its champions maintained, it might be slow, and merchants might chafe under petty exactions and injustices, but in general it was esteemed both in Britain and in Spain, for the complementary character of the economies of the two countries made it a healthy traffic of great value to both. The relations of these two powers since the middle of the sixteenth century show the increasing importance of the trade. Even in the time of Queen Elizabeth the Spanish trade was one of the most valued branches of English commerce, and when for reasons of religion and to maintain the balance of Europe Elizabeth was forced to make war on Spain, the English woollen trade suffered severely. The peace of 1604 was at first popular with British merchants, who hoped to regain some of their trade with Spain.[52] Cromwell's war against Spain, though it was popular as a return to the vigorous treasure-seeking policy of Elizabeth,[53] was disliked by the merchants and was found to be more prejudicial to the cloth and shipping industries than had been expected.[54] As always in a war with Spain, England suffered more than her enemy, since she had more ships engaged in trade and in danger of capture: "were we as successful in captures as heart could wish, we should upon an even lay, lose forty ships before we could take one". Nine-tenths of the merchants trading to Spain were ruined, and the Yorkshire cloth trade was said to be "dead by reason of the wars with Spain". Moreover, English investments in Spain were far greater than those of Spain in England, so here again England suffered.[55]

During this century of wars English industries had been developing and those of Spain decaying, so that, as the religious and political causes of dispute waned or changed, the commercial reasons for friendship became steadily stronger.

With the decline of Spain and the rise of a strong France threatening the Spanish Netherlands, England and Spain chose to compose their differences and unite in opposing the ambition of Louis XIV. This renewed friendship was expressed in the commercial treaty of 1667. That after a century of disputes it was possible to conclude a treaty so satisfactory that it lasted without a change for nearly thirty years, and was used as a classical example in Anglo-Spanish commercial negotiations for nearly a century, shows that the English trade to Old Spain was really to the advantage of both countries.

To study the commercial treaty of 1667 in the light of the humble complaint, laid before His Britannic Majesty at some time between 1660 and 1669 by the merchants trading to Spain, would be to see a vivid picture of the conditions of life among the English merchants trading to Spain in the seventeenth and eighteenth centuries.[56] There fraudulent factors evaded punishment by turning Roman Catholic and seeking sanctuary, monks forced their way in to visit dying heretics, duty was demanded on a cargo of fish even when this was rotten,[57] and accounts, even when they involved sums of over £30,000, had to be kept in a denomination worth less than the third part of a farthing.[58]

From the point of view of the development of Anglo-Spanish trade the treaty of 1667 was of great value for three reasons. It not only secured advantageous terms for the most important branches of English trade, it laid down general conditions concerning how the trade was to be carried on, and for the protection of individual merchants. On all these subjects it became a classic in Anglo-Spanish commercial relations.

Three particular trades benefited specially by the terms of the treaty of 1667. By articles 7, 8, 11 and 12, the carrying trade, which had suffered from the competition of the Dutch, profited by the understanding that goods from the Plantations and from the East

Indies might be brought to Spain as though they were the products of England, and that the part of the cargo that was not sold might be re-exported duty free. By article 1, the fishing industry was exempted from the tax of *milliones* which should have been levied on consumers, but which had too often fallen on the producers because of exemptions granted to such important consumers as municipal officials or the heads of religious establishments. By article 20, the woollen industry profited by the restoration of the trade with the Spanish Netherlands. There had been some discussion as to the possibility of securing for England a monopoly of Spanish wool in return for a Spanish monopoly of English tin, but this scheme had been abandoned because the amount of Spanish wool far exceeded the needs of English industry in the late seventeenth century.[59]

The most important of the general commercial regulations contained in a treaty of commerce might be expected to be those concerning the Customs duties. Yet here the treaty of 1667 achieved little. The English Customs system of the seventeenth century was complicated, but the Spanish duties were a financier's nightmare.[60] There were the customs and the *almojarifazgo*; there were special duties on fish and spirits, and there were the royal monopolies on stamped paper, salt and tobacco. When the import duties had been paid, the merchants were confronted with a further complicated and oppressive series of duties, such as the *alcabalas* and *cientos y milliones*, crushing inland trade. In the seventeenth century these duties differed from one province to another, and merchants were almost entirely at the mercy of the greed, dishonesty and caprice of individual tax collectors.[61]

Article 10 of the commercial treaty of 1667 limited the number of Customs officials that might visit an English ship, so that the master might not be ruined by having to pay and feed them. Article 6 laid down that the Customs duties were to be publicly exposed in the Customs House, but otherwise all duties were left uncertain, and merchants agreed with the farmers as they could.[62] It does not sound very satisfactory, but for thirty years the English merchants found that by means of judicious bribery they could avoid the excessively heavy duties.

With regard to the protection of individual merchants the treaty was more explicit. The chief successes in this sphere were that a special official, a *Juez Conservador*, and also a series of English consuls were set up to safeguard the interests of English merchants.[63] Nearly a century passed before the consular system was working smoothly, but for thirty years the *Juez Conservador* protected English interests. He prevented the inspection of English merchants' books, guaranteed cheap justice and prevented religious molestation. This last was the more necessary because, in Spain, financial exactions were sometimes made under cover of care for religious interests. Because of the high charges for commission, the long delays natural to the Spanish trade, especially the trade to the Indies, and the need for heavy cash payments in advance, it was considered advisable to have a responsible head of the firm continually in residence. For this reason merchants usually traded on a partnership basis; often these partnerships were family affairs. It was, therefore, a serious grievance that, on a merchant's death, his effects were often seized by the court of *Cruzada*, from which no amount of suing could recover them.[64] Articles 32, 33 and 34 of the treaty of 1667 gave protection against this abuse, and, so long as the office was continued, the *Juez Conservador* saw that the treaty was observed in this and every other respect.

That the treaty was conscientiously observed, and that for thirty years English merchants trading to Old Spain suffered few molestations, was due partly to the friendly relations existing between the two courts, but it was also partly due to the fact that the Anglo-Spanish trade was popular in Spain. Conditions were unfortunately not so favourable with regard to the other branch of Anglo-Spanish trade, that which the South Sea Company began to carry on in 1713 under the Asiento contract between the rulers of Great Britain and Spain.

§3

When compared with the flourishing, popular trade to Old Spain, the direct trade which the South Sea Company carried on to the Spanish colonies for thirty-seven years under the Asiento agreement does not appear in any way satisfactory. This trade was thought to embody the most valuable characteristic of the trade to Old

Spain, for it permitted direct contact with the Spanish Indies, and it was thought that it would secure for Great Britain a considerable share in the gold and silver of Mexico and Potosi. It had as its avowed object the supply of slaves to the Spanish colonies, for after the middle of the sixteenth century Spain had found that to supply her colonial empire with manufactures taxed her mercantile strength to the utmost without attempting to supply the colonists with labour as well. As a branch at once of the Spanish trade and the Africa trade the business undertaken by the South Sea Company after 1713 appeared to be promising, but there were aspects of the trade which belied this favourable appearance.

That the slave trade in general was a paying proposition was shown by the large fortunes made by Liverpool and Bristol slavers, and as a branch of this trade the South Sea Company's Asiento was approved by such an economic expert as Sir Robert Walpole.[65] It did not matter to him whether the Company's negro trade was actually showing a profit, what made him support the Asiento was that it encouraged the African trade, which in turn bred sailors. The African trade was not particularly valued as providing a market for British manufactures. There was some demand for woollens in Guinea,[66] and it was claimed that at one time the Royal African Company exported upwards of £70,000 worth of woollens and other manufactures, but although there was always a hope that a market for English cloth might be built up in Africa, it was realised that a district so backward as the Slave Coast and so unsuitable for white settlement could not offer any valuable market for good English cloth. In this respect the trade of the South Sea Company was not much more valuable.

Much was hoped from the permission to send each year to the Spanish Indies one ship laden with merchandise, but this was only a small sideline of the main trade of the South Sea Company. The Asiento had been granted to the English to supply the Spanish colonies with negro slaves, not to carry on a general trade, and although the annual ship has occupied a great deal of attention in subsequent studies of the doings of the South Sea Company, it was actually only an incidental venture undertaken at irregular intervals and involving expenses and profits quite small in comparison with those of the negro trade of the Company.[67]

By the additional article of the Asiento treaty of 1713 the burthen of the annual ships was limited to 500 tons. By the treaty of 1716[68] this was raised to 650 tons. The Company had not been able to avail itself of the privilege of sending out annual ships during the first three years of the Asiento, and the 1500 tons thus lost to the Company were to be made good by the tonnage of the annual ships being increased by 150 tons for the next ten years. Actually the concession was of little use to the Company, for between 1717 and 1727 only four annual ships sailed, and although the extra tonnage was continued, only two more ships benefited by this concession during the whole course of the Asiento.[69] The irregularity of these sailings made it impossible for the South Sea Company to create a steady demand for their goods in the Spanish Indies.[70] The Spanish colonists wanted manufactures and preferred to pay the high Spanish prices, since the silver fleets and galleons were more regular than the South Sea Company's miscalled "annual" ships.[71] If both the Spanish and the legal British sources of supply failed, there were always the Dutch, French and English colonists and merchants ready to supply the Spaniards by way of illicit trade. Even when the annual ship did sail, she might only go to the chief port of the Spanish Indies to which the Spanish fleet or galleons were bound that year, and might only trade there while the Spanish merchants were doing so.[72]

In so far as the South Sea Company succeeded in exporting British goods in the annual ship, these competed with the commerce of the British merchants trading to Cadiz to supply the silver fleet or galleons. It was even believed by influential British merchants, and by Sir Robert Walpole himself, that the "sale of English goods would be increased by the return of the trade to its old channel".[73]

Since 1713 the English share in the trade of the silver fleet and galleons had declined.[74] Although for a time between 1713 and 1719 it had seemed that the English might recover their share in the Spanish colonial trade,[75] the French continued to be the most successful nation in this branch of trade,[76] and there were few English merchants in the factories of Seville and Cadiz. This did not mean, however, that the British trade to Old Spain was decaying because of competition from the South Sea Company's annual ship. On the outbreak of war in 1702 all the English Protestant merchants had retired from Spain, and after the peace of 1713 they did not return, partly because they feared the potential competition of the newly established South Sea Company, but also because they had suffered heavily because of the irregularity of the Spanish silver fleets and galleons during the last years of Charles II, who had oppressed the merchants with taxes. They were also discouraged by the favour which had been shown to their French rivals during the war.[77] But this did not mean that there was no British trade to Cadiz and Seville. When the English merchants had retired in 1702 their Irish Roman Catholic clerks remained behind, and after the war these Irishmen revived the British trade. The French might have obtained the lion's share of the trade of the annual Spanish merchant fleets, but the British soon secured a considerable share of the trade. Cadiz was, during the eighteenth century, the richest and most important of British factories in Spain, and the British trade to Old Spain throve. The South Sea Company's annual ship had not seriously decreased the British trade to Cadiz, but this was chiefly because the trade of the annual ship, though some voyages could show high profits, was in fact very inconsiderable.[78]

The South Sea Company's trade was chiefly prized because of the returns it was hoped to secure in bullion. From the time of Hawkins and Drake, Englishmen had believed that the Spanish Main was a sort of Tom Tiddler's ground. Even in the eighteenth century the Indies were looked upon as an inexhaustible supply of real wealth, and when the idea of founding the South Sea Company was suggested in 1711, it was asserted that the new trade would yield so much bullion that not only would the whole of English trade be increased, manufactures developed and the number of idle poor decreased, but that every class would directly benefit by the trade to Mexico and Peru.[79]

In fact, the South Sea Company had considerable difficulty in obtaining bullion. In spite of their reputation for immense wealth the Spanish Indies were not well supplied with coin.[80] The annual Spanish merchant fleets took off most of the ready money of the colonists, and much of the rest went in taxes to Old Spain. Even in Havana, where the Spanish annual fleets reassembled before setting out on their return voyage, the South Sea Company factor had to accept fruits in payment for negroes. For a time the Company tried the experiment of refusing to accept payment in any form but that of bullion,[81] but even in Cuba this was not a success, and factors preferred to accept fruits rather than add to the number of bad debts.[82] On the Windward Coast not only was there little money, but the fruits were all monopolised by the Guipuzcoan Company which traded to Caracas for cocoa,[83] and the Asientists found it useless to maintain a permanent factory where the planters could only afford to buy slaves after the cocoa harvest.[84] When the South Sea Company did manage to secure payment in bullion it seems to have expended a good deal of this in Jamaica,[85] for the residents in the island declared that the trade had brought great relief to the colony which, until the establishment of the Asiento, had been in "a miserable condition for the want of currency" of which there had been a "deplorable scarcity". But although the Jamaicans liked the little bullion which the South Sea Company managed to obtain, they heartily objected to the fruits with which the Spanish colonists paid as part of the price of the negroes they bought.

Snuff, indigo and cochineal commanded a good market in Great Britain, but they competed with the produce of the British West Indies, and even when Spanish sugars were sent to the Company's agents in Amsterdam and Hamburg,[86] they competed with the export trade in British West Indian produce. Politicians seriously maintained that the produce of the Spanish colonies was so different from that of the British plantations that its presence in a ship could be taken as proof of illicit trade,[87] but the difference was not apparent to the West Indian merchants. If the South Sea Company was not dangerous to the valued West Indian trade, this was again only because the amount of trade the Company was able to carry on was always inconsiderable.

The slave trade when carried on as part of the general colonial trade of Great Britain might be very lucrative, but it was far less satisfactory when it had to be carried on under a Spanish licence. Though the *Asiento de Negros* had always raised the hopes of foreign merchants it had never proved, in fact, to be a profitable undertaking.[88] For two centuries before the attempt by the South Sea Company, Spanish and foreign merchants had tried to make a profit out of supplying the Spanish colonies with slaves, and with one exception they had failed. In war time the trade was liable to heavy losses, and at all times it was strangled by heavy duties. The Spaniards, who had first undertaken the trade in the sixteenth century, were ruined by heavy taxation, and over-minute state regulation. The Portuguese, who took over the trade when Portugal became incorporated in the Spanish empire, had enjoyed the advantage of being free to trade to the coasts of Africa, but even so, their venture had failed because of heavy taxes. When, in the late seventeenth century, Portugal regained her independence, friction with Spain made it impossible for Spanish merchants to trade to Africa, even if in the general economic decline of Spain there had been enough capital to finance the trade. This opened the way for foreign enterprise, and there were always foreign merchants eager to prosecute a trade which put them in direct touch with the wealth of the Indies. By then, however, a new difficulty had developed, for as European nations settled in North America, and the islands of the Caribbean, other nations became interested in the slave trade, and the Asientists had to compete with illicit traders. When the Portuguese once more attempted to carry on the trade through a national company, bad feeling with Spain was too great, and the attempt failed. A French company which next undertook the trade might have had better success, but was under the disadvantage of having to operate in war time.

The English Asientists were no more fortunate than their predecessors. Their trade was interrupted by war, national feeling made their relations with Spain difficult, and they had to bear the weight of heavy taxation. Under articles 2 and 5 of the Asiento of 1713, the Englishmen who supplied the Spanish Indies with slaves were bound to pay the King of Spain a duty of $33\frac{1}{3}$ pieces of eight —or roughly £8. 10s.—each for 4000 of the 4800 negroes annually to be imported. By article 5 the tax on the remaining 800 had been remitted in return for a loan of about £50,000 which the Asientists had made to His Catholic Majesty before they ever began the trade. But this was of little use, as the Company never managed to import the full quota of negroes, and whether many or few were imported the duty of £34,000 had to be paid regularly each year.

From the point of view of British merchants, the Asiento trade in negroes, even when it was supplemented by the irregular voyages of the annual ships, did not justify the expectations of the peace-makers of 1713. From the Spanish point of view it was the duty of the mother country to supply her colonies with labour, and these slaves had to be bought with bullion or fruits. The only way in which Spain could secure any advantage from the transaction was if the trade to the Spanish colonies could be made to appear so potentially valuable that foreign merchants could be persuaded to pay to be allowed to carry on a trade which the native Spaniards lacked capital and ships to undertake themselves.

From the point of view of the British statesmen a direct trade to the Spanish Indies was believed to be potentially valuable, and there was always a hope that the legitimate Asientist trade might be used to cover a steadily increasing amount of illicit trade. Actually the value of illicit trade carried on under the Asiento was small. The South Sea Company as an institution did not smuggle, and the illicit trade of individual supercargoes on the annual ships, of Jamaican agents, of the factors in the Spanish ports, and of captains of slaving sloops plying between Jamaica and the Spanish-American ports, was very little when compared with the illicit trade that went on from the British colonies in the West Indies. Of the colonial smuggling the Spanish colonial governors vigorously complained,[89] though neither they nor the Spanish representative on the Company's board of directors made very serious complaints of the South Sea Company's illicit trade. British statesmen were also interested to encourage the African trade as a nursery for seamen, and since they knew that the Asiento trade supported this trade, and believed that it was a source of bullion and hoped that it might in time prove very valuable, they preferred to retain the trade even in the face of expert mercantile opinion rather than allow it to fall into the hands of the French.

The direct trade with the Spanish Indies, which had raised enormous hopes and for forty years attracted a great deal of attention, was like the famous South Sea Bubble, a commercial delusion. The Spanish colonies needed a supply of slave labour, but the Asiento was not an efficient means of supplying them. It gave rise to a small but costly trade which, because it was regulated by an international agreement between two crowns, was of a semi-political character, and easily became a fruitful source of disputes between Great Britain and Spain. There was no particular reason for the English Asientists to be popular in Spain, for any other trading nation could have carried on the trade equally well, and the French in particular would have been eager to undertake it. British statesmen for the same reason were determined to cling to the trade although it might not prove profitable, and did cause political friction with the court of Spain. The Asiento trade as carried on by the South Sea Company was of small value and a fruitful cause of political disputes, yet for forty years it played a part in Anglo-Spanish relations, sometimes of equal importance and sometimes of even greater importance than did the long-established, reciprocally profitable, flourishing trade to Old Spain.

CHAPTER II

"MONARCHY, CHURCH AND TRADE"

*Events leading up to the outbreak of the War of
the Spanish Succession, 1700–1702*

A trade as valuable as that between England and Spain would
normally make English statesmen reluctant to break with Spain,
but during the uncertain period that followed the death of the
Spanish king, Charles II, it was the English merchants who were
the earliest to decide, and the most energetic to advocate war.[1]
The reason for this behaviour, and the importance of trade considerations in determining the policy of the English government,
form an interesting commentary on the causes which are generally
said to have led to war. The political principles of William III
made him eager to preserve the balance of power in Europe, to
maintain the independence of Holland and prevent the increase
of Bourbon power. The principles of the English politicians made
them passionate in their defence of the Protestant Succession. The
imperialistic designs of far-sighted English statesmen and merchants
made them consider the necessity of defending British trade to
America, where it seemed to be threatened by the alliance of
Spanish rights and French efficiency,[2] but among the motives
which, after eighteen months, led England to declare war on Spain,
was certainly the interest of the merchants trading to Old Spain,
the Netherlands and the Mediterranean.[3]

When Charles II eventually died and, by his will, left all his
territories to the grandson of the king of France, English opinion
was relieved rather than infuriated,[4] and very ready to continue
on good terms with Spain.[5] Ever since his accession in 1665 the
question of the Spanish Succession had been urgent, and during
the last thirty years of the seventeenth century the feeble health
of the Spanish king had frequently alarmed the diplomats of
Europe. The problem of the Spanish Succession had been the

central pivot of the whole reign of Louis XIV, and it had been of supreme importance to William III. Their attempts to preserve the peace of Europe had led to the partition treaties of 1698 and 1700, but the terms of these agreements when they were learnt in England were not at all popular.[6] When it was known that Charles II had left by will all his vast dominions to the young Duke of Anjou and that Louis XIV had abandoned the partition treaty and accepted the bequest, William III had the mortification to realise that "nearly everyone rejoices that France prefers the will to the treaty". Harley declared that the will was "better than we could expect",[7] and when Aglionby was sent as a special English envoy to Spain with the royal condolences he had orders to cultivate the friendship of the new king.

The particular objection to the second partition treaty had come from the numerous class of merchants trading to the Mediterranean. That sea, it was alleged, would have become a French lake, since the treaty would have given to the Dauphin Naples, Sicily, the Tuscan ports and Finale, not to mention Guipuzcoa on the south coast of the Bay of Biscay.

By the will the whole Spanish empire was certainly left to a Bourbon prince, but "the Tories did not care of what family was the new King of Spain, provided that the interests of Spain and France were...kept apart, and that English trade did not suffer".[8] This the Tories and merchants believed would be safe under Philip V for, as he was young, they hoped that, under the influence of native advisers, he might become a good Spaniard.[9]

The attitude of the English politicians was due not only to their hopes of the formative influence of the Madrid court on its new king, but to their fears and suspicions of the conduct of William III at Kensington. The chief wish of the Tories, who in 1700 were in great strength in Parliament, was for peace. The Glorious Revolution had taken place only eleven years before, and the country was still faced with considerable internal problems. The safety of the Protestant faith was of consuming interest in the opening years of the eighteenth century, and not only security for religion but the whole question of civil liberty was bound up in the question of the Protestant Succession which, with the death of the Duke of Gloucester in 1701, was to become as urgent as that of Spain. The

long war against France, which had broken out almost as soon as
William and Mary had been established on the English throne,
had postponed the settlement of domestic concerns, and in particular
had made it impossible to reduce the standing army which had
been one of the most obnoxious features of the reign of James II.
This, together with a heavy National Debt and large foreign
subsidies, the Tories wished to remove. The passionate interest in
domestic problems was strengthened by the prevalent English
hatred of foreigners. Englishmen might detest Louis XIV, but
they also disliked their own Dutch king, and entirely failed to share
his interest in continental politics or his attempts to secure the
United Provinces from French aggression. Until the English could
be convinced that the succession of Philip V to the crown of Spain
was going to be actively injurious to them, they were prepared to
acquiesce in the violation of the partition treaties, about which
Parliament had not been consulted, and approve the succession
of a Bourbon in Spain.

In this attitude they were supported by the Dutch States General[10]
which, though it had better reason to fear Bourbon ambition, was
also prepared to acquiesce in the accession of Philip V. The indifference of the Dutch and English was not shared by their ruler
or the emperor. Leopold considered that his claim to the whole
Spanish inheritance was more just than those put forward by either
the French or the Bavarian candidates, and in this belief he had
refused to come into the second partition treaty. For a time, after
the death of Charles II, it was thought that he might yet adhere to
that treaty, but it soon became clear that he intended to assert his
claim by force of arms, and win at least some compensation in
Italy. William III had spent his life combating the ambition of
Louis XIV. In 1697 it had seemed as if for a time he had been
successful, and when Louis had come into the partition treaties
William had had reason for self-congratulation. Now, with Louis'
recognition of the will of Charles II, William had to suffer the
bitterest diplomatic humiliation of his life, admit himself duped,
and find himself faced with the whole task of curbing the Bourbon
ambition to dominate Europe as if his previous wars had never
been fought. The defeat of his old antagonist and the protection of
his Dutch inheritance made William vehement in his desire for

war, and exasperated at the indifference shown by his English subjects at this crisis.[11]

In December 1700, a month after the will of Charles II had been made known, it seemed as if the English had firmly decided not to engage in any war "no matter what efforts are made to entice them",[12] but it was still possible that this opinion might be altered if events did not bear out the ideas which politicians and merchants had formed as to the effects of the accession of Philip V. This was clearly realised by the French ambassador in London, Tallard, who wrote to Louis XIV on December 21, 1700:[13]

The nation appears to agree to accept the execution of the will, but they may change this opinion if the King of England can manage to make them uneasy by telling them that things will not remain as they are, that your Majesty will come to an arrangement sooner or later with Spain as to the Netherlands, that perhaps France and Spain will combine to conquer Portugal in exchange; that His Catholic Majesty may one day become King of France, since there is only one life between his person and that high honour, and that he would naturally prefer to allow the trade of his country to fall into the hands of a nation from which he is descended, and of which he may one day become king, rather than allow it to be in the hands of foreigners to whom he is indifferent.... They add that your Majesty has already offered troops to enter the places in Flanders, and that it is desired to drive out the Dutch....The nation although it is determined to maintain peace may yet be ruined by the fear of the future which may be instilled into it....Your Majesty cannot take too great pains to exhort the Spaniards not to make any changes in their trade relations with England and Holland nor behave too circumspectly with regard to the security of the Low Countries.

It was obvious that these were the two points most interesting to England. They had been clearly stated at the time of the negotiation of the first partition treaty. Security had been demanded that the crowns of France and Spain should never be united; that Dutch independence should be guaranteed, that some compensation should be made to the emperor in Italy, and that commercial concessions should be made to England and the United Provinces. These terms were repeated during the negotiations at the Hague in March and April of 1701,[14] and the most important security of Holland and the encouragement of trade were stressed in speeches in Parliament, and formed the essential core of the instructions given to Aglionby when he was sent to Madrid in 1701. The instructions to Aglionby were quite explicit:

that it has always been our inclination and desire to maintain and cultivate a sincere friendship with the crown of Spain...and as we are desirous to continue our former friendship and intimate correspondence with the crown of Spain, so we shall be glad to be assured that there is the like disposition on their part...that all former treaties and alliances between us, Spain and the States General may still subsist and remain in full force....We shall look upon it as a particular mark of their intention to live in amity and good correspondence with us if they take care that Flanders continue united to the crown of Spain, and governed so as to cause no jealousy to its neighbours...(and)...the Dutch forces be still continued in those garrisons in Flanders where they are at present, under the orders of Spanish governors.

Unfortunately for the peace of Europe, Louis XIV did not see fit to prevent any fears being aroused with regard to the safety of Holland and the peaceful continuation of Dutch and English trade with Spain. That he had no intention of alarming them is shown by his reply to Tallard, "You confirm the news I had already received concerning the English. I observe that they desire peace, and that the succession of my grandson to the throne of Spain does not, of itself, cause them any alarm. It only remains to quieten the fears the King of England wishes to arouse in his subjects with regard to the Low Countries, their trade and their religion." He added that far from entertaining any wish to annex Portugal so as to have something to offer to the King of Spain in exchange for the Spanish Netherlands, he had actually offered to conclude a defensive alliance with the court of Lisbon; and that he had expressed his willingness to enter into a new treaty of guarantee with Spain, England and Holland. His action with regard to the Spanish Netherlands he defended as being necessary in view of the Dutch attitude:

It is true that I have offered my troops to garrison the places belonging to the King of Spain in the Spanish Netherlands, if this should be necessary; I have even advanced some of my troops on the frontiers of my realm in the direction of Luxemburg, but the conduct of the Dutch made this precaution absolutely necessary, and it is impossible that their designs should not cause suspicion when they refuse to acknowledge the King of Spain, yet at the same time want to remain in his towns.

But in one connection the great King of France showed himself either unable to appreciate the importance of English and Dutch fears, or else determined not to sacrifice the possibility of advantages for French subjects in order to secure the friendly indifference of the Maritime Powers to the succession of Philip V to the throne of Spain. "As regards commerce nothing can disturb it but war, that of the English can sustain no alteration by the succession of my grandson to the Spanish throne except in the case of the two nations breaking with Spain when they would fall into those very evils they are so eager to avoid, and once war has begun it may be that the English and Dutch will never be able to make good their losses."[15] The arrogance behind this threat showed clearly that Louis XIV would never follow the advice of his ambassador, and urge the Spanish court to refrain from making any alteration in the conditions affecting the trade of England and Holland.

In fact, Louis XIV seems to have felt himself so strong in 1700 that he was able to act without considering what effect his conduct might have upon the Maritime Powers. There seemed to be good reason for his confidence. France was assured of the alliance of Savoy, Mantua, Bavaria and Cologne. The negotiations with Portugal were promising. The emperor was weakened by Rakoczi's revolt in Hungary, and the internal disputes among the German princes which had been provoked by the creation of the Hanoverian electorate and the Prussian kingdom. William III, the French king's most energetic and brilliant opponent, was crippled by failing health, domestic opposition and a lack of support even in Holland. In November 1700 Louis had accepted the will of Charles II in spite of having entered into two successive partition treaties. It may be said that in view of the death of the Electoral Prince of Bavaria, the hatred of any form of partition evinced by the Spanish people and the obstinate refusal of the emperor to waive his claims, the execution of the will seemed to be less likely to provoke a war than would have been a strict adherence to the second partition treaty. Louis' subsequent actions appeared to be almost wanton provocation of the Maritime Powers. No sooner had Philip V started for Madrid than Louis XIV issued letters patent, in which he recognised his grandson's eventual right to succession in France. In February 1701, with the consent of the

Spanish authorities, he sent French troops into the Spanish Netherlands and occupied the eight fortresses which had been garrisoned
by Dutch troops. In this way he secured possession of 15,000 of
the best Dutch troops which were only released after the States
General had acknowledged Philip V. During the previous fifty
years torrents of English blood had been shed in defence of these
fortresses, the right to supplement the Spanish defences with Dutch
troops had been a cherished result of the Peace of Ryswick, and
the security of these Spanish fortresses had been a main object of
the policy of the English king, yet to force the Dutch to acknowledge
his grandson the French king occupied the Barrier towns.

The interference with the trade of the Maritime Powers to Spain
though less spectacular, and though it took place partly without
the express desire of the French king, was nevertheless an important
influence on public opinion during most of the year 1701.

At this time the trade to Old Spain and the trade to the Spanish
Indies exercised almost exactly similar influences on the policy of
English statesmen. At the time of the death of Charles II the only
foreigners who might legally trade direct to the Spanish Indies
were the Portuguese merchants of the Cacheu Company, which then
enjoyed the right of supplying the Spanish colonies with slaves.[16]
The only ways in which English or French merchants might trade
with Spanish America were either through joining in the trade of
the annual silver fleets or galleons, or by carrying on a contraband
trade via the West Indies.[17] Both methods were illegal. When
the first partition treaty had been under discussion Lord Somers
had suggested to William III that "if it could be brought to pass
that England might be some way a gainer by the transaction,
whether it be by...an agreement to let us into some trade with
the Spanish plantations, or in some other manner, it would
wonderfully endear your Majesty to your English subjects".[18]
That English statesmen were keenly interested in events on the
other side of the Atlantic was shown by the fact that at the time of
the conclusion of the Triple Alliance, in the autumn of 1701,
Marlborough and Heinsius demanded that the English and Dutch
might be allowed to keep any conquests they might make in the
Western seas.[19] Before the death of Charles II Englishmen had
been negotiating for some share in the trade carried on by a

Portuguese Company under the *Asiento de Negros*.[20] The illicit trade via Jamaica was at this time flourishing[21] and, at the end of the seventeenth century, English merchants enjoyed a rich share in the annual Spanish fleets and galleons; a later British consul at Cadiz stated that "in the galleons which came home in 1692 the interest of the British factories of Seville, Cadiz and Port Saint Mary amounted to above 900 D. per cent. . . . England being then in secure peace and tranquility with Spain",[22] but the fact remains that English merchants only enjoyed a direct trade with the Spanish Indies by illicit means. It was, therefore, particularly galling to find that within a year of the accession of a Bourbon prince to the Spanish throne, French merchants secured a legal right to share in the trade of the Spanish colonies.

During the last decade of the seventeenth century French diplomats as well as English had tried to obtain a share in the Portuguese Asiento trade, and as early as September 1700 French statesmen had hoped that, when the Portuguese Asiento came to an end, similar concessions might be secured for France. In January 1701 Harcourt, the French ambassador in Madrid, had written to his master stressing the advisability of extracting some commercial advantages from the accession of the Duke of Anjou, and suggesting that to obtain the Asiento would be the most profitable means of attaining this objective. Louis had replied that this was no time to think of trade, but three months later, in April, he had told Harcourt that the time had come to obtain the Asiento. In August 1701 Ducasse arrived in Madrid to carry on negotiations for the French Asiento, and it was hoped that the first ship would be able to sail before the end of the year. On September 14, 1701, the Asiento was concluded.[23]

At the same time companies to trade to the South Seas had been established at St Malo and Paris, and although, out of respect for Spanish susceptibilities, these were refused permission to trade in the Pacific with the Spanish colonies, the British merchants were greatly alarmed. A French East India company had been set up as early as 1664, and a China company in 1698 when it was thought necessary to provide employment for the numerous St Malo privateers who had been put out of work by the Peace of Ryswick, and who, because of the failure of negotiations with the

Portuguese, could not be employed in the Asiento trade. In 1698 there had also been founded a South Sea Company, but by 1701 this had proved incapable of prosecuting the trade, so a new South Sea Company was set up at St Malo, and in November of the same year this joined with the existing China company to form the China companies of St Malo and of Paris.[24]

At the same time the English saw their trade with the Spanish Indies increasingly impeded. In August 1701 it was reported that the system of annual Spanish fleets and galleons sailing from Cadiz was to be reorganised, "so that all the profits of the trade are to go to the Spanish and French only to the exclusion of all other nations and especially the English and the Dutch".[25] Not only was the Indies trade by way of Spain molested, but very soon after the accession of Philip V there were rumours that French ships would be used to molest the illicit trade carried on by Dutch and English merchants in the Indies. At the beginning of 1701 Schonenberg was in charge of English interests in Spain. This Dutch minister had been given English powers, and had succeeded Alexander Stanhope when he was suddenly recalled in 1699 because of a dispute between England and Spain. Early in March he reported a number of suspicious conferences between French experts and some members of the Consejo de Indias. These meetings took place at the house of the French ambassador, and resulted in a decision to send French ships to the Indies to accompany the Spanish war ships, and it was later determined that for the return voyage the bullion from Vera Cruz should be embarked on these French ships rather than in the Spanish fleet then trading in the Indies. But such was the suspicion of France that another explanation of the presence of these French ships was seriously sent to the English Secretary of State. "Persons perfectly well informed and of whose good will I have proof tell me that the object of this design is not only to put the Spanish ports in America in a proper state of defence against the invasions of the English and the Dutch, not only to check the trade of these two nations, but actually to dislodge them from some of the islands which they now possess, such as Jamaica and Curaçao which they think the most dangerously situated to threaten the Spanish islands, and prosecute a trade prejudicial to the interests of the Spanish monarchy."[26]

It was not only in their illicit trade with the Spanish Indies that the English and Dutch merchants feared that the accession of Philip V would hamper them. Their trade to Old Spain was long established, sanctioned by treaty and of great value, but here, too, the accession of a Bourbon prince to the Spanish throne was followed by a series of vexatious oppressions which seemed to justify the gloomy suspicions of the English merchants. As the French ambassador had said, it was only natural to suppose that under a French king the French merchants would be treated favourably, and that, in a court dominated by French influence, French fashions and consequently French goods would be preferred above those of any other country. There might not be express orders in favour of French trade, but

there is indeed at Court all countenance given to those who consume the French manufactures; the grandees often appear in that dress before the king which was not so in his predecessor's time. By degrees the *golilla* will be turned into ridicule and with it the use of bays may fall. But whether this be or no, our merchants may assure themselves that henceforward they will meet with little fair dealing or advantage in the Spanish trade, but will upon all occasions be very severely handled not to say anything of the French preference in everything, of which they may be sure.[27]

That English trade to Old Spain really was in danger was shown by the successive complaints of molestations in one after another of the branches of the trade. In May the tobacco trade was reported to be in serious danger, and when the Dutch minister passed a formal office of protest he had little hope of success as the French were certain to oppose his requests, and the Spanish court would not refuse the French anything. When the Spanish reply was made to Schonenberg's memorial at the end of August, it was plain that his misgivings had been justified. The prohibition on the import of Virginia tobacco was to continue, and the only mitigation of the grievance that could be obtained for the English merchants was that the stores of tobacco which they had already introduced, but not yet sold, were not to be confiscated but might be sold to the royal officials who had orders to buy. But this concession was of little value, for the consul at Seville reported that the royal officials would only buy the stores of tobacco at half-price.[28]

By June the English Secretary of State had heard a rumour that the Spanish Council of State had seriously proposed a measure to get English bays laid aside.[29] The English agent in Madrid had heard of no such specific scheme, but the prevalence of French fashions was in itself a serious menace to English trade.

With the vintage in the autumn came news of molestations in the wine trade. At Malaga extra duties were demanded on the export of wine, though this was contrary to an agreement concluded in 1699, and at Corunna English merchants suffered similar injustices. The Spanish authorities refused to answer Schonenberg's memorials on this grievance, and he was led to wonder whether this was "to hide from me their true design of entirely ruining our trade, or to preserve a way for excusing their conduct when it shall be seen what turn events will take".[30]

English merchants were also liable to suffer seizure of their effects on very insufficient grounds. In October the Governor of Malaga publicly sold the effects of the English and Dutch merchants who had refused to pay the wine duty, and although a favourable reply was made when Schonenberg memorialised against this injustice, at first no attempt was made to put the conciliatory promises into effect. This Schonenberg attributed to the influence of the French, "who have most certainly determined to ruin the English and Dutch trade completely".[31] Even though in the case of the Malaga incident the merchants were eventually released and their effects restored,[32] this did not deter His Catholic Majesty's officials from fresh acts of rapacity. There followed a similar action by the administrator of the sugar rents at Seville, and although a sentence against him was obtained by Schonenberg, the minister realised that he could not prevent fresh exactions in future. "As soon as one vexation is at an end these people begin another for they know that in the present situation of affairs the best way to please the Court is to invent successive oppressions upon the trade of the English merchants."[33]

It was clear that the French merchants were trying to exclude English and Dutch trade from Old Spain, and that the new court was not unfavourably disposed towards this effort. As early as April 1701 Aglionby had commented on the blind subservience of Spain to France. "This is not blindness for the want of good eyes, but by the wilful shutting of them",[34] and Schonenberg had repeatedly stressed how dangerous the French ascendency in Madrid would be to the trade of the Maritime Powers. "The predominating influence of France tends increasingly to the total ruin of the small trade which the English retain in Spain. This, together with the blind dependence of this court, which is determined to sacrifice at whatever cost all that is most sacred in public faith and solemn treaties so long as it may please the court of France, has made my efforts unavailing." [35]

Early in September it seemed as if the British fears of the effects of French influence at Madrid were to be completely justified. The Dutch minister reported that His Catholic Majesty had been petitioned by the administrators of the Customs to grant concessions to English and Dutch merchants to encourage the trade which had declined seriously because of the fears of war, so that the Customs revenue derived from that source had sensibly diminished. It was thought that the king had been advised not only to refuse to grant any concessions, but actually to withdraw all the privileges of the merchants of those two countries, that they might prevail upon their governments to cease their opposition to France and Spain. Actually His Catholic Majesty had only refused any new benefit, but it was feared that the French might yet force him to take more violent measures. "I could explain at great length the pernicious effects which threaten the trade of England and Holland in the near future, unless these two powers take speedy and active measures for their defence since friendly overtures must remain unavailing so long as France retains her ascendency in Spain." [36]

The illicit share in the trade to the Spanish Indies and the very valuable trade to Old Spain seemed to be in danger of ruin as a result of the accession of a French prince to the Spanish throne, but these were not the only branches of English commerce which were in danger. The Netherlands trade was in serious jeopardy. In 1667 this had been so highly esteemed that its re-establishment had been preferred to a monopoly of Spanish wool, but with a Bourbon on the Spanish throne and French garrisons in the fortress towns of the Spanish Netherlands, the trade languished. In February 1701 Louis XIV occupied the fortresses of the Spanish Netherlands. One section of the British nation then began to rouse itself, for the bankers began to be alarmed and the merchants feared that the markets of the Netherlands would soon be closed.[37] With French troops in Ostend and Nieuport the London merchants feared that the whole trade of the English Channel might be interrupted.[38]

The trade to the Mediterranean and the Levant was in even greater danger, as Aglionby saw as early as June 1701:

> Many more of this kind (of insult) must be expected, and particularly now they are sure of Portugal with whom France and Spain have signed an alliance offensive and defensive in case of war....It should be a matter for serious reflexion for a House of Commons to consider all these steps made so regularly by France towards uniting the power of Spain to theirs; they seem to carry with them the trade of the whole world; and England will have no place to send a ship to but the East Indies and their own American colonies. There is not already a port between London and Leghorn where we can shelter ourselves in case of war or to refresh; and Leghorn itself is but precarious now so that the Turkey trade is quite out of doors.[39]

In England public opinion steadily became more hostile to France as Louis XIV took each successive step in defiance of the interests and honour of the Maritime Powers, and as it became increasingly clear that a Bourbon on the Spanish throne constituted a real danger to English and Dutch trade. In December 1700 William III had dissolved Parliament, but as yet nothing had happened to modify the originally favourable opinion held by the English as to the will of Charles II, and the Parliament that met in February 1701 was strongly Tory, and fiercely hostile to William personally. The king's speech urged the House to guard against any danger that might arise from the acceptance of a Bourbon as King of Spain. The resolution passed on February 14 in reply was vague and non-committal. The Commons "would stand by His Majesty" and take effectual measures for "the interest and safety of England, the preservation of the Protestant religion, and the Peace of Europe", but even the last watery phrase was only retained by eighteen votes against a Tory protest.[40] By February 20, however, they resolved to ask the king to enter into negotiations for those specified purposes with the United Provinces and "other potentates", and declared themselves ready to honour the treaty of 1678 by which England had agreed to supply 10,000 men to

Holland in case of need. By April 11, when a new appeal from the
States General was laid before Parliament, the Commons agreed
to support the king in taking what means might be necessary to
protect the safety of Holland, but a Whig proposal coupling the
defence of England with that of Holland was defeated.[41] But in
May mercantile opinion was in advance of Parliament. The
Commons' slowness in foreign affairs had

given general disgust to the nation, and particularly to the City of
London, where foreign affairs, and the interest of trade are generally
better understood; the old East India Company, though they hated the
ministry that had set up the new, and studied to support this House of
Commons from which they expected much favour; yet they as well as
the rest of the City saw visibly, that first the ruin of trade, and consequently the ruin of the nation, must certainly ensue, if France and
Spain were once firmly united.[42]

As a result the Kentish petition was made to Parliament, urging
the Commons to change their loyal addresses into bills of supply
"before it is too late". When the Commons objected to this
petition others followed, the most famous of which was the Legion
petition, and on May 9 "the Commons unanimously decided that
they would aid the king to support his allies in maintaining the
liberties of Europe, and that they would provide succour for the
Dutch in accordance with the treaty of 1678". On June 12 the
Commons assured the king of their support in "such alliances as
he should think fit to make, in conjunction with the Emperor and
the States General, for the preservation of the liberties of Europe,
the prosperity and peace of England, and for reducing the
exorbitant power of France".

Before the next Parliament met in the autumn, political events
on the Continent had combined with the increasing fears of the
merchants to make the idea of war less unpopular in England.
On September 7, 1701, the Triple Alliance was concluded between
England, Holland and the Empire, its signature having been
hastened by the victories of the Imperial troops under Prince
Eugene over the troops of His Catholic Majesty in Italy. It was
the intention of the contracting parties to communicate their terms
to Louis XIV in a final attempt to avert war, and adjust the
question of the Spanish Succession satisfactorily, but this was made

impossible by the sudden recall of the English ambassador from France.

On September 16 James II died, and on the following day Louis XIV recognised his son as James III. The gesture was one of courtesy made out of consideration for the ex-Queen of England and for Madame de Maintenon, but it had the effect of touching off the inflammable materials which had been accumulating in England. The city of London drew up the first of many loyal addresses to William III, when a new Parliament assembled, although the Whigs were not returned in such great strength as they had hoped. By then Whigs and Tories were of similar opinions on questions of foreign policy.

Louis' only hope of maintaining the peace was now to frighten his opponents. In November French troops occupied Cologne, through which the attack on Dutch territory had been made in 1672, and in October heavy duties had been imposed on English goods imported to France. By then, however, the merchants were roused, and this new injury only made them more determined to fight in defence of their trade. When William III met his last Parliament he found it ready to support his warlike policy. "I promise myself you are met together full of that just sense of the common danger of Europe, and the resentment of the late proceedings of the French king, which has been so fully and universally expressed in the loyal and seasonable addresses of my people." As the chief causes of the war William III mentioned two. The first was "the owning and setting up the pretended Prince of Wales for King of England" as a threat to "the Protestant religion", and "the present or future quiet and happiness of England which could only be secured by the succession of the Crown in the Protestant line". The second was the menace to trade. "By the French king placing his grandson on the throne of Spain, he is in a condition to oppress the rest of Europe...he is become the real master of the whole Spanish monarchy.... This must affect England in the nearest and most sensible manner, in respect to our trade, which will soon become precarious in all its variable branches." Parliament responded as the king had hoped. A Bill of Attainder was passed against the Pretender, and supplies were voted to pay for 40,000 sailors and 40,000 soldiers.[43] On May 4, 1702, war was declared. The change in public opinion was illustrated by a letter from one Tory gentleman to another:

Indeed I take the state of the question—peace or war—to be very much altered since the last sessions. We have now very potent alliances formed abroad, we had then none, the treaty of partition having broken those that we had. We had then very great effects at sea and in Spain; our merchants since have been so prudent as to bring home or transmit to other parts, those they had there: and this is so inestimable a value, that it now appears what an incredible loss we should have had had we declared (when the town would almost have forced us to it) last winter.[44]

The importance of commercial interests as a cause of the war were emphasised in the instructions given to the English ambassador who was sent to Spain after the end of the war.[45] "The preservation of the commerce between the kingdoms of Great Britain and Spain was one of the chief motives that induced our two royal predecessors to enter into the late long, expensive war."

One of the features of this crisis was that the interests of the merchants engaged in illicit trade with the Spanish Indies were the same as those of the merchants carrying on the lawful trade to Old Spain. The merchants sharing in the trade of the Spanish Indies were united with those trading to Old Spain, the Netherlands, Italy and Turkey in opposing the succession of a French prince to the throne of Spain. Their influence combined with the wishes of the king, and the increasing suspicion of the statesmen, to change the feeling of mildly pleased indifference that had existed when Charles II's will became known into the active hostility which made it possible for Queen Anne to declare war in May 1702, in defence of Monarchy, Church and Trade.

CHAPTER III

"A LAME, BLIND, MISSHAPEN MONSTER"

The Commercial Treaty of 1713 and the negotiation of the Asiento Contract, 1711–1716

§1

The Peace of Utrecht is associated with the triumphant acquisition of the Asiento, which, together with the acquisition of the New-foundland fisheries and two successful commercial treaties, were intended to provide a very valuable encouragement for British trade. The gaining of the Asiento—"the Feather and Flower of our trade"—has made observers overlook the fact that, in 1713, the Tory statesmen also concluded a commercial treaty with Spain, which proved so actively hurtful to trade that within two years another had to be negotiated to make good its shortcomings. The trade to Old Spain was neglected, for the English statesmen negotiating the peace were preoccupied with the problem of obtaining a direct share in the trade to the Spanish Indies.

To obtain such a direct trade had been the ambition of English merchants and statesmen since the discovery of the riches of the New World. When it became obvious that the nearest that foreigners could get to this ideal was to supply the Spanish colonies with negro slaves, English diplomats had tried to get for their countrymen some share in the Asientos granted to other nations.[1] When France had obtained the Asiento in 1701, this had been a serious blow to English commercial ambition, but since French armies had been defeated at Blenheim, at Ramillies and Malplaquet there seemed a real possibility that as a result of English victories on the Danube and in Flanders English merchants might obtain the long coveted privilege of trading to the Spanish Indies.

In 1711 these hopes were strong enough to serve the Treasurer Harley as a bait to offer to holders of £80,000 navy and ordnance bonds in exchange for their holdings.[2] During the Parliamentary session of 1711 the ministers were faced with two pressing needs

—to maintain the war system even in the act of making peace, and to recover the finances. In this difficult situation "Harley's conduct of finance placed him high even in Whig opinion. Faced by an unsecured debt of nine and a half millions, he restored public credit, got the year's supplies and, assisted by the financial experience of Halifax, raised in two lotteries £3,500,000 secured by new duties on leather, hops, playing cards and postage. For the further liquidation of the debt, he pledged the country to a new South Sea Company trading to the Spanish Indies—an arrangement which, incidentally, implied a friendly settlement with the ruler of Spain."[3] The new company was to pay 6 per cent interest convertible by Parliament on its shares. Parliament made no difficulties over appropriating Customs duties to secure the interest on the Company's shares. The bondholders were eager to exchange their holdings for shares in the Company, which thus began its career as a useful financial ally of the British government. From the South Sea trade the shareholders hoped to make far more than their guaranteed 6 per cent.[4] It was, therefore, essential that, in the peace negotiations with the Bourbon powers, the English diplomats should secure the concession of the Asiento, and already in May 1711 this seemed tolerably certain.

When the Whig ministry fell in 1710 both France and England were heartily sick of an expensive war, which could never attain the extravagant objectives which the emperor and some of the English Whigs still wanted. The defeats inflicted by the Bourbon troops in Spain had made it plain that, in spite of Stanhope's victories, it was useless to insist on the claims of the Archduke Charles to the Spanish throne. "Armies of 20,000 or 30,000 men might walk about the country till Doomsday...wherever they came the people would submit to Charles out of terror, and as soon as they were gone proclaim Philip V out of affection;...to conquer Spain, required a great army, to keep it a greater."[5] France was exhausted; England burdened with a very heavy share of the expenses of the war. The peace negotiations at Gertruydenberg in 1709 had been allowed to fail although the French envoys had agreed to astonishingly humiliating terms, and had only refused to order French troops to join in an attempt to turn the French prince off the throne of Spain.

Late in 1710 the English statesmen intimated their readiness to resume negotiations.[6] In April 1711 French proposals were made in answer to the English overtures. In the same month the Emperor Joseph I died and the Archduke Charles became Charles VI, so that it now became obviously impossible for any English ministry to support his candidature for the Spanish crown. This had not been one of the original objects of the alliance of 1701, and when it was dropped an understanding with France became possible. In July 1711 Prior was sent to Paris to discuss preliminaries, and it is significant of the importance of trade in the policy of St John that the terms he was instructed to secure for England included many of purely commercial significance. Some dealt with the Newfoundland fisheries, others with the Mediterranean where it was asked that Gibraltar and Port Mahon should be ceded to England, and that English merchants should enjoy equally all trade privileges conceded by the Spanish government to their French rivals. It was also requested that the Asiento should be conceded to England. Torcy objected that "we asked no less than to be master of the Mediterranean and Spain, to possess ourselves of all the Indies, and to take away from France all that appertains to that crown in America".[7] But Prior only answered, "We are a trading nation and as such must secure our traffic." In August Prior returned to England, accompanied by Gaultier and Mesnager, and on October 8 the preliminaries—"Mat's peace" as they were called by the Whigs—were signed.[8]

In January 1712 the Peace Conference opened at Utrecht to conclude the definite treaties of peace and commerce between the combatants.[9] There was, however, some misgiving on the part of Louis XIV as to the reliability of the Spanish diplomats. Philip V was displeased with the preliminaries signed at London, and under Bergeyck's influence he was inclined to favour a private accommodation with Holland as being likely to result in better terms for Spain. In an attempt to prevent Spanish independence from wrecking the negotiations, Louis XIV prevailed on his grandson not to send his plenipotentiaries to Utrecht. The Maritime Powers refused to admit them till the general conditions concerning Spain had been arranged, and Bergeyck and Monteleon remained kicking their heels in Paris. The English and French plenipotentiaries meanwhile discussed the vitally important question of trade to the Indies. The English demanded real securities in the shape of actual ports. They also wished to be exempted from the tax of 15 per cent on goods from the Spanish Indies exported from Cadiz. In April the English demanded the right to choose the territory on the Plate River, which it was intended to allow them to use. The French negotiators pointed out that it had been particularly difficult to secure the concession of any territory from His Catholic Majesty, and that, if the English wished to increase their demands, this had better be done by direct negotiation with Madrid.[10] This suggestion pleased the English, who perhaps preferred to negotiate direct with Spain rather than with their ancient enemy, and in October 1712 Lord Lexington was sent to Madrid.[11]

The chief object of Lord Lexington's mission was to acquire the Asiento for English merchants[12] and, to facilitate this important negotiation, he was given the help of a commercial expert, Manual Manasses Gilligan.[13] Gilligan, who had been concerned in supplying negroes to the Portuguese Asientists, who was paid a pension by the King of Spain till his death, and whose correspondence with Oxford had disappeared as early as 1715, seems to have been a mysterious person, but he succeeded in negotiating a very successful Asiento contract.

Subsequent legal experts could point out that the English Asiento of 1713 was a marked improvement on the French one of 1701 or the one projected between England and Spain in 1707.[14] The outstanding features were the demand for territory on the Plate River where negroes might be rested after the long voyage, and the demand, new in the history of the Asiento, for permission to send one ship of 500 tons annually to the Spanish Indies to carry on a general trade. But in spite of the satisfactory character of the terms from the English point of view, little difficulty was experienced in obtaining Spanish consent. Gilligan made known his terms on December 25, 1712; in January 1713 the Spanish ministers in charge of the negotiation presented their report to the Catholic king, who instructed his plenipotentiaries to conclude the Asiento on the terms suggested by Mr Gilligan. The Asiento treaty between Queen Anne and Philip V was signed on March 26, 1713. On the next day was signed the preliminary Anglo-Spanish treaty of peace.[15]

§ 2

The preliminary treaty of commerce between the two crowns was less easy to negotiate, and a definite treaty of peace had been concluded at Utrecht[16] by the time Lexington managed to obtain some semblance of a preliminary treaty of commerce on July 13, 1713.[17] The task had not been made any easier by the prevailing interest of the Tory ministry in the trade to the Spanish Indies. Not content with securing a legal share in a part of Spain's colonial trade by the Asiento, they were keenly alert to increase and protect the indirect share of the English merchants in the general trade of the Spanish Indies that was carried on in the silver fleets and galleons that sailed on alternate years to Vera Cruz and Portobello. The merchants had shared the views of the minister, as is shown by the memorials in which they made known their griefs and the privileges which they hoped might be secured as the result of a victorious war.[18] In article 8 of the proposition of the factory of Cadiz they had suggested that English merchants might be allowed to embark "all sorts of goods and merchandise in and upon the Spanish ships that go and come to and from the West Indies...in their own names and for their own accounts, provided they are carried by and go to the consignation of Spaniards". In another paper called "Freedom and Security for the English trading to or in the Spanish Dominions" they had also asked that they might be allowed to "export the silver which comes from the West Indies, coined or uncoined...also the uncoined or bars of gold...which should be granted, because most of the silver and gold from the West Indies is the product of the manufactures and merchandise of other nations".

The ministry was also inconveniently interested in the illicit trade of British colonists with the Spanish Indies. Bolingbroke had declared that the French must be excluded from the West Indies. They "cannot establish at this time a wiser principle than that of curing the world of the jealousy which has been entertained of the designs of France, to let themselves in, not only to the Spanish trade, but the Spanish dominions too in the West Indies".[19] It was this interest in the clandestine trade to the Spanish American coast that prompted Lexington to put forward three impossible

demands in his memorial of July 1713.[20] The first was a request
that the English right to cut logwood on the Yucatan coast at
Campeachy and Honduras might be acknowledged by treaty.
The second contained in articles 2, 3 and 4 of the memorial was that
English ships found on the coasts of Spanish colonies should not be
seized unless they were in a port and actually trading, and in
support of this request it was stated that "some vessels belonging to
the British islands trading to others situate to the windward have
been obliged by reason of strong easterly winds that blow in those
seas, to sail to the next firm land or islands belonging to Spain upon
which account these ships and their loadings have been many times
seized and confiscated". The third request was that British subjects
from the lesser Antilles might be allowed to trade freely "to the
Spanish Caribee coasts, there to traffic, and bring from them all
manner of provisions which they produce, and this shall be understood to be from Paria or Trinidad to the River Unare or Piritu".
The reason alleged in support of this claim was that the British
colonies on the Lesser Antilles were often short of provisions, and
found it difficult to get supplies either from England, Jamaica or
the northern mainland colonies. Such demands could not but
displease the court of Spain, and all that Lexington could obtain
was that they should be incorporated in the text of the preliminary
commercial treaty concluded in July 1713. He had, however, the
mortification of seeing each request followed by a categorical refusal.

This was enough to justify Bolingbroke's angry comment that
the plenipotentiaries had sent "a lame, blind, misshapen monster
from Madrid instead of that fair offspring which was expected".[21]
In form the treaty certainly was misshapen and it seemed far more
of a preliminary negotiation than did the preliminary treaty of
peace. It took the form of twenty propositions with three additional
articles, and four articles concerning the American trade. Each
was followed by a Spanish reply, and those concerning the American
trade were not the only ones that were in the form of decisive
refusals. The requests made in articles 9, 10 and 14 that English
captains might take on board bullion in payment for goods sold
were refused as contrary to the laws of Spain, as was the proposal
made in the second additional article that English merchants might
be allowed to change the cargo of one ship into another in Spanish

ports, and the demand made in article 17 that the treaty concluded in 1700 with the town of Santander might be ratified. Article 13, which contained the complaint that Spanish Customs officers broke open boxes, and the request that merchandise should be examined only in the Customs House and in the presence of the merchants concerned, provoked the Spanish plenipotentiary Bedmar to suggest a counter proposition, but this conceded the essential privilege demanded by the merchants. The request made in article 7 that English merchants should not be forced to pay the duty of *milliones* on bad fish was met by the retort that the duty was paid only on the sale of the commodity, and that no merchants need sell bad fish. In the same way the complaint made in article 6 that the privilege of the most favoured nation, conceded by the commercial treaty of 1667, had not been observed, was answered by the assertion that the privilege had never been revoked, but that if Lexington could find cases of its infringement he might suggest a remedy. Two articles, 11 and 18, were specifically referred to the congress at Utrecht, since they raised the question of the right of English merchants to import African goods to Spain, and their right to elect and pay a *Juez Conservador*.

But on the whole the preliminary treaty had laid a safe foundation for English trade to Old Spain. By article 5 goods seized within six months of the outbreak of war were to be restored, and under article 16 debts to English merchants contracted before the war were to be paid. By article 20 the commercial treaty of 1667 was renewed, and by article 1 English merchants trading to Spain were not to pay heavier duties on export or import than were paid by native Spaniards or other foreigners, and any favourable reduction granted to another nation was to be granted also to England. Article 2 stipulated that a book of rates was to be compiled, and these were to hold good all over Spain. Bolingbroke had been impatient to end the negotiation,[22] and Lexington had admitted that he had not had enough time to do as well as he could have wished.[23] Early in 1713 both he and Gilligan had been ill for some months, and when they resumed negotiations the court had been so much less tractable that they had experienced the greatest difficulty in obtaining any sort of treaty.[24] Nevertheless a preliminary treaty had been obtained, and it could not justly be called a monster.

It was between the time when the preliminary treaty left Madrid and the ratifications of the definitive treaty were exchanged that the Anglo-Spanish commercial treaty changed into an instrument really injurious to English trade. The plenipotentiaries at Utrecht had little to decide, yet by abandoning the claim for a *Juez Conservador* they removed a valuable protector of the English merchants in Spain.[25] With regard to the import of African goods to Spain article 10 of the ratified commercial treaty upheld the right of English merchants to continue this branch of trade, and in so far nothing had been done of very serious detriment to the English trade. But when the treaty was ratified, it contained three additional explanatory articles which had the effect of doubling the duties payable on goods imported. It seems probable that Bolingbroke understood little of the technicalities of commerce, and that he relied on the judgment of Arthur Moore,[26] one of the Commissioners of Trade, who had begun life as a footman. Queen Anne was not interested in the niceties of trade regulations, and on "being given to understand that the three explanatory articles of the treaty of commerce with Spain were not detrimental to the trade of her subjects, she had consented to their being ratified with the treaty".[27] When the House of Lords examined the Commissioners for Trade they found that Arthur Moore had stood to gain 2000 *louis d'or* a year by the ratification of the explanatory articles.[28]

Hardly had the bells stopped ringing for the peace and the Te Deum for the acquisition of the Asiento been ended when the merchants discovered that there was something seriously wrong with both the treaty of commerce and the Asiento. When the trade with Old Spain was officially reopened, it did not recover as in 1697. At first the merchants suspected that the cause was French competition. Under Louis XIV manufactures had been developed in France, and during the twelve years of the war French merchants had enjoyed a virtual monopoly of the Spanish market. It was asserted that there was no market in Old Spain for English goods, for the country was at once overstocked with French goods and impoverished. One merchant pamphleteer wished that "Mercator and his friends (who supported the commercial treaty) saw the French cloth they have here; which if they did they would believe that the French could make cloth". That the commercial situation was really bad was shown by the fact that the export of bullion from Spain could only be maintained by English merchants paying for silver as if it were a commodity of merchandise, with bills of exchange. The contention that much bullion had been imported to England was explained away, partly by the fact that much of this had been bought, partly by the fact that some of it had been exported from Cadiz in a British man-of-war which had undertaken to carry the silver to Amsterdam on behalf of some Dutch merchants. The Lords of the Admiralty had not allowed the vessel to proceed on her voyage, and the money had been landed in England, but was no proof of a favourable trade balance. The conclusive evidence of the small volume of English trade with Old Spain was the fact that the exchange was against England. In Holland and Portugal when the trade balance was in England's favour so had been the exchange, "so until Mercator can show the exchange in Spain is under par of silver, I do assert and affirm, the balance of trade is against us".[29]

The evils of the commercial treaty of 1713 were of two kinds, one relating to tariffs, and the other to the civil rights of English merchants living in Spain. The first of the three additional articles had been supposed by the Tories to express the principle of a uniform light tariff. Unfortunately they did not realise that the rates existing at Cadiz and Port St Mary which had been selected to supersede the various tariffs in force in the other Spanish ports were the highest in the country. "The articles signed by the Bishop of Bristol say, the duties in Spain shall not exceed those in the reign of King Charles II, but the ratified articles have given up this rule." "Now Andalusia is to be the rule for these places and the reign of King Charles II, by the late treaty, is not to be the rule for Andalusia."[30] The standardisation of duties was not in practice beneficial to English merchants, who, in the past, had found it quite easy to secure individual exemptions from the farmer of taxes by means of a little bargaining and bribery.[31] Some merchants considered that the exemptions, or gratias, which they had enjoyed were theirs by right under the most favoured nation clause, and as a compensation for the fluctuations in the value of the Spanish dollar. Even though some realised that "it was not to be expected that such indulgence would be shown to them whenever a wise Prince came to be at the head of the Spanish affairs ", this only made it all the more necessary that the English commercial treaty should have made it quite clear what was the exact amount to be paid. The first of the additional articles in an attempt to unify the tariffs had only increased those payable in the ports of Biscay and the Mediterranean coast. The other two failed to put any limit to the amount that might be exacted in internal Customs duties. The "ratified articles oblige us to pay 10 per cent the first custom... and leaves us to pay his *alcabalas* and *cientos*". They leave "the Prince at liberty to make his *alcabalas* and *cientos* what he pleases,...but what they shall be hereafter King Philip only knows".[32] In fact the treaty had raised the duties payable by British merchants from 9 or 10 to 16 or 17 per cent.

One serious objection to the new duties was that "the new uniform 10 per cent duty would extend to the exportation of the products of the Spanish West Indies, especially to the dyes, cochineal and indigo, the duties on which had formerly been paid by the importer". This, as the merchants of the Turkey Company pointed out, would increase the charge of dyeing every cloth by 10*s*. at least.[33]

The danger of accepting the duties usual at Cadiz and Port St Mary as the basis of a uniform tariff for the whole of Spain had been pointed out by such an expert authority as Sir William Hodges. He had told the Commissioners for Trade, when they were considering the preliminary treaty of commerce in August 1713, that those duties were higher than any others in Spain, since other ports had privileges and so could afford to impose low duties. Sir William said expressly that "it would be a very great disadvantage to trade if the duties all over Spain were upon the same foot", since not only were the Andalusian duties very high, but no nation paid such heavy duties at Cadiz as did the English. He and Mr Mead suggested that, with regard to the Canaries, it would not be sufficient safeguard to say that the duties should be at the same rate as in the time of Charles II of Spain, but that 6 per cent should be laid down as the rate, and these two gentlemen together with Mr Doliffe and Mr Bowles and several other Spanish merchants gave the Commissioners for Trade detailed figures as to the amount of the duties in Andalusia, Aragon and Catalonia, Valencia and the Canaries. But Gilligan's influence was all in favour of the Cadiz duties, "he believed these gentlemen were under a mistake: for that all the English merchants at Cadiz and other parts of Spain (with whom both the Lord Lexington and he have frequently had occasion to correspond) agree that the duties at Cadiz and St Mary are lower than in other parts of Spain".[34] The opinion of Sir William Hodges and the other merchants trading to Spain was disregarded and the treaty, signed on December 9, 1713, and ratified on February 7, 1714, almost doubled the duties.

If the additional articles included in the ratification were injurious to English trade, the Bishop of Bristol's cession of one of the two points referred to the plenipotentiaries at Utrecht had an almost equally bad result. The expert commercial advisers to the Commissioners for Trade had stated positively that it was unnecessary to insist on the old privilege of electing and paying a *Juez Conservador*. When Lexington's preliminary treaty of commerce had been laid before the Commissioners for Trade for their criticism, three gentlemen experienced in trade had been desired to attend to give their opinion on the various articles. Mr James Doliffe, Mr John Mead and Sir William Hodges had accordingly attended, and with regard to the *Jueces Conservadores* the two latter gentlemen had said, "there was no need at all for them for the Governors of the ports are so powerful that Judge Conservadors can do nothing without their leave; that formerly they had one at Cadiz, but they kept him but two years, by reason that they found a more immediate dispatch of their business by applying either to the English Consuls, or to her Majesty's Ministers at the Court of Madrid". The only case in which they agreed that a *Juez Conservador* might be useful was in the Canaries, which were too far from Spain to allow of the British minister at Madrid being of any immediate help to the merchants. But when the trade was resumed in 1714 English merchants were soon complaining bitterly at the inconvenience of having no *Juez Conservador*. The privilege of electing and paying a *Juez Conservador* had not been esteemed in Cadiz, because

our Judge Conservador was always to be one of the graduated lawyers, too inferior a man to contend with so great a man as the Governor of Cadiz, who as the king's chief military and civil officer would hardly be restrained from entering the houses of our merchants. The cost and trouble of keeping him from doing this was so very great, that we rather chose to make the Governor of Cadiz a present of the same yearly salary, and then, though he was above accepting the title of the office, he was contented to act as our Judge Conservador.

The merchants clamoured loudly for the restoration of a privilege which had been ceded because the practice of the Cadiz factory had been misunderstood. The existence of a *Juez Conservador* was one of the safeguards of the export of bullion, and for this reason the merchants were eager that the office should be re-established. The judge would also protect English merchants from many petty abuses, for if it was known that he would try any case involving an English merchant, there was less likelihood that Englishmen would be forced to take onerous and tiresome public office, that their goods would be seized "for the necessary dispatch of the armadas", that guards would be put in their ships at the owners' expense, that proceedings would be brought against them for selling rotten fish, or that they would be subjected to religious persecution. It was found that even the concession of a *Juez Conservador* in the Canaries showed a tendency to limit the powers of that official to protect English merchants, since he was to have cognizance of cases only at the first instance. As the treaty stood there seemed very little hope that English merchants might recover their privilege, for although it was stipulated that they should do so if the right of electing a *Juez Conservador* were granted to anyone else, it was rumoured among the merchants that the French already enjoyed the substance of the privilege, and did not wish the form as, in that case, their advantage would have been shared with the English.

In May 1714 the commercial experts who, nine months before, had asserted that there was no need to retain a *Juez Conservador*, came before the Commissioners for Trade with advice as to what instructions should be given to the new ambassador for Spain.

In discourse these gentlemen desired that my Lord Bingley might have instructions to endeavour that conservadors may be appointed in Spain as formerly; for without it they could not pretend to trade there but with the utmost hazard both of their persons and estates, being for want of such an officer liable to the several courts and jurisdictions of that kingdom, and even to the inquisition itself.[35]

When the effect of the treaty came to be considered in Parliament, even the Tory character of the House was not enough to prevent some protests. The queen in her opening speech announced, "the ratifications of the treaties of peace and of commerce with Spain are exchanged, by which my subjects will have greater opportunities than ever to extend and improve their trade. Many advantages formerly enjoyed by connivance and procured by such methods as made a distinction between one British merchant and another, are now settled by treaty, and an equal rule is established." The Lords' address of thanks expressed "the greatest pleasure, and the utmost gratitude" for the news that the ratifications had been exchanged, but the Commons were less satisfied. Sir Peter King had suggested "that they ought not to act by a spirit of divination, and return thanks for the treaty of commerce with Spain before they knew whether it was advantageous or no", and the Commons' address finally took the form of a congratulation "on the conclusion of the treaties of peace and commerce with Spain whereby your Majesty is pleased to declare that you have procured new benefits to your subjects". In the debate in the Lords on April 16, 1714, on the treaties of peace and commerce with Spain, "the Whig lords being apprehensive that if any debate arose about the Spanish treaty the other party would propose an address to the Queen approving of that treaty, which they thought absurd, they therefore agreed to say nothing against the treaty that might lead them into a debate". Lord North and Grey tried in vain to elicit objections, but after he had finished speaking there was silence for a quarter of an hour. Lord Clarendon then proposed an address of thanks since "no objection can be raised against the Spanish treaty". This at last provoked a reply, and Lord Cowper declared that "this is the most barefaced attempt, that ever was made by this or any other ministry, to secure themselves, by endeavouring to get the sanction of this House". "I cannot remove my finger from the original cause of our misfortunes 'the cessation of arms'. We were then told that if a blow had been struck it would have ruined the peace. Would to God it had ruined this peace." The Whig lords' attack on the peace was vehement, but as yet they concentrated their criticism on the political treaty, and their only comment on the treaty of commerce was that "as for the pretended advantages...it was plain they were no more than what had been stipulated before by the treaty of 1667". As was natural the Commons were quicker to realise the evils of the commercial treaty. When the Lords invited the Lower House to concur in an address of thanks for the treaties, although the Tory majority agreed to do so, some eminent Whigs were in a dissentient minority. Mr Aislaibie spoke of "so precarious a peace", and Mr Ward—an eminent merchant—objected to the duties. By July the Lords gave the merchants trading to Spain an opportunity of expressing their grievances. In a debate on the commercial treaty with Spain Lord Nottingham showed that, because of the three additional articles regulating duties, "it was impossible for our merchants to carry on that trade without certain loss". In support of this statement Sir William Hodges and thirty more eminent merchants came before the House, and declared that "unless the explanations of these three articles were rescinded, they could not carry on their commerce without losing twenty or twenty-five per cent". The House demanded all the papers relating to the treaty, and the names of those persons who had advised the queen to sign it.[36] The Commissioners for Trade were examined, and opinion began to set in the direction of redrafting the treaty. When, with the death of Queen Anne, the Tories fell from power the Whigs carried this determination into action.

§3

But the merchants trading to Old Spain were not the only section of the commercial interest to be discontented and disillusioned after the conclusion of the treaties in 1713. The South Sea Company was finding the much-coveted Asiento by no means as profitable as they had expected.

The Asiento treaty of 1713 had not granted nearly as many privileges as merchants and ministers had hoped in 1711. The very name of the South Sea Company had become a mockery of unrealised hopes, for the general trade of the Company had been limited by article 10 of the Asiento treaty to those shores of Spanish America that are washed by the Atlantic. Under the treaty the

Company might trade in the Pacific with negroes, but this might only be done in ships hired there. No ship might sail round the Horn from England, or from one of the British colonies in the West Indies, and, in fact, the South Sea Company does not seem to have ever traded in the South Seas. This was not, however, the only unwelcome limitation of the merchants' ambitions.

Instead of having secured a right to carry on a general trade to all the ports of the Spanish Indies, they had obtained, by the additional article of the Asiento treaty, the right to send one ship of 500 tons each year to the port which was to be visited by the silver fleet or galleons. The ship might only trade in the port where the annual Spanish merchant fleet was doing business, and at the same time. Yet this slight concession had been thought an adequate equivalent for the English abandonment of the claim to an exemption from the 15 per cent export duties at Cadiz.[37]

The privilege of sending an annual ship had been thought by the Spaniards to be such a generous concession that they had stipulated that in return no illicit trade was to be carried on, but to many British merchants this seemed a very dangerous promise. Richard Harris, an African merchant, who provided the Commissioners for Trade with some valuable information concerning the Spanish trade,[38] put clearly the merchants' case with regard to the promise to abstain from illicit ventures:

'Tis a very great doubt whether that will not be interpreted to be a national agreement to extend to all His Majesty's subjects besides the South Sea Company who do carry on the logwood trade or other trade with the Spaniards called clandestine trade, and if so whether or not that being the condition of granting the licensed ships, the Spaniards will not take that advantage to make us comply with our agreement before they suffer us to dispose of their cargoes....[39]

The value of the illicit trade, and particularly of the logwood cutting, had been emphasised by Mr Harris in his "Plan for preventing a trade being carried on from France to the South Seas":

'Tis presumed that under the name of this clandestine trade is also understood our logwood trade, against which this proposal seems directly pointed which is so essentially necessary in dyeing our manufactures that it would be of the last and worst consequence to be deprived thereof —forasmuch as the Spaniards made us pay £100 per ton and upwards for it before we found it out and cut it ourselves which now costs us nothing but the fetching, employs a good number of ships and seamen and proves a great help in the balance of trade abroad...if dyeing becomes dear or difficult the manufactures do so too and our great rivals the French who have licences for fetching the commodity would thereby be enabled in all respects to outdo us in the colours of dyed goods...it seems rather absolutely necessary to support this pretended clandestine trade and our logwood cutters who are near 2,000 men by all necessary methods than on any account whatever to give it up.

The limitations and conditions hampering the trade of the annual ship were not the least of the disappointments that confronted the English Asientists when they knew the terms of the treaty concluded by Lexington. They were sadly disillusioned when they found that, instead of being allowed to carry on a general trade in English merchandise, the business of the Company was limited, like that of all its predecessors, to supplying negroes to the Spanish colonies. If the South Sea Company was to trade in any considerable quantities of English merchandise to the Spanish America, this would have to be by illicit means. Bolingbroke had said clearly that he considered the value of the Asiento to be that it could be used as a shield for such illicit trade:

> The French, the Dutch and other nations would claim the same indulgence, and would make the same use of it which we proposed to do, when we asked it. By this means they would insensibly let themselves into a direct trade with the Spanish West Indies in common with the queen's subjects. Whereas we shall have this advantage solely to ourselves, if we make a discreet use of the privileges obtained by the Asiento Contract, and if we constrain ourselves to concur with the Spaniards to debar others from making any alterations in the old laws and customs by which all nations are excluded from the Spanish West Indies.[40]

But the illicit trade carried on by the Company made it most unpopular with the British colonists of Jamaica, who had carried on a thriving illicit trade with the Spanish Indies before 1713. They had hoped that with the return of peace this illicit trade would flourish but, after the treaties had been concluded in Madrid and Utrecht, they found the ports in the Spanish Indies closed against them. *Guarda Costa* ships molested British trade,[41] and the South Sea Company, by establishing a depot at Jamaica, discouraged all illicit trade but its own. Before the new Asientists had had time to organise their trade and get it into some system, the Jamaicans sent home vehement complaints:

This island (is)...now likely to become the meanest of all your Majesty's colonies in America, since we have lost the benefits of sending dry goods, the manufactures of Great Britain, and the produce of your Majesty's northern colonies, as well as negroes to the subjects of Spain in America by the Asiento lately settled. We therefore humbly assure your Majesty that if an exclusive Company for the trade to Africa should prevail it must wholly discourage all persons from coming to settle in this island and put your Majesty's subjects now here upon thoughts of abandoning their estates and removing to some other places where they may labour for themselves and not for an exclusive Company...many years' experience under an African Company even before the Asiento was in the hands of the English has shown us that if they should be re-established we must certainly be ruined.[42]

§ 4

This then was the situation as it confronted the statesmen of 1714. The longed-for peace was little esteemed, and the trading privileges with which Bolingbroke had hoped to crown his negotiations at Utrecht caused active dissatisfaction among a large section of the trading population. The South Sea Company had not yet sent an annual ship, the illicit trade by way of Jamaica had declined, and even the trade to the Indies by way of Old Spain was crippled by high duties, while the trade for native Spanish products was equally unsatisfactory.

It is small wonder that the instructions given to the first English ambassador intended for Spain after the conclusion of the peace dealt principally with commercial privileges.[43] But Lord Bingley never went to Spain, for on August 17 Queen Anne died. With the accession of George I the Whigs, under Townshend and Walpole, replaced the Tories, and in turn were confronted with the problem of re-establishing the lucrative trade with Old Spain and the Spanish empire.

When the new Parliament met in March 1715 the House of Commons instituted an enquiry into the Spanish trade and the South Sea Company. The secret committee that undertook an enquiry into the negotiations that led up to the commercial treaty of 1713 sat under the chairmanship of Robert Walpole. It had some withering comments to make on the work of Gilligan, Lexington and Arthur Moore. It censured the preliminary proceedings by which valuable commercial privileges had been surrendered, and was of the opinion that the negotiations for the commercial treaty had been mismanaged. Concerning the three explanatory articles included in the English ratification the committee's comments were damning:

> For want of the papers which passed between them (Gilligan and Oxford) upon this subject, your committee is likewise at a loss to find what motives could induce the British ministry to admit so essential an alteration of the treaty of commerce, signed by the queen's pleni-potentiaries, as is made by the three explanatory articles, as they are called, which are added to the said treaty, and are, in unprecedented manner, inserted in the ratification of it; notwithstanding it doth not appear, they had ever been consented to, much less signed, by any of the queen's plenipotentiaries;...By whatever management these articles were ratified, and how legal and warrantable it was to affix the Great Seal to articles so pernicious in their contents, and so irregularly offered, your Committee must submit to the consideration of the House.

The House showed its opinion of the matter by impeaching Oxford.[44] But the trial was long delayed, and when it eventually took place the impeachment was dropped.[45]

In the meantime the Whig ministry, like the Tories before them, had prepared instructions for an ambassador to go to Spain and remedy the grievances of which the merchants complained.[46] It was in these instructions that there occurred a passage showing how important trade appeared to the Whig ministry of 1715:

> The preservation of the commerce between the kingdoms of Great Britain and Spain was one of the chief motives that induced our two royal predecessors to enter into the late, long, expensive war, and one of the principal benefits expected by our people from the conclusion of a peace after such a glorious and uninterrupted course of successes, and is of the greatest importance, to the interests of our subjects, and to the riches of our dominions.[47]

The much coveted Asiento was proving less profitable than had been expected, and statesmen and merchants turned their attention once more to the trade with Old Spain. Of this, two branches at this time occupied the attention of British statesmen. It was necessary to revive the mutually beneficial trade with Old Spain by which wool, oil, wine and fruits were exchanged for woollen cloth, fish and metal manufactures; it was also the wish of the ministry to revive the indirect trade with the Spanish Indies which had been carried on clandestinely through Seville.

To restore the trade to Old Spain it was necessary to restore the duties to the scale that had been in force at the end of the seventeenth century, and to recover the protection of a *Juez Conservador* in the ports frequented by British merchants.

To recover the share which English merchants had previously enjoyed in the trade to the Indies was less simple. It was first necessary to oust the French who, during the war, had been granted licences to send single ships to the Spanish Indies. "We are of opinion that while the French carry on a trade from France to the Spanish West Indies directly or indirectly the trade from Great Britain to Spain must be of no benefit to Great Britain...the greatest part of our commodities formerly sent to Cadiz being for the use of the Spanish West Indies from whence the trade is hereby removed to France."[48] The French trade was carried on by way of Cadiz, direct from France, or from the newly established French colony on Española.[49] An attempt had been made at Utrecht to check the trade carried on from France. By article 8 of the treaty of peace concluded with Spain on July 13, 1713, it had been stipulated that His Catholic Majesty should grant no trading privileges to the French, and in the treaty of peace concluded with the French on April 11, 1713, it had been agreed that His Most Christian Majesty would not "hereafter endeavour to obtain, or accept of any other usage of navigation and trade to Spain, and the Spanish Indies, than what was practised there in the reign of the late King Charles II of Spain, or that what shall likewise be fully given and granted, at the same time, to other nations and people concerned in trade". Yet in 1714 the French ambassador approached the English court with a suggestion that England and France might take joint measures to prevent the seizure in the Spanish Indies of ships belonging to their nationals which had sailed thither from European ports for the purpose of trading.[50] But the West Indies were still flooded with French goods, and French ships still sailed from Cadiz under licence. In the West Indies the French position was strong not only commercially but strategically. Española, being to windward, could command the trade of Jamaica, and the French colony of Louisiana could threaten the trade that passed homeward-bound for Europe through the Gulf of Florida. The sailing of French ships under licences could only be prevented if the Spanish colonial trade could be carried on as before by annual Spanish fleets trading on alternate years to Vera Cruz and Portobello.

During the war the sailing of the annual Spanish fleets had been interrupted, and one of the objects of British diplomacy after 1713 was to re-establish the Spanish colonial trade in its pre-war form. As the merchants trading to Spain had plainly informed the Commissioners for Trade early in 1715,

it would be more for the advantage of Old Spain to carry on their trade as formerly to their northern ports in the West Indies than to carry their goods directly to their ports in the South Sea, because the dispatch of their galleons was regulated upon their advices according to the consumption and demand of goods in those parts. Whereas the frequent supplies of goods now sent by the French glut their market and ruins their trade. Provided that the Spanish West India trade be carried on as formerly from Europe by Spaniards only, we presume we shall be on as good a footing as other nations.[51]

Some English commercial experts, like Richard Harris the African merchant who was consulted by the Commissioners for Trade, believed that the French were so securely possessed of the lion's share of the trade to the Spanish colonies that was carried on through Old Spain, that it was useless for the British to try to obtain advantageous conditions in that branch of trade. In his "Plan for preventing a trade...from France to the South Seas" he advocated instead that British statesmen should support the clandestine trade with the Spanish colonies that had been developed from Jamaica and the other British colonies in the West Indies:

By the articles of peace France is debarred from trading in the South Seas or otherwise than on the foot trade was carried on in the time of King Charles II; whereby it is meant the method of trade by the galleons and *flota* in which the English and other nations had their share. But there is no provision made to deter the English or all or any other nation from trading in the Spanish North Sea where it hath been carried on by most European nations during the time of King Charles II...and if measures were taken to prevent the English from trading in that manner, the consequence would be that the English traders with their estates, vessels and effects would remove to Curaçao under the Dutch or St Thomas's under the Danes, a free port to all nations, and carry on the same trade from there as they used to do from our colonies.

Another adviser of the Commissioners for Trade, Mr Bannister, gave the same advice, specially stressing the need to support the valuable logwood trade,[52] and the official representatives of the Island of Jamaica supported this advice with another complaint as to the evil state of that colony owing to the suppression of the illicit trade with the Spanish colonies. "Many of our sea-faring people have been and still are obliged for want of employ, to leave this island, and the vessels lie useless for want of men."[53]

The British government, however, preferred to concentrate on an attempt to restore the English trade with the Spanish Indies that had been carried on by way of Old Spain. When Paul Methuen was sent out to Spain as minister plenipotentiary in 1715, although his instructions did not contain any reference to the desirability of His Catholic Majesty's refusing to grant any more licenses to French trading vessels, he was ordered to make a special study of the state of Spanish feeling towards France, and to represent "that the ancient manner used by the Spaniards in their navigation to the West Indies seems to be the most advantageous to trade".[54] Methuen did succeed within two months in eliciting from the Spanish minister, Cardinal Giudice, a promise that the French trade in licensed ships should stop, but the English merchants reported that no change was noticeable in practice.[55]

With regard to the other branches of the English trade with Old Spain, Methuen at first made light of the alleged evils of the commercial treaty of 1713, but soon his tone changed to one of gloomy despondency. That British trade was seriously hampered was certain, but any alleviation of the merchants' grievances seemed impossible in the political atmosphere of 1715. The Spanish court was unfriendly towards the English who had supported the Austrian pretender for a dozen years of war, and this dislike had only been increased by the death of Queen Anne and the fall of the peace-making Tories. England was weak diplomatically because of the precarious hold of the Hanoverian dynasty on the throne. Spain was, moreover, supported by French influence in her determination not to suffer any alteration of the treaties concluded at Utrecht. When Methuen returned home in the autumn of 1715 he saw no hope of retrieving the blunders of 1713–14 but by beginning a fresh war.[56]

That Bubb was able to secure an eminently satisfactory treaty within six months of arriving in Spain was due principally to a change in the political situation. When Bubb went out, there did not seem much hope of his succeeding any better than the more experienced Paul Methuen. Orford had written to him: "I wish you good success in your negotiations, though by all I can learn, there is very little appearance of restoring that trade in the manner it formerly was. However, you will do the best you can."[57] Bubb did his best, he "threw himself into the coil with abundant energy...it may be doubted, in fact, if Spain ever housed a more truculent Englishman until George Borrow invaded it on behalf of the British and Foreign Bible Society".[58] He established a jovial correspondence with Lord Stair in Paris, with the commander of the Mediterranean squadron, the ponderously funny Governor of Gibraltar, and the despondent Governor of Minorca, and he entered with energy into the negotiations begun by Methuen with the Spanish court.[59]

All Bubb's energy and youthful enthusiasm would, however, have been of little use if changes had not been taking place in the political situation. At the beginning of his negotiation Bubb had acted in co-operation with the Dutch ambassador, Ripperda, and together they had pressed Cardinal Giudice for a favourable answer to the complaints of the merchants. But soon Bubb reported on Ripperda's authority that Alberoni, the Parmesan envoy, who had absolute control over the queen and whose only object was money, would procure the treaty for £9,000—that is 14,000 pistoles.[60] At first Stanhope, the Secretary of State in charge of the negotiation, demurred. The bribe was a large one, and Alberoni was not even an official minister of the crown of Spain. However, by October, Stanhope could report that "out of regard for the person for whom I have a singular respect having been personally acquainted with him some years ago" he had been able to persuade George I to grant him 10,000 pistoles. In a postscript Stanhope added, "I would not advise you to break off for 4,000 pistoles more."[61] Alberoni swept Giudice aside, and before the end of November

Bubb was in direct communication with him. Alberoni, and the new Queen of Spain whom he served, were both Italians interested in the recovery of the Spanish dominions in Italy that had been ceded in 1713, eager to recover the lands that had belonged to the queen's Farnese relations, and proud to save Italy from the government of the emperor. Spain was in a position to pursue such ambitions. Louis XIV was dead, and a sickly child had succeeded him. It was improbable that the French court could continue to exercise its predominating influence over the court at Madrid. Philip V was interested in warfare, and ready to follow the suggestions of his energetic consort. But if the Spanish court wished to oppose its late Austrian rival in Italy, it did not wish to find the emperor supported by British subsidies or a British fleet.

Alberoni wanted an Anglo-Spanish alliance or at least a friendly understanding, and he was ready to pay for this with commercial concessions. Late in September Ripperda had been summoned to court and had interviewed Alberoni. At first they had discussed questions concerning Holland, then Alberoni declared that Philip V wanted to live in amity with George I, and asked Ripperda if he would act as go-between to the English envoy. On October 11 Bubb was able to send home proposals for a commercial treaty that were so satisfactory that the British minister and commercial experts could think of little to add. The negotiations were not all easy, however, for there was a bitter conflict between Alberoni and Giudice, and what Bubb got from the king in the morning Giudice tried to get taken back at night. But the negotiations were quickly ended, and proved so satisfactory that almost the chief of Bubb's grievances was that the treaty was drafted in "the worst piece of Latin that ever appeared since the monks' time".[62]

The business was begun like a theatrical intrigue, and it finished in the same style. On the Spanish side it was difficult to find a suitable person who was ready to sign. Alberoni could not be thought of, as he had still no other position at the Spanish court than the envoy of the Duke of Parma. At last the Marquis of Bedmar, a suitable and charming person but without any political influence, was given the necessary power. At the time he was seriously ill so the signing of the treaty took place at his bedside.[63]

On December 14, 1715, the treaty of Madrid, or Doddington's treaty, was concluded,[64] and considering the youth and inexperience of the diplomat, and the fact that Secretary Stanhope had been too occupied with the Jacobite rising to criticise his efforts, its terms were eminently satisfactory. The Commissioners for Trade approved the treaty at once;[65] and the government esteemed it so highly that Bubb was made a plenipotentiary, and his salary raised by £3 a day.[66]

The chief result of the treaty of 1715 was that by its first article the Spanish duties were put back to what they had been in the time of Charles II of Spain. By article 5 the English were to be the most favoured nation and this in itself was a serious blow to French competition, and by article 4 it was also agreed that the English should pay no more in duties than did the native Spaniards. His Catholic Majesty's representative in the discussions had demanded a similar concession for Spanish merchants trading to England, but this Bubb had refused even to consider, and the refusal of reciprocity showed clearly the contrast between the trade of the two powers. Finally, by articles 6 and 7 the innovations in Spanish trade regulations and the obnoxious additional articles that had been included in the ratification of the commercial treaty of 1713 were abolished. Philip V had desired that someone might tell him what were the innovations said to have been made in Spanish trade, but Bubb had turned this aside by saying that to enumerate all the innovations it would be necessary to give the king lectures for two or three hours daily for six months.[67] Article 5 of the treaty restored the privilege of electing and paying a *Juez Conservador*.

Beyond the clauses protecting the English trade to Old Spain there were two other curious privileges. By article 2 the treaty concluded between the British merchants and the magistrates of Santander in 1700 was confirmed, though this may have been due to a slip on the part of Bubb. It was this article that was, thirty-five years later, to bring Anglo-Spanish negotiations almost to a standstill. A second curious concession was made in article 3 by which British subjects might gather salt in the Island of Tortudos, a West Indian privilege which at first sight seemed out of place in a treaty dealing primarily with the trade to Old Spain, but Doddington's treaty, as is shown by the Preamble, was also intended to make good the deficiencies of the peace treaty of 1713. In the autumn of 1713 the question of the English right to gather salt at Tortudos was attracting considerable attention.[68] The colonists of Massachusetts and the Sugar Islands, especially those of Barbadoes, had been much dismayed by the seizure, since the end of the war, of some English ships engaged in the salt trade. The agent of Massachusetts, Mr Dummer, presented a memorial to Bolingbroke. When he and several other gentlemen were summoned before the Commissioners for Trade, they declared "that they could prove that the English had gathered salt on the island of Tertuda without interruption for above 45 years past, and that they doubted not but they could find some old West Indian here in England that would be able to prove that we gathered salt there before the year 1667".

They added in discourse that, if the New England men were prohibited trading of salt there, it would be an unspeakable loss to them, for that then they should be obliged to buy it of the Dutch for the curing of their fish; that Barbadoes in particular would suffer very much by such prohibition, the people of that island getting all their salt from Tertuda; that all the islands being supplied with fish from New England for the food of their negroes, the said fish must be sold considerably dearer, if the New England men were obliged to buy their fish of the Dutch.

At a later interview it was again asserted "that if the Spaniards should continue to take our ships gathering salt there it would not only be of very great prejudice to our governments on the Continent, but entirely ruin...our sugar plantations, more especially... Barbadoes, for that the planters could not maintain and provide for their negroes without the salt mackerel and scale fish from New England". The right obtained by Bubb's treaty was, therefore, much esteemed, but it was not won without a struggle, and Bubb complained that this one point had caused him as much trouble as if he had been demanding a Spanish province.[69] From the Spanish point of view he was asking for a right which might be used to cover a great deal of illicit trade. It shows how eager Alberoni and the queen were to conciliate the British court, and how little they were interested in the Indies or in trade that they were prepared to grant the privilege Bubb asked.

§ 5

Bubb's success in repairing the mistakes of 1713 had been so complete that it would have been a pity not to take further advantage of the accommodating temper then prevailing at the Spanish court. Bubb even went so far in the spring of 1716 as to suggest to his chief that it would be wise to conclude an Anglo-Spanish alliance. He pointed out that the emperor would certainly provoke His Catholic Majesty in Italy, that it was not the interest of Great Britain to allow the emperor to become too strong, and that it was now possible for His Britannic Majesty to become the protector of Spain, thereby separating that country from France permanently. He also pointed out that as the result of a political alliance with Spain, English merchants would obtain better trade concessions than could be won by war, and that it might even be possible in this way to recover all the losses of the last four years. Commercially the idea was sound, but Stanhope turned it down because it was contrary to the essential aims of British diplomacy. He explained that such an alliance would revolutionise the diplomatic system of His Britannic Majesty's government, and that England was not prepared to risk war over Italy. In conclusion he added that English policy with regard to Spain had never aimed at more than commercial advantages.[70] Now that the question of the Succession had been settled, British statesmen thought that Spain had once more relapsed into the position of a second-class power. Stanhope reckoned without the energy and ambition of Elizabeth Farnese, and the reforming force of the French spirit which had come into Spain with the new dynasty. It was to put Spain on her feet and make her stagger through an energetic part in European politics for a hundred years at the call of Elizabeth Farnese and her son Charles. In 1716, however, British statesmen had not realised the strength of this new spirit that was beginning to animate Spain, and thought of her only as a valuable customer.

The new complacency of the Spanish court and the luck of the British plenipotentiary were only used, therefore, to remedy some deficiencies in the Asiento treaty of 1713.[71] That treaty had disappointed the hopes of the English merchants; it had also proved obscure, and difficult as an instrument regulating trade. When, therefore, Stanhope sent Bubb the ratification of the commercial treaty on January 9, 1716, he informed him that for a perfect peace to subsist between England and Spain it was necessary to settle the questions raised in executing the Asiento treaty. Shortly afterwards, in February 1716, Bubb received from the South Sea Company a memorial, which, like all the documents of that nature produced by the Company, was of prodigious length and great complexity. Bubb considered the Asiento treaty was "one of the worst I ever saw and most effectually calculated for captiousness and chicane", but he was ready to try to remove some of the inconveniences of which the directors of the Company complained. The difficulties which were chronicled in the Company's memorial were of two kinds, the most important concerned the annual ship, but there were also some disputes as to the date from which the Company was to pay duties to His Catholic Majesty. The Company complained that they had expected to begin their trade as from May 1, 1713, whereas this had not been permitted till the treaty of peace had been concluded. With regard to the annual ship the Company complained that in fact no ship had sailed in 1714 or 1715, that if a ship were despatched it might only sell its goods in the port to which the annual Spanish trading fleet was bound, and while the fair intended to provide a market for the merchants from Old Spain was actually in progress. During the first years after the peace, the Spanish trading fleets had not been re-established, and the South Sea Company directors were as eager to see Spanish colonial trade restored to its old methods as were the British merchants trading to Cadiz. In fact, the directors were so eager to see the trade of their annual ship securely established, that they informed Secretary Stanhope that they were prepared to put down two, three or even four thousand pistoles if the revision they wanted would be made easier by "a present well lodged". Stanhope informed Bubb secretly that he might pay Alberoni the same sum as had been exchanged during the negotiation of the commercial treaty, but Bubb demurred, "that way of negotiating being too ticklish for a man of my age and inexperience to engage in". He had begun to suspect that the 14,000 pistoles he had paid to ease the negotiation of the commercial treaty in 1715 might have been wasted. When in 1718 Stanhope hurried to Spain in an attempt to avert war, and had an interview with Alberoni, the cardinal said that he had been accused of having taken money to conclude the treaty but that this was untrue. Bubb certainly had never obtained any receipt, and it is possible that Ripperda found his office of go-between lucrative.

In 1716, Bubb was able to conclude a second successful treaty,[72] and on this occasion no English money was used to secure advantages. With regard to the duties it was decided by article 7 that the Company need pay them only as from 1714. The trade of the annual ship was made less uncertain, since by article 2 the Spanish government guaranteed to hold fairs regularly each year at Vera Cruz or at Cartagena and Portobello. By the same article it was laid down that if for any reason it was found impossible to hold these fairs the South Sea Company ship might sell its goods after a certain specified time. By article 3 the Spanish authorities were to inform the South Sea Company of the date when the annual Spanish trading fleet was to set sail. If it was not ready to sail by June the Company's annual ship might leave, and if the Spanish fleet had not arrived in the Indies after four months the South Sea Company's ship might sell its goods. To recompense the Company for the losses it had suffered by not having been able to send an annual ship to the Indies in 1714, 1715 or 1716, the lost 1500 tons were divided equally by article 8 of Bubb's Asiento treaty among the ten ships that were to sail between 1717 and 1726, each of which was to be of 650 instead of 500 tons burden. In this way the wishes of the Company were granted by the Asiento treaty of May 26, 1716, and Bubb was highly complimented for his second successful negotiation.[73]

§ 6

It seemed in 1716 as if British merchants were to enjoy their familiar trade with Old Spain and a certain amount of direct trade with the Spanish Indies. The privileges that English merchants had enjoyed in Old Spain before 1700 and which had been abandoned when the Tory negotiators obtained the Asiento, had been recovered in 1715, because of the changed political situation that had followed the rise of Elizabeth Farnese and Alberoni.

The acquisition of the Asiento did not, in fact, prove hurtful to English trade in Old Spain, but that trade did not flourish between 1713 and 1718. At first merchants had feared that this was because of the mistakes or dishonesty of the men responsible for the negotiation of the commercial treaty of 1713. The mistakes were rectified by Bubb's treaty of 1715, but still trade suffered many vexations, for the treaty of 1715 was not executed. In March 1716 Consul Herne at Alicante complained that "the late treaty as yet is not taken notice of or put in practice",[74] and Messrs Reynolds and Hervey, merchants of Bilbao, reported about the same time that, in the independent provinces of the north-west, "the articles of peace and commerce are disregarded by the natives of Bilbao in all such matters as they comprehend disagreeable to their particular interest, and by the great inequality of justice strangers are wronged, and impositions continued".[75] As late as 1718 Consul Russell at Cadiz reported that the Peace of Utrecht had never any solemn publication.[76] In Cadiz and Seville, as late as 1717, special war-time taxes had not been abolished.[77] Duties throughout Spain remained high. Consul Herne at Alicante declared at the end of 1717 "that instead of abating in our customs they raise them every day",[78] and in general, as Consul Russel complained, "the ministers interpret the Articles of Peace and observe them or not observe them as they please, and it's their conveniency and in conclusion we are in all respects on a worse foot than the trade was before the late war".[79] It was even suggested by several of the consuls that the new Spanish ministers, and especially Patiño, then beginning to make a name as a financial expert in his position as Intendant at Cadiz, wanted[80] to ruin the whole of English trade. From Cadiz Russell reported, "the plan they have laid and are practising to straighten the commerce upon all accounts, and the conveniencies the British trade enjoyed by the Spanish trade is reduced to less advantage than before the late war they enjoyed, and from the prospect I have of affairs I fear it will be every day worse".[81] Consul Blakeley at Alicante came to the same conclusion; no attempt was made to reduce the excessive duties, and fresh obstructions were put in the way of British merchants, "this with the continual vexations they give us (who live amongst them) makes it plain they have a further design".[82]

Several important branches of English trade to Spain suffered severely. The woollen manufactures were in no position to fight French competition, and Consul Blakeley at Alicante reported sadly, "they have already loaded our woollen goods with such excessive customs that hath rendered them almost unvendable, and as the merchants in England have for some years past found no profit in sending them, their consumption here is almost out of date". In 1718 there was a scare that the fish trade might be extinguished, for an order was sent to the Customs officials that in future they were to admit no commodities from the Indies in any but Spanish ships. It was feared that this might be aimed at the trade in salt fish—or Poor Jack—and although the Spanish Intendant believed "that Poor Jack will be excluded by said order, it not coming from the Indies, be that as it will, the other part of the order will cut off a great branch of our trade, and if the fish be included in the said order, we shall have nothing left to trade upon".[83]

Another indication of the disinclination of the Spanish government to encourage British trade was the determined attempt between 1713 and 1718 to diminish the powers of the British consuls.[84] During the seventeenth century the privileges of the consuls had been vague but considerable. They had assumed office either after having been elected by the factory, or having been nominated by His Britannic Majesty. In either case the consul had received a royal patent, and no one had questioned his right to serve as consul even if he were not of British nationality. Often the consul had been helped by a vice-consul, and in a ceremonious country like Spain it was found useful to have a subordinate to do routine business, such as visiting ships to inspect their papers, or helping British masters to pass their goods through the Customs. This assistant had been sometimes elected by the factory, as at Cadiz, and sometimes chosen by the consul, but in neither case had any formality been involved. The consul had usually presented his deputy to the local governor, and this reception had served as official sanction. When, in 1714, the British merchants returned to Spain, they found the formalities increased and the privileges greatly diminished. During the war the French consul at Cadiz had injudiciously extended his power in a way very repugnant to the Spaniards. When peace was restored, a vigorous attempt was made to limit the power of the foreign consuls.

In September 1714 and February 1716 orders were issued curtailing the foreign consuls' jurisdiction, so that at last they were empowered to act only as agents and solicitors. Another change which seemed far less irksome, but caused far greater protest, was that no consul might appoint a vice-consul unless he was empowered to do so by a special clause in the *cedula* of approbation issued to each consul in the name of the King of Spain. It was also laid down that vice-consuls must be formally approved by His Catholic Majesty, and that they must be native subjects of the king they served. This attempt to diminish the power of the foreign consuls remained a source of dispute till diplomatic relations between England and Spain were broken by war in 1718, and reappeared as an English grievance even as late as after the treaty of Seville in 1729.

Other molestations under which English trade to Old Spain suffered between 1713 and 1718, though not so serious as the failure to reduce the high customs, and the attempt to curb the powers of the consuls, were nevertheless very vexatious. In two ports in 1714 and 1716 large donations were demanded from the English factories,[85] and when the merchants of Cadiz refused to pay, soldiers were billeted in their houses, and notaries were forbidden to take their evidence. In Alicante a similar refusal was followed by the seizure and public sale of the merchants' effects, so that as Consul Herne wrote despairingly, "they do with us what they will". At Alicante Mr Merrett reported, in the spring of 1716, "the continual impositions we have daily put on us is incredible...and since our consul has been deprived of acting as such, our governor obliges the commanders to pay him more consulage than ever the consul received".[86] This consulage the governor continued to receive while the dispute over the consul's *cedula* of approbation went on. Embargoes were laid on foreign shipping whenever His Catholic Majesty needed transports, and at this period it was done with quite unnecessary harshness. At Alicante, "our Intendant embargoed two English ships" in August 1717, "and would have forced the captains to deposit as much money as was two months' pay, as a security...but said captains alleging they had no money to make such a deposit, were instantly sent to prison and after being maltreated some days to force them to give what they had not got, were freed".[87] Merchants and captains alike objected to the loss that would result from such embargoes, but with no effect. At the beginning of 1718 Consul Herne wrote, "they have laid a general embargo on all the coast of Spain, so that a full stop is put to our commerce, and when it will be over I cannot tell, but the worst of it is, they pretend to freight our ships at 3 dollars per ton per month when they formerly paid 4, and although some ships may afford to serve them so, yet our galley built ships cannot, but they will hear no such argument, but force them to go".[88] British consuls noticed these many interruptions to the trade with Old Spain, and feared that they had but one purpose, the total ruin of the English trade, which object they thought had been almost attained in spite of the commercial treaty of 1715.

The English trade to Old Spain would not necessarily have suffered because of the acquisition of the Asiento. The concentration of the Tories on obtaining this long-coveted means of carrying on a direct trade with the Spanish Indies had made them neglect to safeguard the trade with Old Spain, but the interest of the Asientists had combined with the energy of the wool, wine and fish merchants to correct the mistakes by the commercial treaty of 1715. If English trade to Old Spain was still in some danger after 1715, it was because political relations between Madrid and London were less cordial than Bubb and Alberoni would have wished, and this is equally true of the period after the restoration of peace in 1720. It was not till 1739 that the interests of the South Sea Company provoked a war which for nearly ten years paralysed the English trade with Old Spain; until then, and after the re-establishment of peace in 1748, Anglo-Spanish trade was a barometer registering changes in the atmosphere of diplomatic relations.

CHAPTER IV

"THAT UNWIELDY, UNTOWARD POINT OF THE WEST INDIES"

The Depredations Crisis, 1737–1739

In the autumn of 1737 began a crisis which, in spite of the efforts of English and Spanish statesmen, ended in 1739 with the outbreak of war between the two countries. The cause of the dispute was the seizure in the Caribbean of some British ships which were suspected by the Spanish authorities of having been engaged in illicit trade with the Spanish colonies, and since the illicit trade of the South Sea Company has become notorious, the Company has often been held responsible for the war. That the policy of the directors in 1738 was one of the chief causes of the failure of the efforts of British statesmen to maintain the peace is shown, by the reports of the Spanish minister, to have been perfectly true. In this case, as in the peace negotiations of 1713, the interests of those persons concerned in the direct trade with the Spanish Indies that could be carried on under the Asiento were found to conflict with those of the merchants who preferred to enjoy the benefits of indirect trade carried on through Cadiz, and with those who were concerned in the trade and the markets of Old Spain itself. But it was the financial policy of the South Sea directors, not the Company's illicit trade, which ruined the hopes of preserving the peace in 1738, and for the original outbreak of the crisis in 1737 the Asientists were very slightly if at all responsible.

§ 1

The importance of the illicit trade of the South Sea Company seems to have been considerably exaggerated. In the eighteenth century smuggling was a familiar feature of the trade of almost every country. With the introduction of tariff systems copied from

Colbert's model by inferior economists, smuggling became the only way in which natural economic forces could operate. In England wool went out and French brandies and laces came in; in Spain, Virginian tobacco went in and bullion came out "in spite of the laws", though "it is death to export it",[1] and at Cadiz there was even an organised corps of half-recognised smugglers. On the other side of the Atlantic the British colonists from the mainland smuggled sugar and rum from the French West Indies in spite of the Molasses Act and the fury of the British West Indian planters, both mainland and island colonists joined in the illicit trade to the Spanish islands for mules, and to the Spanish American mainland for bullion. The Spanish colonists were equally ready to take advantage of this contraband trade of their neighbours, or smuggle Chinese goods brought by the Acapulco galleon among themselves. In this atmosphere the fact that some private trade should have been carried on by the servants of the South Sea Company was not likely to cause serious international friction.

The attitude adopted by the Company was not such as to aggravate the offence. The Company hardly ever smuggled corporately or officially, for such flagrant misconduct could not have secured the approval of the general court of the Company's shareholders, or even that of the court of directors, for there the official representative of His Catholic Majesty was always in attendance. One of the Spanish representatives, the Chevalier d'Eon, had been bribed to connive at the mismeasurement of the two permission ships, allowed to sail to the Indies at the beginning of the Asiento under article 12 of the Asiento treaty as a special favour to Queen Anne, but this irregularity had not had the approval of the whole board of directors.[2] Officially the Company not only refrained from smuggling itself, but declared its intention of punishing any of its servants who might be found guilty of such an offence. The attitude throughout the service was simple, there was nothing immoral in private trade, but if goods were introduced which competed with those sold by the Company, or in such large quantities as to irritate the Spanish authorities, then the practice was evil. After 1735–6 the Spanish officials became more strict,[3] and the South Sea Company's Jamaican agents, who were responsible for sending the necessary supplies of negroes to the factories in the Spanish colonies, were at great pains to discourage the captains of the negro sloops from engaging in illicit trade. Until 1737 it had been usual for the same captain to trade regularly between Kingston and one particular Spanish port,[4] and that they all took advantage of this encouraging opportunity for illicit trade was shown by the angry outburst of Captain Fennel whose private cargo was seized at Vera Cruz in 1736 although "no vessel since the establishment of the Asiento had carried so small a quantity of provisions and liquors as he did".[5] In fact, the captains were all prepared to risk the dangers of private trade, and the factors were bitter against them for trying to smuggle in goods unknown both to agents and factors, and then applying to the factors for help if casks of blue paint were discovered under the ballast and the captain was in danger of being sent a prisoner to the *Casa de Contratación* in Old Spain.[6]

The Company's agents at Jamaica after 1736 took great care to prevent the captains of the negro sloops from being charged with smuggling. Merewether "always told our masters that if we found them concerned in dry goods to ever so little a value so that the Company's affairs by that means met with the least embarrassment they might depend on being employed no more".[7] On his return each captain was asked by one of the agents whether he had met with any embarrassment, and beyond this personal supervision the agents had devised a more formal scheme for preventing smuggling which, in view of the new strictness of the Spanish colonial officials, had become dangerous. "We have for some time past inserted in our certificates everything we have sent to the factors, and for what they have ordered for the chief of the Spaniards we have given our masters a liberty to take it on board by way of letter. By which means we on our part keep to the exact letter of the charter party, and keep the masters in awe."[8] The agents did not object to private trade as such, but they did not want to risk allowing the captains to carry this on at the discretion of their greed. They wanted to control the volume and nature of the trade, so as to cause as little disgust as possible to the directors in London and the Spanish officials. The attitude of the Jamaican agents is summarised in Merewether's statement, "The Masters are all kept in that awe, that they dare not bring even any money from the

Factors but to our consignement. . . . Where it is in our power we will know what is doing."[9]

The Company's agents in Jamaica were not, in fact, averse to making some profit themselves by way of private trade with the Spaniards, but they were careful to be discreet. Mr Pratter was said to have suggested a scheme to the Company by which several hundred pounds' worth of dry goods and provisions might be introduced into Havana under cover of fetching home some of the effects of the Company. The directors turned down the suggestion, but Pratter acted upon it, and a formal complaint was made against him by Don Thomas Geraldino, then representing the King of Spain on the Company's board of directors. This was "the third representation Sir Thomas has made against Mr Pratter for the like practices".[10] At that time the cellar of the Jamaican agents was "full of war and other proper goods for the Spaniards which had lain there some years", but on Merewether's advice these were shipped off at once to the owners. Pratter and Merewether had a share in 300 barrels of flour that were carried in the *Lyon*, but the captain, on this occasion, took on many more goods unknown to the agents. These were got from a Bristol store, and consisted chiefly of mercery, and had Merewether been consulted they still would have been sent for "the factors are never denied what they asked for themselves or for some top Spaniard".[11] But

Pratter knew nothing of any dry goods going in that ship, for his constant rule was, long before I was joined with him, not to be concerned in any dry goods himself, or to suffer more to go than what necessaries the factors wrote for on their own accounts, or to oblige some top Spaniard, and those goods were but mere trifles. Mr Pratter might be imposed upon for he was not apt to suspect, but when he found that any person dealt falsely with him, he seldom forgave them, his resentment proceeded more from prudence than passion.[12]

After Pratter's death Merewether continued to indulge in some private trade but always with discretion. He frankly informed the sub-governor, Burrell, and asked for his support. "150 barrels of flour...makes up the quantity of 200 barrels that I have been concerned in to any place since Mr Pratter's death. . . . This and a trifle of private money which we receive to forward home bounds the Agents' transgressions for which give me leave to ask your favour in case we should ever be attacked on this head",[13] and it was clear that he realised the dangers of too blatant a manner. "Neither shall Mr Manning or I be concerned in one barrel flour or any other sort of provisions in the ships we are now sending out. The times in prudence will not admit of it, the Spaniards...are too severe."[14]

The factors in the ports of the Spanish colonies were more dangerously reckless in this private trade, and sometimes provoked the Spanish local authorities to take action to suppress it, or the representative of His Catholic Majesty on the Company's board of directors to protest, but even so the illicit trade of the Company's factor did not lead to serious international friction. In some cases, the factors were even tolerated by the Spanish authorities, who were at times ready to use the Company's negro sloops to carry a few private commissions for themselves.

At Buenos Ayres the Spanish governor had a 25 per cent share in the factor's private trade. On one occasion the governor asked if a captain might bring a cargo of goods for him,[15] and at another time he was allowed by the factor to send a private cargo of hides to England, on one of the Company's ships, when he particularly wanted money to lay out at court to defeat his enemies. The chief cause of friction at Buenos Ayres, as in the other ports, was provided by captains of negro sloops or provision ships who tried to smuggle independently and on too large a scale, but although some of these suffered severely the Company's factor could report, "Had the ministers on the shore been of the same mind as the marine gentry...I am afraid poor Bennet and Fisher would have made a much worse figure than Dumaresq, but they really have been particularly indulgent."[16]

In other ports the relations between the Spanish officials and the Company's factors were less intimate and friendly. In Panama the Spanish authorities objected so strongly to the private trade carried on by one of the factors that the whole factory was expelled to Portobello.[17] In this particular case the contraband goods had been brought to Portobello in one of the Company's ships, carried across the Isthmus by a Spanish merchant engaged in the trade of the yearly galleons, and sold in the streets of Panama by factor Johnson's servant, so alienating the small pedlars as well as the large merchants. The case was scandalous, and aroused a great deal of opposition to the Company. Perhaps it was the most outrageous of any attempt at private trade made by one of the factors, but it could not serve as a pretext for seizing or searching British ships on the high seas. In general the factors' chief vice was not so much that they engaged in private trade as that they demanded bribes.

The illicit trade carried on by the supercargoes and other members of the crews of the annual ships made more noise because the Spanish merchants of the silver fleet or galleons were on the watch, and in any case the trade was more concentrated.

Some of the cases of this illicit trade were particularly striking. In 1725 the *Prince Frederick* sailed to Vera Cruz, accompanied by the negro sloop *Prince of Asturias* full of additional goods.[18] In 1730 the *Prince William*, on her way to Portobello, took in an extra cargo from the negro sloop *St James* to fill up the space left by the provisions and fuel which had been consumed on the voyage.[19] In 1725 the *Royal George*, on her way to Cartagena, endangered her safety by taking on board an extra 150 tons of goods at St Kitts. She was then so heavily laden that it would have been impossible to use her guns had she been attacked by a pirate.[20]

The Spanish ministers knew of the illicit trade of the Company, for at the Congress of Soissons the Spanish plenipotentiary had managed to bribe two of the Company's servants to make very full and quite damning revelations,[21] but such a well-informed expert on colonial and trade matters as Patiño had believed that the illicit traffic carried on under cover of the negro trade was greater than that carried on in the annual ships.[22] Even together with the legal trade of the Company the competition offered by the annual ships to the silver fleet or galleons was inconsiderable. The illicit trade was used as an excuse by the authorities in Old Spain to delay granting the necessary licences for the annual ships,[23] but the whole private trade carried on under the Asiento did not exasperate Spanish colonial governors as did that of the interlopers from the British and Dutch colonies in the West Indies.

§ 2

Against the Company Spanish coastal patrols could do little. That traffic between Jamaica and the ports of the Spanish American mainland or islands was legally permitted by treaty. Cargoes of Spanish money or fruits were also perfectly permissible on the return voyage, and if the negro sloops had been found to be carrying provisions or dry goods in addition to their ordinary cargoes on their outward voyages, these might have been for the use of the Company's factors or "to oblige some top Spaniard", in which case it would have been highly indiscreet for the captain of a Spanish coastguard ship to interfere. The private trade of the Company was usually carried on with considerable regard for the susceptibilities of the Spanish colonial authorities, whom the Company's servants were eager to conciliate; the trade of the interlopers was for the profit of the traders and the satisfaction of such of the Spanish colonists as wanted cheap goods at a time when neither silver fleet nor galleons was in the Indies. The interlopers had little consideration for the authorities of the Spanish colonies, and were often the bane of their lives. Complaints from the Governors of Havana, Cuba, Porto Rico and Santo Domingo all show that the illicit trade which provoked them to fit out guard ships was not that of the South Sea Company, but that of the British and Dutch interlopers.

Before this time the amount of contraband trade carried on by English and Dutch colonists with their Spanish neighbours had been considerable. Unlike the illicit trade with the French colonies, it was thought economically healthy and therefore encouraged by the British authorities. Between 1670 and 1700 this trade had developed in toleration. As Horace Walpole the elder explained the situation, "a strict friendship and union subsisted between the Crowns of Great Britain and Spain both in Europe and America, and a flourishing trade...between the English and Spanish plantations...was carried on to the great advantage of the nation...by connivance and indulgence on the part of Spain".[24] That there had been little Spanish opposition to this state of affairs is suggested by the fact that when in 1739 the Spanish royal archivist was ordered to find papers concerning prizes taken in American waters from 1670 to 1700 as a result of illicit trade in contravention of the

English treaty of 1670, he had to report that no such papers could be found. "I have examined the papers of the Archive with the greatest care and am unable to find any *expediente, despacho* or *consulta* dealing with the subject."[25]

During the war of 1702–13 British subjects had at first been forbidden to trade with the Spaniards,[26] and the Jamaicans had concentrated on prizing Spanish vessels. "The repeated success of the men-of-war and privateers during this war was incredible, not a day passed but prizes were brought in...the people of this island were intent on nothing so much as encouraging the privateers...the island became richer than it had been since the days of Morgan."[27] But even this brisk warfare did not entirely stop the trade with the Spanish colonies. In 1704 the prohibition against the trade was removed, and in 1708 a zone in which Spanish trading ships might not be attacked was created by Act of Parliament.

After the peace of 1713 and the acquisition of the Asiento for the South Sea Company, the Jamaican colonists complained bitterly that their trade with the Spanish colonies had been ruined. They said that the Company used six ships, whereas before 1713 the trade had employed twenty-five,[28] and that the Jamaican illicit trade in negroes was, in fact, ruined seems clear from the contempt for it shown by the South Sea Company agents:

> It is these cargoes which are not fit for the honourable Company or this island that give rise to the illicit trade, and some of these will be sent to the South Keys and Española. The consignees would choose to sell their negroes here, but as they cannot they are forced to send them out, and oft times to take part in them themselves to help forward the voyage so that the illicit trade hence to Cuba is founded on distress and necessity, and the voyages for the most part turn out accordingly.... The sloops in these voyages being liable to be taken are fitted out in a defensible and expensive manner...the private trade...had been on the decline for some years past, and is now at a very low ebb, so low that when I see a person entering largely into it I think him to be in no good way....At our past Quarter Sessions I was surprised to see a Jew one of the top supercargoes in the illicit trade for negroes, and dry goods, making application to be relieved in his taxes by reason of his poverty, and he had an allowance. It may happen that there may be a hit in the illicit trade, but it is like getting a great prize in a lottery.[29]

The agents for the South Sea Company pointed out that the Jamaicans were beaten in this trade by the Dutch "who employ persons fit for the business which the traders here do want",[30] and that "the reason why there is not so great an illicit trade as formerly is solely owing to the new and severe regulations of the Spaniards ".[31] It seemed, however, to the Spanish governors that the new and severe regulations had very little effect, and that even if the illicit trade in negroes had declined, the trade in provisions and dry goods carried on from Jamaica was still very considerable. As late as 1787 Florida Blanca could speak of Jamaica as a "terrible hangnail".[32]

The Spanish islands in the Caribbean suffered most continuously from the attentions of the contrabandists. The ports on the Spanish main, except in the less frequented places such as the peninsula of Yucatan or the windward coast, attracted foreign contrabandists less. The great ports of Vera Cruz, Portobello and Cartagena were certainly where most bullion was to be found, for it was collected there in readiness for the trading fleets that sailed each year from Old Spain,[33] but these ports were too public to suit the Dutch or British private traders. Even the coast between Vera Cruz and Cartagena was unsuitable for illicit trade, for there sailed the guard ships of the Indies, the Barlovento squadron maintained by the King of Spain.[34] Conditions in the Caribbean were far more favourable to the illicit traders. There the colonies of the various nations were so intermixed that it was easy to trade from one to another unnoticed.

Geography abetted the contrabandists, for the prevailing winds and currents made the normal trade routes from any of the foreign colonies in the Windward Islands either to the British colonies on the American mainland, or home to Europe, pass close to the great Spanish islands of Porto Rico, Española and Cuba. The prevailing winds were the North-East Trades which let a ship do the voyage from Barbadoes to Jamaica in a week, but made the return journey take three months, and for this reason even ships bound for the Windward Islands from Jamaica might prefer to sail westwards and northwards out of the Caribbean, and come back with the help of the south-westerly winds that prevailed off the Virginian coast. The usual course for most of the traffic of the Caribbean, whether British, French or Spanish, was to enter between two of the small Leeward Islands, or in the north between Cape St Nicholas and Cape de Cruz or perhaps the islands of Saona and

Mona. The return voyage was usually between Jamaica and the southern shores of Española and Cuba, turning north at Havana and passing through the Bahama Channel,[35] thus exposing Española and Cuba to a great deal of illicit trade.

After 1713 the successful retention of the Spanish throne by a Bourbon prince caused a change in the political situation in Europe, and introduced a reforming energy into Spain which produced a vigorous attempt in the Spanish Indies to check the activities of the foreign contrabandists. Jamaican merchants who had hoped that peace would allow them to resume their lucrative illicit trade with the Spanish islands were speedily disillusioned. As early as the beginning of 1714 the Governor of Bermuda complained, "The Spaniards from several of the ports here in the North Seas, arm out sloops with commissions to seize all English vessels in which they find any Spanish money, any salt, cacao or hides, for which reasons any vessels that trade in these ports, from port to port, are certainly prizes."[36] In the days of the buccaneers such conduct would have led to the issue of letters of marque, but by 1714 a new era in West Indian relations had begun, and the Commissioners for Trade gave it as their opinion that "the only and proper way for relief" would be by way of representation through the diplomatic channel.[37]

This was the beginning of a negotiation which was to be the despair of a succession of British diplomats throughout the eighteenth century. After the two wars between England and Spain which broke out in 1718 and 1727, disputes over prizes naturally increased, for merchants complained that their ships had been seized before hostilities had begun, or after they should have ended. Contentions over prizes delayed the conclusion of peace preliminaries in 1727,[38] and embittered Anglo-Spanish relations until as late as 1732.

From 1727 to 1728 was a time of mistrust and bad faith over the delayed execution of the peace preliminaries of 1727; 1730–1 was one of suspicion over the non-execution of the treaty of Seville, and in both periods British West Indian trade suffered. In the first it was harassed by "Spanish pirates with Commissions only from the Spanish Governors".[39] In the second the merchants of Jamaica presented a petition on the "melancholy prospect still of the

insecurity of our navigation, of loss of our trade in this island, that
without some speedy and effectual remedies this island...must
(by the continual losses, and difficulties of coming to and going
from it in safety) be reduced to the most deplorable condition".[40]
The only satisfaction that could be got from Spain took the form
of orders to restore ships unjustly prized, and in these the agents
sent out to the Spanish Indies to recover the merchants' effects had
little faith. "In these ports if you get 20 *cedulas* for the restitution,
the Spanish governors mind them no more than blank paper, and
will always put off such demands with evasive answers, and saying
there is no money in the King's Chest, so that the British merchants
may give up for ever any hopes of satisfaction...there will never
be restitution or satisfaction made in that Government (St Marta)
nor any other to the value of sixpence. Notwithstanding the peace
they threaten to fit out as much as ever."[41] Old prizes were not
restored, and new depredations were committed with dismal
regularity. As the British minister at Madrid said, "If it be
remarked that one of my letters to this Court is too like another,
I have nothing to say for myself but that if you strike the same
string you must expect the same sound."[42]

In the late summer of 1730, when the sugar trade was at its
busiest, the trade was so much molested that the Duke of Newcastle,
then Secretary of State for the Southern Department, took the
decisive step of ordering Admiral Stewart, the commander at the
West Indian Station, to make reprisals.[43] That a serious conflict
was averted was due to the wisdom of the admiral. He wrote:
"The losses the trade has met with that have come within my
knowledge since my being in these seas are so trifling that except
this vessel of Benson's I know of no other damage except two or
three vessels that have been plundered of bread and necessaries
which I am sorry should occasion all this clamour."[44] Stewart
did not make reprisals and the situation was eased by diplomatic
developments in Europe, which improved the relations between
England and Spain, and led to the curbing of the activities of the
guarda costas, or coast guard ships.

It is a curious indication of the character of the coast guard
system as it existed in the Spanish islands of the Caribbean, that
even in this period, 1720–32, when the Spanish governors were

encouraged by the court to check foreign contraband trade, the most famous of the *guarda costas* should have been such a man as Henriquez of Porto Rico. "The Grand Arch Villain", according to a report by one of the South Sea Company's factors,[45] began life as a slave, and later became a shoemaker. He betrayed a gentleman to the Inquisition, and so got money. With this he took to privateering; as the result of giving presents to the royal officials and even to His Catholic Majesty this mulatto ex-slave was given a gold medal and the title of Don. Thereafter he was known as Don Miguel Henriquez Cavallero de la Real Effigea, and he was also given the title of Capitan de Mar y de Guerra, y Armador de los Corsos de Puerto Rico.[46] "This infamous wretch from so mean a beginning has raised himself to be in effect King, at least more than the Governor of Porto Rico, for he that is called Governor there is obliged to be little better than a creature of Henriquez's... all such as are sent to that island have positive orders from His Catholic Majesty to protect and support the armaments of this accursed villain...the very President and *Audiencia* of Santo Domingo dare not contradict him they having suffered severely for it once, by one of their members (an *Oydor*) having had his nose cut off, and his face slashed by one of this fellow's dependents for having once determined a cause against him." [47]

Even though it was known to the Spanish colonial officials of the island that Henriquez had acted illegally in taking several merchant ships, "none of which was from among those that infested the shores of the island", and had divided the spoil among the captors without regard to the claims of the royal treasury, no attempt was made to punish him. The privateer had the protection of the Governor Mendizabal, and was actually encouraged by that official to make unjust prizes since the governor shared in the proceeds. In 1728 the governor even went so far as to issue privateering patents ordering the seizure of all British ships simply because of their nationality.[48]

In this particular instance the Governor Mendizabal was certainly out to make as great a private fortune as he could regardless of the effect of his conduct on international relations, and Henriquez may have been a desperado, but, unfortunately for the peace of the Caribbean, it was only such men who were prepared to undertake the risks of doing coast guard duty. Only off the coast of the

Spanish Main could the Spanish government afford to keep up a regular, official squadron to check illicit trade. In the islands the governors had to prevail on public-spirited or ambitious, adventurous men to fit out guard ships to sail with a patent from the governor to try to intercept and capture some of the foreign contrabandists. Too often the patents were taken out by men who were risking everything in the hope of taking a rich prize. In such cases, a man might even be his own guarantor and outfitter as well as captain, and in this case it was useless to demand damages and satisfaction from him if, after a ship had been condemned as a good prize in the Indies, this verdict was reversed on appeal to Old Spain. By then the prize money would have been shared out among officers and crew, and spent on wine and gambling. Such sailors of fortune were not so much interested in preserving the theoretical trade monopoly claimed by the merchants of Old Spain as in taking as many and as rich prizes as possible. The attitude of the lower-deck members of the crew was made clear when the South Sea Company factor at Cuba lodged a complaint against one of Henriquez's subordinates, Morales, for having taken a ship with negroes. When the crew learnt that they might only take ships engaged in illicit trade they ran away saying: "What, must we not take any vessel we can overcome, that is not Spanish? If this is the case our Captain is a villain, and we'll go a-privateering no more."[49] It was not surprising, therefore, that unjust seizures were numerous so long as relations between England and Spain were unfriendly.

After 1731, however, the Spanish authorities really made a determined effort to check these acts of violence. The second treaty of Vienna,[50] negotiated between the King of England and the Emperor, was a step towards executing the treaty of Seville, and after Don Carlos had sailed for the Italian duchies, accompanied by a British squadron,[51] the Spanish behaviour towards Great Britain in the West Indies became more friendly. In the spring of 1731 energetic steps were taken to suppress piracy as distinct from privateering. One pirate from Porto Rico was hanged, and Don Manuel Pintado, commander of the galleons that year trading to the Indies, was given orders to co-operate with Admiral Stewart to suppress piracy.[52] This commission Admiral Stewart showed no reluctance to execute, and on this occasion even went further than his instructions and "used my endeavours with His Majesty's ships under my command to hunt those vermin called *guarda costas* as common robbers".[53] A serious attempt was also made to prevent the coast guard ships from causing further disputes. Orders were sent to the Governors of Havana, Porto Rico, Santo Domingo and Trinidad to stop the depredations of the coast guards, and even illicit trade was to be no excuse for seizures.[54] In July 1731 the Governors of Porto Rico and Santo Domingo were recalled and charges were made against them.[55]

In February 1732 His Catholic Majesty particularly prohibited attacks on British trade,[56] and in July 1733 the privateering regulations were revised to make it more difficult for Spanish guard ships to prize innocent ships.[57] In future proper security was to be given either by the privateers or by their outfitters; all proofs of prize cases were to be sent by the governors to Old Spain, and the old regulation that prizes might be taken only to the port from which the captor had fitted out was reiterated.

In 1732 there was a hope that the dispute over the depredations might be ended by the commission set up under the treaty of Seville.[58] Claims dating back to the war of the Spanish Succession were examined, and long memorials were exchanged between the British and Spanish commissaries, but the British minister soon realised that the whole thing was solemnly preposterous. The secretary of the British Commission brought him "a bag full of claims" and Keene soon reported ruefully that he was

really blind with poring into old *autos*, one's understanding ought to suffer as well as one's eyesight in reading such stuff, besides the greatest part of them is imperfect, and I defy Doctors' Commons in the lump to comprehend them, and set them in a good light. They are the sweepings of old escritoires and counting houses, things that would never have seen sunshine if His Majesty's goodness and desire to satisfy his subjects had not paid the expense of the legalisation as it is called. In short never was there such a heap of mangled confusion, we shall be laughed at by our adversaries. For example, what man in his senses can ask for reparation for a quarter deck blown up in the defence of his ship in time of open war? Yet one Mr Chitty has done it in the most formal manner, and the support of this notable claim is an ill spelled letter from the Captain who gives an account of his having beat the privateer and got away from him, *ex pede Herculem*.[59]

The commission of Seville did not settle the conflicting claims of England and Spain before it gradually sank out of existence,[60] but for five years there were appreciably fewer disputes over depredations committed in the West Indies.

From 1733 to 1735 the Spanish officials in the Indies treated the British tolerantly, "that is during their joint war with France and Sardinia against the Emperor, they thought fit to manage us lest we might be provoked to declare for the Emperor". From 1735 to 1737 the temper in the West Indies was the same, though for a different reason. "As soon as a separate peace was concerted between the Emperor and France unknown to Spain, this latter crown in hopes that we might be brought into measures to disappoint it showed all imaginable regard for our trade in the West Indies." Horace Walpole the elder stated that "from 1734 to 1737 they made few or no captures upon us in America";[61] actually during that period Keene reclaimed twenty ships seized in the Caribbean.[62] In 1735 the Governor of the Leeward Islands wrote that "the Spaniards of Porto Rico have in a manner declared open war against the subjects of the King my Master".[63] But this seems to have been an exaggeration, and from the reports of the Spanish colonial governors it appears that most of the British ships seized at this time had been guilty of illicit trade. "There are...several reasons for considering them good prize. Most of them were taken at Santa Cruz laden with wood....The one laden with salt is also good prize, for this is a known product of Tortuguilla...and the collection of this salt is prohibited to other nations....The fifth prize was taken near the island of Culebra, and from the position of her boat it is to be thought that she had come to take in mules." Of another English ship the Governor of Porto Rico wrote in the same letter: "Even the English factor who defends every prize hotly gave up the *Friends' Adventure* when he saw the mules disembarked."[64]

During the period 1733–7 the unjustified depredations against British trade in the West Indies were considerably checked for political reasons, but the Spanish governors complained that they were then unable to defend their coasts against the contrabandists.

To check the excesses of the coast guards without discouraging men from the service was very difficult. To try to recover the value of a prize if the verdict condemning it were reversed on appeal was to ruin the privateer, and even if a governor limited his activity to restoring conscientiously every prize that seemed doubtful, and punishing the privateers concerned, he was likely to destroy his district's one defence against foreign contraband.

It was also very difficult to determine when a prize had been guilty of illicit trade or not. The privateering regulations which had been drawn up by the ministers in Old Spain since 1674 were excellent in theory.[65] By article 17 of the 1718 regulations any foreign ship met in a suspicious course was to be stopped, and her papers and cargo examined. If the cargo was of commodities which might have come from a Spanish colony, and were not satisfactorily explained by the papers, the ship was to be taken. Two of the crew were to be detained as witnesses and all the papers were to be sent to the port from which the privateer had originally sailed. There under article 5 of 1674 and article 1 of 1718 the case was to be tried. Unfortunately it was as difficult to decide what fruits proved illicit trade with the Spanish colonies as it was to decide what was a suspicious course. The English claimed that "Spanish dollars...are the only coin in all the West Indies", and that "There are many things which are growth of the Spanish plantations, that are likewise produced in those belonging to the English, such as logwood and other dyeing goods, as well as cocoa and almost everything besides silver."[66] In 1738 even the experts in Old Spain admitted that "they found matters were much altered since the signing of the Treaty in 1670 as we had now a permitted commerce to the Spanish possessions in America by the Asiento contract, and consequently neither the Spanish coin nor the fruits of their countries could pass as proofs for condemning an English vessel of having been guilty of illicit commerce".[67] In fact, the only course open to the Spanish colonial governors when the policy of the Spanish court forced them to deal gently with foreign contrabandists, was for them to discourage the coast guards from taking ships, which in a different political atmosphere would certainly have been declared good prize. This deterred men from fitting out as coast guards, and as a result foreign contraband throve.

During this period of enforced toleration of foreign contraband the Spanish colonial governors were bitter in their complaints that it was impossible to maintain enough privateers to protect their shores against the swarm of illicit traders. It had never been easy for the governors to persuade the Spanish colonists to fit out guard ships. Not only was the business expensive and dangerous, but most of the colonists were more ready to trade with the foreigners than to fight them. A Governor of Cuba reported that the colonists "complain bitterly of the financial burden of maintaining the guard ships, not that this is true but simply because they hamper the illicit trade".[68] When an earlier Governor of Cuba had tried to get some privateers to seize an English ship to get information "they all hid".[69]

From all the Spanish islands came complaints of the indifference of the Spanish colonists in the matter of preserving any defence against the foreign contrabandists:

Since I became Governor I have kept you informed of the state of the privateers—I told you the little enthusiasm which existed for the work, the lack of crews, ships and money to maintain it.... Dn Miguel Henriques, Capitan de Mar y de Guerra, was the only person who supported them, and he has now ceased to do so for he has suffered great losses until he is almost without resources.... Porto Rico... is the centre of many valuable trade routes, such as those of the Maracaibo Registers and the ships of the Guipuzcoa Company, therefore please help us by giving us a guard ship, or by helping us to maintain a couple of privateers to defend the island against illicit trade.[70]

The Governor of Cuba complained in 1730 that "this island is so poor that it cannot adequately protect its coasts against the illicit traders".[71] In 1737 his successor was still begging the Secretary for the Indies to give him some help to stem the tide of contraband. "This island is very convenient for catching illicit traders for they all go back to Europe by way of the Bahama Channel. A guard ship cruising from here to Mantanzas could do much to check this deeply rooted contraband trade.... There are numbers of ships that pass here with no legal cargo.... I work with all my might to eradicate the evil."[72]

When the governors did succeed in overcoming the colonists' selfish sympathy for the foreign contrabandists, and prevailed upon one or two of them to fit out a guard ship, it was in great danger of being taken by the English or Dutch. As the Governor of Porto Rico related in 1735:

The privateers of this island conform strictly with the instruction and subsequent orders as to the manner in which they are to cruize to check the illicit trade. If they exceed these limits I punish them. On February 17 of this year Dn Juan de Elola left this island with a patent signed by me. On March 12 and 15 he sent back five English ships, but these have not yet been condemned as good prize for Elola himself has been prevented from returning to port by an English man of war and two other English ships fully armed which began to cruize off this island to watch for him. Elola went to Maiaquez to refit, and Sr Gonzalez, who had originally fitted him out, sent a small ship thither with stores. This, on its coming out of Maiaquez, was seized, taken to S. Kitts, and condemned as a corsair. In May of this year an *aviso*...was attacked by an English ship, and only escaped because the Parla fort opened fire in her defence....The English minister objects because the corsair was too far away from this island, but the privateer must sail to windward to catch the illicit traders on their return voyage....Your Excellency will see that the Porto Rico privateers do not deserve the English complaints, rather do the English deserve our complaints for having armed themselves to cruize against our privateer, and for having actually seized an innocent Spanish ship, and the little one sent to help Elola refit.[73]

Other details of the violence of the foreign contrabandists were reported by the governor in another letter:

Since about June of last year our foreign neighbours have been very aggressive. The French took a corsair fitted out from Margarita by Dn Josef de Zunega. I, therefore, prevailed on Captain Andres Antonio Gonzalez of this port to fit out a privateer. He took a few prizes but as soon as this was known English ships from St. Kitts arrived in May of this year to look for him, not finding him they took a merchantman of this island, and I believe are still on the watch for Gonzalez.[74]

In March 1737 the Governor of Porto Rico wrote:

At Santo Domingo a Dutch merchantman seized a Spanish ship, imprisoned the crew in the hold and sank her. The English man of war, now off Aguada, is said to have caught the Spanish privateer fitted out from Santo Domingo to chase the Dutchman; and it is said that all the crew have been murdered, but of this I have no certain information. What is certain is that whatever privateer they do catch they treat with the greatest possible barbarity, though I have assured them that any ships brought in here and not proved good prize shall be restored, as I restored an English ship in November of last year. Although our privateers certainly do not restrict themselves to the limits prescribed by the royal instruction it is obvious that the foreigners hold them in such hatred that they almost compel our privateers to illegal practices.[75]

The foreign contrabandists were very bold in the way they carried on their illicit trade among the Spanish West Indian islands. Apart from the trade in provisions and dry goods they gathered prohibited salt from the island of Tortuguilla. "Sometimes as many as thirty ships are there at once in a convoy especially about the month of April. They make themselves masters of the island, and even set up clusters of huts." In the same despatch the Governor of Porto Rico added that the trade for mules was "very prevalent, and not a day passes without some foreign ship touching at a Spanish colony for these animals. So zealous are they to pursue this illicit trade that one mule ship burnt and destroyed a Spanish privateer from Margarita off Ponce in July 1732."[76]

This illicit trade may not have been so serious a menace as the logwood settlements on the peninsula of Yucatan, which had only been moved, not destroyed by an attack in 1716,[77] or the persistent though usually tactful contraband of the South Sea Company, but it did more to provoke the Spanish governors in the fourth decade of the eighteenth century. The logwood cuttings were far removed from any seat of Spanish authority, and the private trade of the servants of the South Sea Company was carried on so as to give as little offence as possible to the Spanish officials. On the contrary the contraband of the West Indian and mainland colonists with the large Spanish islands of the Caribbean was a perpetual source of intense annoyance to the governors. The moderate policy of the Spanish government since 1733 had only encouraged the contrabandists, and in March 1737 the sorely tried governor of Porto Rico wrote: "The foreigners have become very bold and never omit an occasion of insulting a Spanish ship."[78]

In desperation the governors prevailed on some of their colonists to fit out a few more privateers. In the course of 1737 these captured about a dozen English ships. Two years later, the dispute thus reopened led to war.

§ 3

At the end of 1737 when the new crisis over depredations in the West Indies began, relations between the courts of George II and Philip V were on the whole cordial. Great Britain had effectually helped to establish Don Carlos in Italy and had not joined in the

War of the Polish Succession. Even if this was not enough to make the two courts friendly, the Spanish court was so disgusted with the French court having concluded a separate peace in 1735 that it was prepared to cultivate the friendship of Great Britain.

The course of British trade in Old Spain had reflected the increased friendship between the two courts. During the period between the end of the war in 1727 and the establishment of Don Carlos in his "expectatives" in 1731, British merchants trading to Old Spain had suffered continuous molestation. Even after the conclusion of the treaty of Seville in 1729, the privileges granted to the British merchants by the commercial treaties of 1667 and 1715 were not observed. The consul at Alicante expressed the views of British merchants all over Spain, when he said as late as 1730, "hitherto we are in these parts in all respects as before the peace under great impositions of exorbitant duties and taxes and go increasing them upon us".[79] The dispute over consular privileges raged until 1731.[80] The trade of foreign merchants had been twice forcibly inspected, once at Alicante in 1727, when a judge was sent by Patiño to investigate Customs frauds, and again at Malaga in 1732 when search was made for prohibited printed calicoes.[81] The quarantine set up from 1728 to 1730 because of an outbreak of plague in the Morea was administered so as to provoke bitter complaints such as had not been made over the quarantine of 1721, when political relations between Great Britain and Spain had been more cordial. Merchants complained that the health regulations were made an excuse for exactions, and that plague in Turkey was made a pretext for detaining ships from Cork till their cargoes of Irish butter went rancid in the July heat at Cadiz. The quarantine was even used to oppress British merchants, while French merchants did not suffer. Fish from England or Newfoundland, or wax and copper from Africa, were detained or denied entrance, while such highly infectious cargoes as cotton from Malta, or even from the Levant, were admitted.[82] British merchants had also suffered from having their ships embargoed to provide transport for His Catholic Majesty's soldiers to Italy or Africa. In 1730 this evil had been chronic. Ships were even delayed because the crews had been pressed into the service of the King of Spain,[83] though such action was expressly contrary to the treaty of 1667.

After 1732, however, the number of complaints had declined. The question of the consuls' privileges had not been settled, but it gave no further cause for friction for some years. The quarantine had ended and, with the end of a vigorous Spanish policy abroad, the cause of the embargoes was removed. In 1732 there was an alarm over a proposal to establish a Spanish Philippine Company,[84] but this did not constitute a real danger. As Keene said, there was no real cause for jealousy of a Spanish Company and "the want of faith and credit will do more to make it miscarry than Mr van Hoey, van der Meer or I together".[85]

The one serious commercial cause of friction between Great Britain and Spain during the period 1732 to 1737 was the question of the tobacco duties. "The tobacco rent is one of the best branches of the Spanish revenue", and it was natural that the reforming ministers of the new Bourbon king should extend the high Castilian duties to all the ports of Spain. It was also natural that they should take energetic measures to prevent any attempt to evade these duties by way of contraband. Foreign ships carrying tobacco, as for instance British ships from Virginia, were liable to be seized even if they only put into a Spanish port on their way to another country. The complaints of the merchants increased when, late in 1731, the tobacco guards claimed to search small ships, for though this would molest the French more than the British it would interfere with the small craft of Port Mahon and Gibraltar.

Between 1733 and 1736, however, even the attempts to stop illicit trade in tobacco gave few occasions for complaint. In 1733 there was a struggle between a British warship and the tobacco guards at Cadiz, and two of the guards were killed, and in 1736 the consul at Corunna grew angry at the seizure of one of the crew of a British packet boat, and declared that "an article of peace is esteemed here as a thing made more for ceremony than for observance".[86] But neither event led to a crisis.

The dispute did not become serious until 1737, when Torrenueva, who had been for many years at the head of the *junta* for tobacco rent, became Minister of Finance, just when political relations between the two courts became less cordial.

In 1737 several other commercial grievances developed. The old question of the safety of the Moors travelling in British ships was revived.[87] "The pernicious practice of the Irish officers in the service of this Crown in debauching our sailors and engaging them to enlist themselves into their regiments"[88] also caused considerable annoyance. The dispute over the consular privileges was renewed, and threatened to end so badly that one consul lamented, "No vessels that put into any of the ports of this coast can expect to meet with anything but bad usage since it has been made a crime for any person to take their part or assist them though it be under the appellation of friend or acquaintance."[89]

Towards the end of 1738 there was a danger that the clandestine export of bullion might be investigated in connection with the exceptionally flagrant smuggling from the last *flota*. A judge was sent to Cadiz to enquire into this smuggling, and it was announced that he intended to examine not only Spaniards, but also foreign merchants. In serious alarm the consul wrote, "If the Court of Spain once insist upon entering into disquisition of this kind, and molest the commerce in the point of exportation of the species of the kingdom...they may as well prohibit all further trade from abroad, and order every foreign merchant out of their country, since without that exportation either permitted or connived at, no trade can be carried on with them."[90]

Late in 1737 all foreign trade was seriously molested by the imposition of a new duty "for the better support of the Infant Don Philip in the office of Grand Admiral of the naval forces of this Kingdom". The duty oppressed the British carrying trade, and although in the spring of 1738 it was finally conceded that the tax need only be paid once, and then only by ships that actually traded in the port,[91] by then the fear of impending war had made the merchants reluctant to engage in the trade.

The molestations of trade that became more frequent after 1737 do not seem to have been made, however, with the object of goading Great Britain into war, for at this time the Spanish court and ministry were pacific, and in their treatment of the depredations crisis showed a surprising degree of friendliness and patience.

§ 4

In 1737 the Spanish monarchy was too weak to be aggressive, and until the end of the depredations crisis the Spanish ministers tried as hard as Sir Robert Walpole to avert war. At this period neither Philip V nor Elizabeth Farnese was as bellicose as in the earlier part of their reign. The king was momentarily recovered from his hypochondriac melancholia with its absurd and disgusting details, but he was indolent concerning state affairs, and the British minister believed "that he was frequently incapable of giving attention to them". The queen was as alert and ambitious as ever in spite of her greatly increased weight, which kept her almost always indoors; but she was not interested in colonial affairs, and most of her attention was now devoted to preparing concerts to be performed by the Infantes to divert their father. In May the British minister had remarked that "everything here is in perfect inaction",[92] and this atmosphere of calm had continued into the autumn.

Neither the favourites of the king and queen, nor the ministers were such persons as to disturb this peace.[93] Scotti, who controlled the privy purse, was "a man of as bad morals as parts, of neither common sense nor common honesty". The Marquesa de las Nievas was an "ill-natured old Spanish woman, who brought nothing good from Paris but a hatred of the French", and the character of these favourites was summed up in the British envoy's criticism of their companion Cervi who "has nothing at heart but his interest, and does no good nor hurt to any foreign power". These were not likely to inflame the king's passion for military glory or rouse the queen's momentarily quiet ambition.

In such a court the ministers had a great opportunity to influence policy, and in 1737 the ministry's aim was to keep the peace. Patiño had died before he could enjoy a period of peace long enough to allow him to effect administrative reforms in the departments of the Marine, Indies and the Treasury,[94] but his successors were equally eager to avoid war, though for different reasons. La Quadra, who had become chief minister on Patiño's death in 1736, was "an honest, timid, indolent man, who being diffident of his own force did not solicit his employment and now he is in it does not take upon himself the least imaginable without positive orders". Torrenueva, the Minister for Marine, was "a weak, embarrassed timid man, without any bad or good intentions towards us, but not having much experience in affairs of the Indies is led away by those he consults",[95] particularly Quintana, "the enemy of all strangers" with "his head full of Spanish smoke" and than whom "a more difficult, tenacious, disputable antagonist never was met with, starting and stumbling at the most trivial punctilios imaginable".[96] But Quintana was not likely to exert too great an influence over Torrenueva, for that minister's own "interest requires in a particular manner that he should avoid a rupture between the two Crowns, for if he has so much pains to keep himself in place under the difficulty he meets with to furnish money when he is in peace it will be impossible for him to hold it if we should cut off his communications with the Indies".[97] Even the Conde de Montijo, the one minister of heat,[98] who had proved troublesome as ambassador in England from 1732 to 1735, and who had recently become President of the *Consejo de Indias*, seemed no longer animated by a dislike of England. When the crisis over the depredations had developed Keene described him as "the most reasonable and most instructed person I meet with". In short, the experienced and judicious Keene was of the opinion that

it is hardly to be conceived that a country destitute as this is at present of foreign friends and alliances, deranged in its finances, whose army is in a bad condition, its navy in a worse if possible, without any minister of heat (unless Montijo should get the reins into his hands), to push their Catholic Majesties on to any extravagant enterprise, or of capacity enough to re-establish their affairs, I say, it is hardly to be conceived that such a country, in these circumstances, can have any premeditated design to fall out with us at present.[99]

Keene's opinion as to the pacific character of the Spanish court and ministers in 1737 was proved correct by the fact that, in answer to the British minister's memorials complaining of the unjust seizure of British ships in the West Indies,[100] La Quadra went "a step farther than ever this Court yet took towards discouraging and chastizing the fomentors and authors of such unjust and cruel practices",[101] and within seven months of the first complaint gave one of the most conciliatory answers ever known in the long negotiations over depredations.[102]

The details concerning the ships that caused the crisis of 1737 suggest that the Spanish authorities were not only lenient in their treatment of the British claims, but that they were more injured than the clamorous English merchants. Five ships seem to have been captured by pirates,[103] for no trace seems to remain of them among the papers of the Spanish colonial governors. Two of these ships caused the complaints that began the crisis when, in July 1737, the governor of the Leeward Islands wrote to the Commissioners for Trade and Plantations that "the Spaniards have begun again their depredations and cruelties within this Government from Porto Rico", and reported that the *Hopewell* and a Bristol ship had been taken to that island.[104] In a memorial of October 30, 1737, Keene reclaimed these ships, but in answer to the Spanish minister's enquiries concerning these ships and two others, the *Fanny* and a Nevis ship which had been reclaimed by Keene in April 1737,[105] the governor of Porto Rico replied, "At the time of the seizures no Spanish privateer was out of this port, nor have the prizes been brought in here. The Spanish brigantine must have armed at St Marta, Cumana or Caracas."[106] Yet there seems to be no trace of the autos concerning these ships among the papers of those districts. Three ships, though they had been stopped and plundered on the high seas, had escaped. In his memorial of December 10, 1737, Keene included a demand for compensation for this molestation of the *Sea Horse*, *Neptune*, and *Caesar*, but they had not been actually prized.

Six ships might be justly supposed to have been guilty of illicit trade. La Quadra informed Keene in a paper of December 19, 1737,[107] that the ship of Captain Hinslow, which had been reclaimed by Keene on October 30, had been declared good prize in the Indies. In a letter of May 26, 1738, La Quadra stated that the captain of the *George*, reclaimed by Keene on December 10, 1737, had had 400 Mexican dollars hidden in a barrel of *bacalao*, had thrown some of his cargo, probably cocoa, into the sea before the Spanish guard ship could come up with him, and was provided with licences from Jamaica which allowed him to trade to ports in that island, but did not permit him to go out of sight of the coast. In a letter of the same date La Quadra informed Keene that the *Prince William* had carried a cargo of brasiletto wood, of which there was no mention in the captain's clearance certificate from St Kitts, and the *Consejo de Indias*, at least, believed that it had been obtained from the Spanish instead of from Providence. The *Dispatch* and *Loyal Charles*, which had been reclaimed by Keene on December 10, 1737, had had cargoes of dye wood and papers which did not satisfy the Governor of Cuba. The *St James*, reclaimed by Keene on November 8, 1737, had been taken close to the shore of Porto Rico, and the captain and crew had fled in the long-boat.

The Spanish ministry showed their honest desire to maintain peace by returning conciliatory answers in every case, and by not upholding a single condemnation. Concerning the five ships which presumably had been taken by pirates, nothing could be done except to make investigations, though as La Quadra informed Keene in his letter of December 19, 1737, the governor of Porto Rico would be punished. The three ships that had only been attacked but not captured were also difficult cases, as here again the Spanish authorities had no news of the molestations, and in his answer of February 21, 1738, La Quadra could only promise to investigate. But in the case of the *St James*, which had really been taken to Porto Rico, and the four ships that had been prized at Cuba, the vessels were actually in the possession of His Catholic Majesty, and the Spanish ministers took special care to make their treatment of these vessels exemplary. As La Quadra informed Keene in his answer of December 19, 1737, orders were given that the value of the *St James* should be restored, and the governor of Porto Rico fined. In his answer of May 26, 1738, La Quadra stated that the *Loyal Charles* and *Dispatch* were to be restored, and the privateer who took them was to be punished, as they had been seized too far from the Spanish coast, and their cargoes of dye wood appeared to have been taken in at Jamaica. The reason for this revocation of the original condemnation of the ships as good prize at Cuba is given in the *consulta* of the *Consejo de Indias*, which explained that "even if some suspicion of illicit trade remain, the prevention of illicit trade should never make Spanish officials lose sight of the need for good harmony with the other powers of Europe".[108] The *Prince William* was also to be restored, although the proof of the captain's illicit trade had been so strong that the *Consejo de Indias* had not been prepared to accept responsibility for revoking the original sentence in the Indies, and had referred the case to His Catholic Majesty who, La Quadra told Keene on May 26, 1738, "as a proof that the king's justice can give way to favour, when the latter may be bestowed without offending the former", declared that the ship had been illegally prized. Even in such clear cases of illicit trade as those of Captain Hinslow's ship and the *George*, La Quadra could inform Keene on December 19, 1737, and May 26, 1738, that it was decided that if the captain chose to appeal the cases should be heard.

Most unfortunately for the cause of peace the conciliatory answer concerning the four ships taken to Cuba was only given to Keene on May 26, 1738, five months after his serious complaints about the seizures on December 10, 1737. In the interval British indignation had been rising, and Keene had been instructed to support his complaints of October 30, November 8, and December 10 by laying before His Catholic Majesty details of all cases of West Indian depredations for which no satisfaction had been obtained. On February 28, 1738, Keene presented a memorial of the ships for which satisfaction had been ordered by His Catholic Majesty, but had never been obtained by the owners. These were seven in all: the *Anne Galley* taken in 1731, the *Woolball* taken in 1732, the *Hopewell*, the *Mary*, the *Three Sisters* all taken in 1733, and two other ships. On March 1, 1738, Keene produced another memorial, this time of ships concerning which His Catholic Majesty had never given an answer to his memorials. The British minister mentioned nine such cases specifically together with five others which were reclaimed by Captain Wimble. The ships were the *Endeavour* taken in 1724, the *Richmond* 1728, the *Robert* 1729, the *Pheasant* 1730, the *Prince William*, Captain Ivy, 1731, the *Friends' Adventure* and the *Thomas* both taken in 1734, a ship commanded by Captain Adams, and a brig from Bermuda.

It was more difficult for the Spanish authorities to offer any effective satisfaction concerning the old depredations for which satisfaction had been ordered but never obtained. La Quadra could only say in his answer of May 26, 1738, that the relevant papers had been destroyed in the palace fire, but that His Catholic Majesty had repeated his orders for the restoration of the value of the ships. Only in the case of the *Woolball* La Quadra showed no disposition to be helpful. In his answer of May 26, 1738, he said that this ship had not been restored only because the owners had refused to accept it. They had made frequent voyages to the Spanish Indies under the pretext of negotiating the recovery, but in fact to carry on illicit trade.

Concerning the old depredations for which no satisfactory answer had even been received, the Spanish ministers were again able to offer very little practical comfort. La Quadra stated in his answer of May 26, 1738, that the five sloops reclaimed by Captain Wimble had all been taken in time of war, two during the war of 1727–8, and three in the war of 1718–20, so any satisfaction for them was out of the question. The *Pheasant*, La Quadra stated in his answer of May 26, 1738, had been reclaimed before the commission of 1732, when it had been decided that no judgment could be given until more proofs were submitted. This had not been done by Keene in his memorial of March 1, 1738, and there seemed no proof that the Spanish court had ever been asked to request the Governor of Porto Rico for any papers that he might have, so again there was nothing that could be offered to the owner of the ship. In all the other cases La Quadra asserted, in his answer of May 26, 1738, that the Spanish ministers found the proofs insufficient, and had written to the governors of the Spanish colonies, where the prizes had been condemned, for papers, although one case at least was suspicious, since it was asserted that the ship —the *Richmond*—had been taken in 1730, yet she had not been reclaimed before the commission of 1732 nor was there any reference to an office passed by the British minister. In the circumstances the Spanish ministers could do no more. They could not give judgment on inadequate evidence, and to have offered compensation from a wish to preserve peace, irrespective of the rights of the case, would have involved a heavy expenditure for His Catholic Majesty's treasury, since even if the ships had really been condemned as good prize in the Spanish Indies, all the money had been distributed and spent long ago. In fact the Spanish ministers had been practically helpful and unusually generous with regard to the prizes recently made, and still actually in the possession of the Spanish officials in the Indies. They could do nothing, however, to allay British annoyance over the majority of the cases of depredations which had been produced during the course of the dispute. Public opinion in England grew steadily more angry.

It is curious to observe that among the prizes reclaimed by Keene during this crisis there is no mention of the *Rebecca*, whose captain's ear gave its name to the war to which the crisis led. The *Rebecca* had been stopped and plundered of clothes, bedding, candles and mathematical instruments as long ago as 1731.[109] Keene had represented against the unlawful proceeding, and the Spanish minister had replied that the Governor of Havana had been sent orders to try to identify the pirates, and "the most precise and positive orders" had been sent by every *aviso* to the Indies, to stop these unlawful proceedings. The case was among the many that had been considered by the commissioners of 1732, but it had seemingly been forgotten by 1738, till it was revived by the British merchants who, in great indignation, laid before the committee of the House of Commons details of some of the most notorious examples of the cruelty and injustice of the Spaniards in the Indies. Captain Jenkins seems to have attended,* and to have repeated his story. He had been on his way to England when he had been becalmed near Havana. There a Spanish guard ship had approached him and demanded his papers. These he sent over for inspection, but his boat returned full of armed men. These searched the ship for contraband goods, and finding none tortured first a mulatto boy and then the captain himself to extract a confession of illicit trade. Jenkins had been hoisted three times to the yard arm and dropped upon the deck with such violence that the last time, when he fell into the hold, he lay like one dead. He had also had his ear slit and cut off and, considering his later good record, there seems no reason to suppose that the fragment if brought to the House in a bottle had really been cut off in the pillory. The Spanish guard ships, or pirates posing as privateers commissioned by a Spanish governor, certainly committed barbarous acts of violence. In the same year 1731, the *Robert* had been taken and her captain "Story King, his officers and men were basely treated and abused

---

* The Journals of the House of Commons show that Jenkins was summoned to appear on March 28, 1738, but on the day when he should have given evidence the Journals only record that the House went into Committee. The Spanish minister, however, reported in a letter of April 1, 1738, that Jenkins had told his story before Parliament, so it would seem that he really appeared.

in a most barbarous and inhuman manner by having lighted matches tied between their fingers, and their thumbs put in hand vices and screws". The surgeon and two cabin boys were "tied down severally with their breast to the bowsprit, and beat...with a cutlas of six pounds with great cruelty on their back", and these "base practices they continued on the body of...Story King for three days successively"[110] to force a confession of illicit trade. It was only by chance that the war of 1739 became known as that of Jenkins' Ear and not of Story King's Thumbs. Such stories of "violences...carried to a height of inhumanity unknown even in times of open war"[111] were very common in the spring of 1738, and just at this time public opinion in London was still further inflamed by the news that thirty-one English sailors were even then languishing in a Spanish gaol.

In March 1738 it was learnt by the public that the sailors who had been in the four ships prized off the island of Cuba had been forced to work their passages back to Europe, and were now rotting in chains in a Cadiz prison, herded with robbers and felons, and fed "on nothing but bad biscuit and *bacalao*". It was not realised that the usual way of dealing with prisoners, taken in contraband ships, was to send them to Old Spain in a man-of-war, and then employ them in a Spanish dockyard. In this particular case, as the British consul at Cadiz later explained, the Spanish Intendant had used the prisoners very well. He had sent them to the dockyard at Carraca because it was healthier than the prison in Cadiz. As for the food, about which the sailors had complained bitterly,

their provisions might very possibly be indifferent, for the provisions of the lower sort of people in the country are in general so, and what they live upon will no doubt both in quantity and quality appear extremely bad, and little to English sailors, who are for the most part accustomed to much better and of a more substantial nature. But by all the information I have been able to get their provisions were not so bad as they have represented them. All the workmen in the yards here I am assured eat the very same bread the sailors had, and the same fish and beans, and dressed in the same manner they complain of and call with water, and I must do the Intendant the justice to say that I really believe he gave orders as he promised to me he would, for their having the usual allowance of provisions and of the same sort given to the Spanish sailors and others belonging to the yards....As for the chains they were nothing more than a shackle on one leg which three or four of the sailors had brought upon their fellows by trying to escape.

Unfortunately for the cause of peace this explanation did not reach England till the middle of May 1738, by which time the story of the sailors' hardships had considerably increased the fury of mercantile public opinion and the parliamentary opposition, so that the sailors had been welcomed home like heroes. The public had been more stirred by the story of their sufferings than by the seizure of a dozen ships in the West Indies.[112]

In this state of opinion La Quadra's conciliatory reply of May 1738 did not appear very satisfactory. In the majority of cases it only promised to consider the claims further if more proofs could be produced. On the general principles involved, it showed no change in the Spanish belief that His Catholic Majesty was the owner of the Spanish Indies and the American seas, and that foreign ships might only sail directly to and from the islands which had been conceded to other sovereigns by treaty. Unable to calm the noisy irritation in Parliament and in the City by obtaining practical satisfaction for the merchants' losses, the Duke of Newcastle vented his feelings by composing a "stern" answer to La Quadra's conciliatory promises of February 21, 1738, that the complaints should be investigated, and that when His Catholic Majesty was in full possession of the facts justice should be done. Already in the memorial delivered by Keene on December 10, 1737, and composed by Newcastle on November 15, the duke had laid down three principles: that English merchants had "an indisputable right" to a free navigation in the American seas, and to a lawful commerce in those parts; that the examination of British ships by Spaniards on the high seas was unlawful under article 14 of the commercial treaty of 1667; and that the manner of examining, the confiscation of that part of the cargo that was not contraband, and the imprisonment of the crew were all contrary to articles 15 and 23 of the same treaty.[113] These views had been flatly contradicted by La Quadra in his answer of February 21, 1738, and had even been criticised by the British minister in Spain.[114] In his "stern" reply of March 28, 1738, the duke modified his arguments and shifted his ground.[115] He was at pains to show that the Spanish assertion that British ships were only free to sail direct to the colonies of His Britannic Majesty was contrary to article 10 of the treaty of 1670, which permitted the ships of one nation to shelter in the ports of another, and that since article 15 of that so-called American treaty admitted of no visitation of examination, the visits of the Spanish privateers guarding the coasts against illicit trade must be regulated by the commercial treaty of 1667. The argument for extending the privileges of the treaty of 1667 to the Indies is unconvincing, and indeed what seems chiefly to have interested the Duke of Newcastle was not so much the actual situation according to international law, but which of the two treaties could be twisted to provide the most protection. "By grasping at too much we may lose all, and by resting singly upon one general article in the treaty of 1670, because custom has called it the American treaty, lose the benefits and stipulations of the treaty of 1667, which would answer all our merchants propose."[116] But such discussion of the principles regulating navigation in the West Indies was less likely than the consideration of particular cases of unjust prizing of illicit traders to provide the practical satisfaction for which the West Indian merchants, then at the height of their power,[117] were clamouring with increasing noise and heat.

During the spring of 1738 the long-standing irritation of the merchants found angry expression, and pamphleteers and many members of Parliament echoed their denunciations of Spanish barbarities and inhuman villainies. In 1737 they had memorialised and complained of the events in the Indies.[118] Since then the Duke of Newcastle and Sir Robert Walpole had tried to restrain the merchants, and had succeeded till March 1738, when the news of the imprisonment of the thirty-one British sailors at Cadiz became known. Then London, Bristol and other great trading cities had memorialised Parliament. Long lists of depredations were laid before the House, and much emphasis was put on the case of Mr Bonham who, in spite of His Catholic Majesty's orders in his favour, had made eleven unsuccessful applications in the Spanish Indies for the restoration of his ship, the *Anne*.[119] The opposition had made the most of this popular discontent, and Newcastle had become thoroughly alarmed.

An attempt was made to quieten the outcry by allowing the merchants to take prizes in return, but as Sir Robert Walpole's ministry wanted at the same time to avoid giving offence to Spain, the measure was so half-hearted that it gave no satisfaction to the merchants. The Spanish minister put the situation quite briefly:

I had heard that reprisalia patents had been offered to the owners of those ships which had been lately seized and taken to Havana. The Duke of Newcastle told me that His Britannic Majesty had simply done this to quieten the merchants.... I was privately informed that the reprisalia offer had not been mentioned (in Parliament when the merchants' memorials were presented), and I thought it absolutely necessary to discover the reason. I then found that the offer had been made on the condition that each merchant who took out a patent, should give £40,000 as a guaranty. For this reason, the merchants will not accept the offer, and so no mention has been made of it in Parliament.[120]

Parliamentary interest in Anglo-Spanish affairs increased. The House even demanded, and, contrary to all expectation, seriously examined, the papers relating to the dispute between the King of Spain and the South Sea Company, for it was suspected, though wrongly, that the present crisis was due to the Company's ill-founded pretensions which the ministry had failed to check.[121] Each day increased "the clamour and influence of those, who, feigning a zeal for the common good, had as their true object, the embarrassment of the ministry".[122] When Newcastle was composing his stern answer of March 27, 1738, the merchants were again laying before Parliament twenty-seven of the most striking cases of depredations. Sir Robert Walpole pathetically asked the Spanish minister not to pay any attention to what was said in the House, "as it was of no value till it had been passed by a majority".[123] Peace seemed to depend on the chief minister's ability to keep a majority, and that majority melted in the blaze of indignation roused by such stories as that of Captain Jenkins. The House even decided upon the unusual step of memorialising the king,[124] and Walpole was only able to moderate the language:[125] he could not prevent a resolution to take up 10,000 extra sailors and allot £500,000 for their pay.[126]

In the crisis, Sir Robert Walpole exerted himself to bring the dangerous dispute with Spain to an end. He modified the force of Newcastle's "stern" answer by sending a separate letter to the British minister, telling him "to moderate the meaning of his office by his manner of passing it". This he told the Spanish minister, who "understood from this hint that what was sent officially might be examined by Parliament, and that it would oblige the English minister if no reply were given to the official paper until after the end of the parliamentary season".[127]

That Walpole was prepared to go even further to safeguard peace was shown by a curious story which Geraldino, the Spanish minister, sent to his chief at the same time as he sent the news of Sir Robert's having modified Newcastle's stern office:

> Mr Arthur Stert was one of the Sevillian Commissioners, and is now a member of Parliament, in the confidence of the ministry. Since his return from Spain, he has visited me from time to time, and on one of these visits we spoke of the present noisy crisis. He expressed the view that our present differences were easy to accommodate, and I did not discourage him from explaining this further. The next day he returned with two papers about claims, and said that if I would lay them before His Catholic Majesty he would not fail to represent them to the English ministry. I suspected that this was not entirely his own idea, but when I asked him he assured me that it was, and that he had mentioned it only to one particular friend of his, Admiral Wager, who had advised him to bring it to me. I replied that his zeal was commendable but that I could not touch a matter of such importance without better authority.
>
> The same night he returned saying that he and Admiral Wager had been to see Sir Robert Walpole, who had not turned down the plan, but had decided that it must be shown to the Duke of Newcastle. This I understood was nothing more than a precaution of Sir Robert's to prevent any trouble arising through the jealous disposition of the duke. . . .
>
> On the following day—the 22nd—I saw the duke. When I arrived Mr Stert and Admiral Wager were in the anteroom, and they went in before me. The duke called me in without dismissing them, and asked me my opinion of the plan. When I replied that as yet I was ignorant of its details, he replied that if I would see Sir Robert Walpole he would enlighten me.
>
> Later in the same day Mr Stert brought me the plan. He said that he had given a copy to Sir Robert Walpole, and that the minister would receive me at nine in the evening. At the appointed time I waited upon the minister who began the interview by telling me how the resolution of the Commons had embarrassed him since Mr Keene's offices must conform with it, although he—Walpole—was firmly decided against a rupture. He went on to say that Mr Stert's plan was entirely his own. The details of the plan were briefly that £200,000 should be paid to the merchants to satisfy their claims. It had not yet been laid before His Britannic Majesty for his consent, because Sir Robert had wanted first to discover whether it would be admissible to Spain.
>
> I thereupon made two objections, firstly that whereas Mr Stert had put forward the English claims in full, he had reduced the Spanish

claims to £60,000.[128] Secondly, I declared that His Catholic Majesty would not enter into this negotiation until the dispute over the Florida limits had been settled.[129] To this Sir Robert Walpole replied that England would not ruin the negotiations for want of lowering the sum required of His Catholic Majesty, and that with regard to the second point his master had already agreed to adjust the limits by a commission, and was even ready to agree to the demolition of a fort erected by Colonel Oglethorpe on his last voyage.

I replied that I would inform the king my master, and asked that Mr Keene might not be told of the negotiation till I had received an answer. But concerning this Sir Robert could give me no promise, though he assured me that no order had been given to Mr Keene formally to touch the matter. This answer made it clear to me that Mr Stert had not spoken to me quite by chance.

As to the manner in which the money was to be paid, it had been admitted by the treaty of Seville that the South Sea Company owed His Catholic Majesty £68,000 for his share in the annual ships, and because of the difference in the value of the dollars in which the negro duties had been paid. This might be used to pay part of the sum. The balance might be made good out of what is believed to have been deposited in Havana from the last three ships that were prized; though perhaps this had better be paid in some other way, lest the public should come to know that it was being paid with its own money. In that case a fifth part of the annual negro duties might be ceded.[130]

This plan had several considerable advantages, as Geraldino was at pains to make clear to La Quadra.[131] The British ministers had shown their goodwill by proposing to pay part of the £200,000 that was to satisfy their merchants and, as Geraldino pointed out, "Mr Stert's plan is advantageous to Spain for several reasons. It preserves the dignity of His Catholic Majesty by making unnecessary the examination of all the merchants' claims in detail. It wipes out all the English claims which are of great value, and could never be otherwise totally extinguished, and it provides that the sum remaining to be paid shall be provided by the South Sea Company."[132] In the light of subsequent events the advantage of this last point seems very doubtful but, before the South Sea Company was to disturb the negotiations, other diplomatic difficulties harassed all those who hoped that the plan if it were accepted would avert war.

In May 1738 Sir Robert Walpole surprised Geraldino by saying that "only prompt Spanish answers could check the English naval preparations". Geraldino replied that he had supposed Sir Robert not to want the Spanish reply to Newcastle's "stern" letter till a reply could also be made to Stert's plan, and Walpole admitted that "if Spain would accept Stert's plan for an accommodation the whole question of the depredations would be at an end".[133] Geraldino soon learnt, however, that a final reply concerning the actual prizes was needed because the ministers "want an excuse for suspending their naval preparations, for these must be financed out of the sum which by Mr Stert's plan was to be used to satisfy the claims of the merchants, and that while the Spanish answer is delayed these moneys will be exhausted in preventive preparations".[134] A squadron under Haddock was actually despatched, because, as Sir Robert Walpole admitted, "he...had managed to defeat the prize and privateer bill introduced by Mr Pulteney, and there he asked me not to misuse his frankness for Mr Keene had before written some things that he had said to me, and all that minister's despatches were read at the Privy Council".[135]

When La Quadra's answer of May 26, 1738,[136] reached London, although it was one of the most favourable and conciliatory ever given to a British diplomat in Spain, it sadly disappointed Sir Robert Walpole. Concerning particular cases of recently prized ships, which had really been taken to a Spanish colony, it was unprecedentedly lenient, but with regard to old cases it only offered to order a search for further proofs, on the principles of the right of search it was as uncompromising as ever, and it contained no reference whatever to Stert's plan. However, this omission was soon explained when Geraldino asked if Mr Keene had not reported that La Quadra had made it known verbally, when he delivered the answer, that His Catholic Majesty would be always ready to enter into a just arrangement to preserve the peace. This assurance, he said, had not been included in the written answer since the question as to the admissibility of Mr Stert's plan had been verbal.[137] Sir Robert Walpole at once declared himself ready to offer the plan officially and in writing, and when "the Duke of Newcastle came in and said that no answer would be given definitely till His Britannic Majesty's opinion was known, Sir Robert replied that he already knew his master's views, which answer seemed to surprise the Duke not a little".[138] On July 3, 1738, Stert's plan was officially despatched to Spain.[139]

When, however, the plan reached Spain, the political situation had altered so much for the worse that Keene found it impossible to conclude any agreement without lowering the British demands. A perceptible difference appeared in the tone of the Spanish ministers' conversation, and the harassed Keene hoped "the accounts they receive from a neighbouring court may not have been a principal motive of this sensible alteration".[140] It was known that the Spanish envoy at Paris had made overtures for a treaty with France ten days after the conciliatory English plan had been officially despatched.[141] Newcastle's injudicious orders of June 1 [142] that Keene should "secure the safety" of His Majesty's trading subjects increased ill-feeling, "since the English merchants are always the first to disclose such warnings".[143] With Haddock's squadron in the Mediterranean, the Spanish ministry had good reason to suppose that the British Parliament intended to force war upon them. La Quadra was only ready to abuse Geraldino.[144] In this crisis Keene bravely risked exceeding his instructions, and took upon himself to reduce the sum demanded of His Catholic Majesty from £140,000 to £95,000.[145] Keene "explained" the financial details of Stert's plan, and reduced the Spanish and English claims proportionately.

Walpole had been awaiting the Spanish reply with almost feverish anxiety.[146] "He said he regretted that the Spanish delay forced him to spend money on preventive measures. He then began to reckon the time that should have been taken by the courier...from this I gathered the anxiety of this minister, who knows how the Duke of Newcastle and his supporters opposed the plan, and fears the use they may make of his faith in the plan if it is not accepted. They might even destroy his credit with his Master."[147] When the counter-project arrived it seemed as if Sir Robert's fears had been realised,[148] and "Newcastle said dryly that Mr Keene's explanations had been *motu proprio*".[149] However, by a great effort, Walpole managed to get the proportional reduction approved by the Privy Council.[150]

It was at this point that the directors of the South Sea Company began to exert on the negotiation an influence which was ultimately to lead to its failure. As His Catholic Majesty had been pleased to order the restoration of so many of the prizes recently taken in the Caribbean, it had become necessary to assign the whole of the

£95,000 on the South Sea Company for payment. This was in no way unusual, for the Company normally discharged its negro duties by paying the salaries of His Catholic Majesty's ministers, pensions or even ordinary bills.[151]

But in 1738 the directors were ready to refuse to discharge even such a piece of routine business for, at that time, the Company was on particularly bad terms with its royal shareholder. When the directors found themselves at last in a strong position, they decided to use this to obtain the satisfaction for which they had been clamouring for ten years. On the outbreak of war between Great Britain and Spain in 1718 and again in 1727, the South Sea Company had suffered considerable losses by the seizures of their effects in their American factories. Article 40 of the Asiento treaty, by which eighteen months were to be allowed for the removal of the Company's effects in the event of war, had been disregarded. According to one estimate the Company had lost £482,241 odd by the first of these seizures alone.[152] The Company had demanded several times to be reimbursed for this loss, and the directors determined to use the crisis of 1738 to secure satisfaction at last from His Catholic Majesty.

The sum of £68,000, which it was admitted the Company owed the King of Spain, had only been determined after five years of dispute,[153] during which the trade of the annual ships had been virtually suspended,[154] so that the directors were disgruntled and in no mood to pay the sum over to the King of Spain. The Spanish agent on the board of directors had been watchful of the negro duties, since these formed the most valuable part of the Asiento from the point of view of His Catholic Majesty. Soon after his arrival Geraldino had begun to object to the rate of exchange at which these duties were paid.[155] In 1725 there had been an attempt to reform the Spanish currency, and the old silver *real* had been withdrawn from circulation in His Catholic Majesty's European dominions. In 1726 it was found that there was a shortage of small change in Old Spain, so the silver *real* was reissued but in a debased form, so that ten instead of eight now went to make up the *peso* or dollar. The Company when it was paid in coined money in the Indies received old silver *reals*, but claimed to pay His Catholic Majesty's negro duties in a *peso* made up of eight of the new silver *reals.*[156] The difference on each *peso* was about 10*d.*, the Company valuing the coin at 3*s.* 4*d.* and the Spaniards at from 4*s.* 2*d.* to 4*s.* 8*d.*, and as the Company had to pay 33⅓ *pesos* on each of 4,000 negroes every year, the difference was considerable enough to encourage the Company to persist in the fraud almost to the end of the Asiento. Sir Robert Walpole had pronounced the Company's contentions delirious, but had declared himself unable to influence the directors,[157] and only when it became quite clear that the Spanish ministers, though they would not prohibit the Asiento, would in fact prevent the sailing of the annual ships, did the sub-governor, Peter Burrell, begin to try seriously to end the dispute.[158] In 1737 an agreement was reached by which the dollar was to be valued at 4*s.* 4*d.*, and the sum which the Company was held to owe His Catholic Majesty at £68,000, a little over half of this being for the difference on the negro duties since 1731, and the rest being His Catholic Majesty's share in the profits of the *Royal Caroline*. "The only condition required by the Company is that the king my master shall order the accounts of the reprisalia to be settled as far as they are liquidated by the Spanish officers' accounts and give proper orders for the Company's reclaiming satisfaction of the balance thereof, either in New or Old Spain in a reasonable time to be limited for that purpose, in such a manner as shall be satisfactory to them."[159]

Now, in August 1738, when Stert's plan had been accepted in Spain and the Spanish modifications had been accepted by the British Privy Council, the directors of the South Sea Company brought the whole negotiation to a stand. They "refused to pay the money unless they should be given satisfactory *cedulas* for the restoration of their effects seized during the reprisalia".[160] To make good their losses they requested that the Asiento should be prolonged, but this Geraldino considered "quite new and quite inadmissible". Walpole thought the whole plan ruined "because the Ministry had only managed to lower the English demands on condition of prompt payment".

The Duke of Newcastle...said the same thing as Sir Robert but with more heat. He suggested that Spain had arranged to pay out of a fund which was known to be non-existent....I replied that even the Governors of the South Sea Company did not deny that the fund existed; but they insisted on mixing other interests with it. I forbore to point out that it was from England that the suggestion had come to make the payment this way, for I knew his dislike of Sir Robert Walpole who had originated this idea.[161]

The directors were firm, and Walpole and Geraldino in despair. The English minister even invited the diplomat to his country house for a conference and violated the sacred idleness of the English week-end, but in vain.

At last Geraldino risked his personal credit in an attempt to preserve peace,

fearing that the whole negotiation might be destroyed...thought that I owed it to the honour of the king our master to say that for him the sum in question was of so little importance that he would be prepared to order the £95,000 to be paid in some other way, if he did not see fit to grant the Company the *cedulas* which the directors requested. The ministers asked for this assurance in writing; I replied that I could not treat in writing before the plan was signed. However, they urged the need of written proof to move the Privy Council, and as they offered to let me have my paper back after it had been shown to the Council, and even to pretend that I had never treated in writing before the Plan was signed, I agreed.[162]

On September 9, 1738, a Convention was signed.[163] His Catholic Majesty agreed to pay £95,000 to satisfy the British claims for ships unjustly prized in the West Indies, and the principles of navigation and other causes of dispute were to be adjusted by plenipotentiaries who were appointed by the same Convention. The Convention was not well received by the Spanish ministers. La Quadra made up in determination for the age and scarcity of his arguments,[164] and declared that Geraldino had exceeded his instructions by signing the Convention.[165] But as it was thought that the King of Spain's prestige and finances would suffer least if the money were paid through the South Sea Company,[166] La Quadra decided, after a month of angry abuse, to send the Company the *cedulas* requested for the recovery of their effects seized in 1718 and 1727. These Keene thought seemed "indeed strong and precise" and he pointed out that the Spanish ministers had now gone all the lengths they would go towards avoiding war, and bringing about reconciliation between the two crowns.[167] Castres, the British consul at Madrid, who had been nominated with Keene as one of the British plenipotentiaries, believed that the crisis was now in a fair way to be solved. "For several days after Haite's arrival, I would have given up any plenipotentiariship for half a crown; it has risen considerably in value since that time, and if we have so much success in our commission as you have had in the Convention, I think we shall have made a very good bargain of it."[168]

The hopes of a peaceful settlement were soon dashed. The governors of the South Sea Company found four objections to the *cedulas*, on whose complete acceptability depended the continuation of peace. They objected to the regulation that claims for satisfaction should be accompanied by a certificate from a Spanish official, that accounts had to be explained and proved by the Company, and were to be presented within six to eight months, and that the Asiento was to end in 1744. Both Geraldino and Sir Robert Walpole impressed on the governors "that on the result of their deliberations depended the restoration of a good harmony between the two countries".[169] But they remained firm in their refusal either to lend His Catholic Majesty £27,000 or pay him the £68,000 they admitted to be owing.[170]

This action of the South Sea Company made it impossible for the British ministry to accept the Spanish ratification of the Convention of September 9, 1738, for, in the ratification, La Quadra had stipulated that if the Company refused to pay the whole £95,000 His Catholic Majesty would be compelled to annul the Asiento.[171] The British ministers were of the opinion that "this would be to annul one treaty to conclude another", and this they would never be able to justify to Parliament. That the ministry was more concerned with appearing in a favourable light before the Opposition than with protecting the interests of the South Sea Company, was shown by a suggestion thrown out to the Spanish minister by Walpole. He said "that the English ministry had not taken official notice when *cedulas* for the despatch of the annual ship had been withheld during the dispute over the negro duties, but that it could not ignore an official declaration annulling the Asiento".

It was Sir Robert Walpole himself who "hit upon the idea of drawing up another treaty confirming entirely the king our master's ratification, except that it shall contain no mention of payment being made through the Company". Sir Robert also suggested that by the new Convention His Catholic Majesty should agree to make the payment, and if the South Sea Company would not act for him, he would not annul the Asiento but merely refuse to issue a *cedula* for the annual ship, and so bring pressure to bear on the directors.[172]

So it happened that within two months of sending home the ratifications Keene, instead of sitting on a commission to adjust colonial boundaries and discuss principles of navigation in the West Indies, was trying in desperate haste to conclude another Convention to avert war. At the same time he was trying to accommodate the grievances of the South Sea Company separately, so that the £95,000 might after all be paid as an assignment.[173] In January 1739 the second agreement, the Convention of the Pardo, was concluded.[174] It was a monument to the sincere desire for peace that had animated Sir Robert Walpole, the two diplomats, and the weak Spanish ministry. Its chances of success were, however, considerably weakened by the fact that La Quadra joined to the convention a declaration to the effect that the agreement had been signed only on condition that the South Sea Company paid at least the £68,000 which was admitted to be owing to the King of Spain.[175] The British ministers disliked the declaration as much as they liked the Convention,[176] but on February 6, 1739, the ratifications were exchanged.[177]

As late as the end of February 1739 the Spanish envoy had faint hopes that the South Sea Company might pay the money and the crisis be averted, but the fury of the parliamentary opposition made all hopes of accommodation vain. As in the previous spring "the merchants of the City, and those engaged in colonial trade memorialised the Commons asking that Parliament may protect trade". "The Opposition has stirred up all the trading towns of England...London, Bristol, Liverpool and the Directors of the colony of Georgia memorialised Parliament ostentatiously.... Every day pamphlets are published by the opposition to inflame the people as though to rebellion." Geraldino seriously doubted Walpole's chances of maintaining a majority for "the fury of the opposition was such as had never before been known".[178]

It seemed clear that the attitude of the opposition would confirm the South Sea directors in their resolve not to pay even the £68,000 owing to the King of Spain.[179] At the same time, the popular outcry against the Convention forced the British ministry to a step which made it impossible for the Spanish ministry to make the payment of £95,000 in cash, even if such an abject step had been considered by La Quadra. On February 9, 1739, after the exchange of ratifications, orders had been sent to Admiral Haddock "forthwith to return to England".[180] A month later the popular clamour was so furious that, on March 21, the ministry felt itself forced to countermand the order. When Geraldino taxed them with having done so, the Duke of Newcastle at first denied having sent any such order, but Walpole explained "that this was a precaution which they had felt to be absolutely necessary in face of the unpopularity against them which had been stirred up in the public by the influence of their opponents".[181] This might not have been enough to move Walpole, who had proudly declared that he was resolved not to let popular clamour get the better of what he believed to be for his country's good, but he was forced to approve of the counter orders by the news of a French marriage which had been concluded for Don Philip. A martial union was a natural deduction from the marital one. Hence while fear of the mob in England drove Newcastle, fear of the Cardinal drove Walpole to this momentous decision. With a hostile fleet threatening his shores where he had already stopped work on the fortifications,[182] His Catholic Majesty would not weaken his prestige by paying £95,000 in cash to a power which might be an active enemy within a few months, nor would he show himself more accommodating than before in the long-standing dispute with the South Sea Company, so that there was now no hope of the directors reconsidering their decision and paying the £68,000, still less advancing the £27,000. The Spanish ministry became less friendly. On March 7 Torrenueva had been made a councillor of the Indies and had been replaced in the departments of Marine and the Indies by the difficult and tenacious Quintana.[183] This change had been brought about by the nationalist Uztariz, and La Quadra had not opposed it. The time appointed for the payment of the £95,000 passed. The Convention had failed, and the fury of the opposition seemed entirely justified.

The interests of the merchants trading direct with the Spanish Indies by clandestine methods had provoked a crisis in which long-standing friction between the South Sea Company and His Catholic Majesty defeated all the efforts of Sir Robert Walpole and the Spanish ministry to preserve peace. The trade to the Spanish Indies carried on through Cadiz and the legitimate trade to Old Spain had been sacrificed because the illicit traders in the West Indies had secured the sympathy of the parliamentary opposition, and the protection of the contraband trade of Jamaica, Bermuda and New England had been made to seem the defence of national honour. The desire to carry on a direct trade with the Spanish Indies had begun a war, and the interest of the peaceful trade to Old Spain had not been strong enough to preserve the peace.

CHAPTER V

"THE CLAIMS OF THE
SOUTH SEA COMPANY...KILLED"

The Peace of 1748 and the Commercial Treaty of 1750

In 1750 the English Asiento was extinguished, and a commercial treaty regulating the British trade with Old Spain was signed. After thirty-seven years the attempt to secure a direct and legal, though very limited, trade contact with the Spanish Indies was given up, and English statesmen contented themselves with protecting the lucrative trade to Cadiz, Bilbao and the other parts of Spain in the Mediterranean or the Bay of Biscay. The policy which had been foreshadowed by Hawkins and finally expressed by Harley was abandoned. The Asiento had failed to justify the international friction which it had occasioned.

§ 1

After thirty years the English Asiento seemed to have proved as unsuccessful as the Asientos which had gone before it. The Spanish authorities found it objectionable and not sufficiently profitable, the British shareholders found it actually unprofitable, and even the British government did not think it worth while to sacrifice a commercial treaty to try to obtain an extension of the Asiento. The few persons who wished to retain the Asiento stressed its potential profits rather than its past gains.

Among the servants of the Company the high hopes of 1711 never entirely vanished. Some criticised the existing conditions of trade, but added that if only the commerce were reorganised upon a new footing according to a scheme which they had prepared, large profits might be made.[1] The directors were reluctant to see a trade end which gave them importance and an opportunity for some private trade.[2]

The British government approved of the Asiento trade since it trained seamen, encouraged the African trade, and introduced some bullion. It might not be actually very profitable, but it was still much coveted, and no minister could choose to give up a trade which might prove more profitable when carried on by the French.

Only the shareholders were firmly convinced that the Asiento trade was a dismal failure. As early as 1732 they had decided to try to get rid of the privilege in return for an equivalent.[3] The enquiry into the Company's affairs which had followed the Bubble scandal in 1721[4] had not stressed the commercial aspect of the Company, and the shareholders had hoped that the trade might improve with time. When no great improvement was shown after the reforms following the peace of 1729, the Spanish member of the board of directors urged his colleagues to lay a true statement of the trade before the shareholders.[5] When informed of the facts, the shareholders were despondent, and prepared to consider favourably Geraldino's proposal that it would be more to their advantage to accept an equivalent from His Catholic Majesty and to extinguish the trade. Such a suggestion had been made early in 1732 by William Tyrry, a Cadiz merchant, in an unofficial letter to Sir John Eyles, the sub-governor.[6] At this time the trade was in process of reformation, partly to make good the interruptions of the late war, and partly because of the organising energy of Sir John Eyles. This was also the time when a commission had been set up at Seville to discuss Anglo-Spanish commercial and diplomatic difficulties, so that such a suggestion as that of Tyrry seemed well timed. The directors, however, were merely surprised at such an unexpected and irregular overture and nothing was done.[7] When His Catholic Majesty's representative on the board took up the case, and made the same suggestion five months later,[8] the directors were no more enthusiastic. Early in 1733, a general court discussed whether to memorialise His Britannic Majesty for permission to treat for an equivalent,[9] but the year passed and nothing more was heard of the matter. At the beginning of 1734, the consideration of the Spanish proposal was again postponed,[10] and the Spanish representative, suspecting the motives of the directors, began a propaganda campaign among the shareholders to defeat the directors' vested interests. The shareholders had no desire to retain an unprofitable trade, and Patiño would have been glad to see the English Asiento extinguished.

In April 1734 Geraldino làid a memorial before his fellow-directors, pointing out the disadvantages of the trade as it had been carried on during the last twenty years, and urging the acceptance of an equivalent.[11] This paper he suspected would not be laid before the general court by the directors, so Don Thomas took the precaution of giving copies to several of his friends among the shareholders.[12] When nothing was said of the matter in the general court, one of these shareholders pointedly asked if Geraldino had not renewed his master's offer of an equivalent.[13] Once more the consideration of the proposal was postponed, but the Spanish representative had the satisfaction of seeing a new memorial decided on to ask His Britannic Majesty's permission for the directors to treat of an equivalent.[14] In July this memorial was presented.[15]

Again, long delays followed, but Geraldino knew that the equivalent was generally popular.[16] The shareholders were, however, uneasy at the delay, and feared that a *cedula* might be granted for the next annual ship, and the trade be carried on in spite of their wishes.[17] In December 1734 the British minister in Spain was ordered to apply for two such *cedulas*.[18] Geraldino was surprised, but not defeated. He knew that many of the shareholders sincerely wanted to exchange the Asiento for an equivalent, and on these he impressed the need for energetic measures to overcome the obstinacy of the directors. When at the general court, in February 1735, no mention was made of the fate of the last memorial to His Britannic Majesty, "the proprietors complained acrimoniously at silence on a point of such importance". It was decided to prepare a second memorial to ask for a speedy answer to the first.[19] This elicited a reply from the British ministry, but in such vague terms that it "neither refuses nor allows the company to accept the offer of an equivalent". Geraldino believed that this was done "to make it impossible for them to resolve to accept an equivalent",[20] but the shareholders decided otherwise and took the vagueness of the official reply as a tacit permission.

The next two months were full of uncertainty and agonising delays for Geraldino, but slowly the shareholders seemed to have become firmly decided in favour of accepting an equivalent. The directors waiting to know whether a *cedula* for the annual ship would be granted or not, omitted no opportunity of postponing the negotiation. At times the Spanish representative gloomily doubted whether his friends, the shareholders, knew what they wanted,[21] but at the end of April 1735 a general court empowered the directors to receive offers to sublet the trade. It was legally questionable whether the Company had the right to do so, but Geraldino was too astute to raise this point, and thus play the directors' game by causing further delays.[22] He concentrated his attention on drafting a proposal to take over the Asiento in such terms as would be acceptable both to the directors and to the King of Spain. There was no time to apply for instructions, for the offer had to be made within fifteen days. The directors wanted only a temporary agreement which would save them the expense and danger of sending out an annual ship at a time when war between Spain and Portugal seemed to be threatening, and there was danger of Great Britain becoming involved. His Catholic Majesty, on the contrary, would not consider offering the Company anything in the nature of a temporary arrangement. He wished not to save the Company loss in any particularly difficult year, but to end absolutely the negro trade which was considered in Spain a menace both economically and politically.[23] At last Geraldino succeeded in drawing up a proposal that satisfied both parties. The Company was offered 2 per cent of the profits of each year's galleons or *flota*.[24] As a pamphleteer pointed out this was about £80,000 per annum, and represented an increase of one-third on the usual profits of the Company.[25] Patiño, on the other hand, considered the sum moderate, since it was less than the profits of the *Royal Caroline*.[26] By this time the directors were unanimously opposed to the equivalent, but the shareholders were as decidedly in its favour, and a general court agreed to memorialise His Britannic Majesty for permission to accept the offer.[27]

In May 1735 Keene sent home a *cedula* for an annual ship,[28] and this might have ruined the negotiation for an equivalent, but Geraldino delayed the despatch of the ship by asserting that she must carry no foreign goods.[29] The shareholders were also firm in their reluctance to risk an annual ship in the disturbed state of

Portuguese and Spanish relations.[30] The shareholders remained faithful to the scheme, and as late as August 1736 some of them still wanted to get rid of the Asiento for a fixed annual payment.[31]

That the equivalent was never accepted was due largely to the opposition of the British ministers, who frowned on the scheme and did their best to accommodate the disputes between the Company and the King of Spain so that the trade might go on.[32] By the agreement of July 11, 1737,[33] the King of Spain's share in the profits of the *Royal Caroline* and the arrears due to him on the negro duties, which had been paid at too low a rate of exchange, were to be made good, and the proposal for exchanging the whole trade for an equivalent was dropped.

The shareholders were not, however, enthusiastic at the re-establishment of the trade in 1737. They regarded it as uncertain and difficult, and as early as 1732 had converted three-quarters of the capital into annuities, leaving only one-quarter for trading stock.[34]

The misgivings of the shareholders seemed quite justified by the condition of the legal trade of the Company. The negro trade had proved to have many considerable difficulties. The source of supplies was distant, so that it was impossible to select the goods that were to be sold. The directors could not supply a well-chosen cargo from a London warehouse but fitted out ships for the Guinea trade, and left the captains to slave as best they could; too frequently this resulted in a ship reaching the Indies with a cargo of which only two-thirds were suitable for the fastidious Spanish buyers.[35] Not only were cargoes of mixed quality, but freight and demurrage were high, and even the best negroes were liable to deteriorate in value during the horrors of the long voyages. The number of actual deaths during the voyages was small, but there was always a danger that negroes might die after they had been landed on Spanish soil, and if this happened after fifteen days, the Company had to pay full duty on the negro. Even those slaves who survived often looked too weak and ill to appear satisfactory bargains at £60 a piece.

The market was as distant as the source of merchandise, and was, moreover, a peculiarly difficult one. As the directors of the East Indian or the Royal African companies knew, it was difficult to keep efficient control over factors and agents thousands of miles away, and slackness and dishonesty were frequent among the servants of the South Sea Company. In the Indies the Company had to compete against illicit competition from British and Dutch colonies.[36] Of the Jamaican interlopers, the South Sea agents were merely disdainful,[37] but the rest of the trade was considerable enough to be a nuisance.

A far more serious difficulty was that the Spanish colonists were often unable to pay for the slaves they needed.[38] In spite of their reputation for wealth, the Spanish Indies were often unable to produce ready money to pay for slaves as well as goods purchased from the annual Spanish trading fleets, and to pay taxes. Money circulated in the great ports where the *flotas* and galleons traded, but in these the only South Sea factory which always showed a profit was at Portobello.[39] In spite of Dutch competition, the factory at Cartagena managed to do good business,[40] but the third focus of Spanish colonial trade, Vera Cruz, was not a good market.[41] There the demand for slaves was small, as cheap labour was supplied by numerous tribes of subject Indians. Havana, where the Spanish trading fleets reassembled for their return voyage, was the only considerable market for the Company's goods in the West Indies, and even there the returns were made not in coin but in fruits.

When the trading centres of the Spanish Indies offered such poor prospects, it is not surprising that the other factories were not very profitable. The windward coast was not only poor, but its fruits were monopolised by the Guipuzcoan Company.[42] The general poverty of the place was almost proverbial, and colonial officials in more wealthy places said that the Governors of Maracaybo or Santa Marta would readily condemn any foreign ship as good prize for the sake of the money that this would provide for the royal treasury.[43] The South Sea Company found that it was useless to maintain a permanent factory in a district where "it is impossible to sell negroes between crops, for the inhabitants have no money".[44]

The factory at St Iago de Cuba had, at times, to be combined with that at Havana.[45]

The factory at Buenos Ayres proved little more satisfactory, although it could provide valuable hides for the return cargoes, and offer a promising market for negroes, since from Buenos Ayres were supplied large districts in Southern Peru, and even Chile. That the trade was not more successful was due partly to the illicit competition from the Portuguese colony of Nova Colonia. The other cause of the failure of the Buenos Ayres factory was the irregularity in the arrival of the slave ships from Guinea. They were sent out from England regularly in pairs, but reached Buenos Ayres either alone or in a bunch of as many as two years' ships at once. There too an attempt to do business for ready money only proved very disappointing.[46]

The Company tried several expedients for overcoming the difficulties of the negro trade, and eventually succeeded in eliminating the long voyages to Guinea except in so far as they were needed to supply the factory at Buenos Ayres. In 1729 the experiment was tried of getting the negroes needed at Buenos Ayres from Madagascar,[47] but this did not prove a success. The supplying of all the other factories from a central agency at Jamaica, though this was difficult to establish, proved quite satisfactory after a time. It was useful to have a depot where negroes could be refreshed before being offered to the Spanish colonists, and where those unsuitable for the Spanish market might be sold. "If Jamaica belonged to the Spaniards, it might still be a question if it were not to the Company's advantage to trust them with their principal factory, by reason of the conveniency it had in its situation above every other place."[48]   From Jamaica to Cartagena took only fourteen days, to Portobello took twenty-one, to Havana thirty, and to Vera Cruz only a little over a month. The only disadvantage was the duty on negroes, and although in 1717 this became so oppressive that the Company sent its cargoes to Barbadoes,[49] where it afterwards continued to have an agency,[50] the superior advantages of Jamaica's position led the Company to keep its chief agency at Kingston during the whole course of the Asiento.

In 1721 the directors tried the experiment of buying negroes in Jamaica.[51] Instead of hiring ships in England to trade to Guinea, the Company built a few sloops to ply between Jamaica and the factories in the Spanish Indies. In 1723, however, it was necessary for the Company to send six or seven hundred negroes to Jamaica.[52] In 1724 two new sloops were built,[53] but there was "a great want of negroes at Jamaica for the supply of the Asiento trade",[54] and the Company had to revert to its previous system. In 1729, however, when the trade was reorganised after the war, the Jamaican experiment was tried again,[55] this time with success, and the Company continued to buy its negroes at Jamaica till the end of the Asiento. The only subsequent change was that as the Company's sloops wore out they were replaced by ships hired for the voyage.[56] But as in fact the same ships were hired regularly this meant hardly any change in the methods of the Company's trade.

The administrative ability of the directors and governors could not, however, overcome the other difficulties in the way of the Asiento trade. It could not improve the market in the Spanish Indies, nor could it rid the Company of the contract by which it was bound to introduce 4,800 slaves into the Spanish empire each year, and pay duty on 4,000 whether there was a demand for so great a quantity or not. This prevented any elasticity in the trade as well as involving the Company in a steady outlay each year.

Internal difficulties among the Company's servants were only made worse by vigorous supervision on the part of the directors. The personnel in the factories changed fast enough because of ill-health, or other natural causes, and if the directors tried too energetically to stop illicit trade, this only caused the removal of factors, and made it increasingly difficult to establish the trade on a secure, habitual basis.

The Company found its relations with the King of Spain irksome in several other ways. Disputes over the actual negro trade were not numerous and led to only two important restrictions on the trade, both in 1724 when the right of "internation", that is to take negroes inland to sell them, was refused,[57] and the factory at Panama was expelled.[58] But disputes between the Company and its royal shareholder had unfortunate effects on the trade in general, and political disputes between their Britannic and Catholic Majesties always had an adverse effect on trade, on two occasions involving the Company in considerable losses.

Between 1731 and 1736 the negro trade showed a less unfavourable balance,[59] partly because of reforms for which the Spanish director, Geraldino, claimed the credit,[60] but even so it did not work at a profit. According to the accounts of the Company about

£100,000 was spent annually to supply the Spanish Indies with negroes, and only about £60,000 was received in return.

The privilege of the annual ships did little to counterbalance the unsatisfactory nature of the main branch of the South Sea Company's trade.[61] In some ways, the trade was easier than that in negroes, and it was generally admitted that there was a great demand for European manufactures in the Indies,[62] but although the annual ships traded at a profit of 2,000,000 Spanish dollars altogether, the trade was so uncertain, and so full of causes of dispute between the Company and the King of Spain, that the shareholders rather feared to incur further loss than hoped to secure any profits.

Even when the Company and the King of Spain were on good terms, the routine regulating the annual ship's trade bristled with difficulties. Before the ship could be got ready the directors had to be sure whether the *flota* or galleons would sail that year, and before the ship could be despatched a special permit had to be obtained from His Catholic Majesty. If relations between the Company and their august shareholder were at all strained, this permit could be obtained only after a long and delicate negotiation, which sometimes threatened to develop into a diplomatic crisis. While the ship was in the Indies, there was always the danger that a threat of war might cause its seizure, or that rumours of illicit trade might cause a crisis. Even after the ship had returned, there was always a danger that the Spanish member of the Board of Directors might complain of illicit trade, or demand that his master's share of the profits might be paid at once. Altogether the privilege was so full of difficulties that it was almost a nuisance.

Both the permission ships, allowed to sail in 1714 as a special courtesy, were involved in the first reprisalia on the outbreak of war in 1718. This naturally decreased their profits. No annual ship sailed during the first three years of the Asiento, and when the *Royal Prince* was sent out in 1717, she was also involved in the first reprisalia, and was able to show a profit of only 5 per cent. The voyages of the *Royal George* in 1721, the *Royal Prince* in 1723 and the *Royal George* in 1724 were more satisfactory, and showed a profit of about 100 per cent each. In spite of being involved in the second reprisalia in 1727, the *Prince Frederick* was nearly as successful as was the *Prince William* in 1730, while according to the accounts the

Royal Caroline in 1732 beat all records. But six profitable voyages in nineteen years were not enough to encourage the shareholders to continue the trade.

Since the ships sailed so infrequently, it was impossible to create a steady demand for the Company's goods in the Indies.[63] The Spanish colonists certainly wanted European manufactures, but they preferred to pay the high prices of the *flota* and galleon merchants since their goods were more certain to arrive than were those of the South Sea Company.[64] If both these legal sources failed, there were always the English and Dutch contrabandists.

As for the illicit trade of the annual ships, it may have enriched some individuals, but did not compensate the shareholders for the lack of regular trade. The chief result of the illicit trade of the supercargoes was that often accounts were purposely confused so that it was difficult to discover what the expenses and returns really had been.[65] The illicit trade caused some protests from the Spanish authorities,[66] but it was disputes concerning the financial aspect of the negro trade that caused the trade of the annual ships to be totally suspended after 1732.

Altogether the trade of the Company was too uncertain and too liable to become involved in international disputes for it to be popular with the shareholders. They found the negro trade unprofitable and the annual ships irregular, and the failure of the Company to show an adequate profit on its negro trade made it unpopular with the King of Spain, just as with any less exalted shareholders. Even when the Company could show a profit as on the seven annual ships, His Catholic Majesty had found it almost impossible to extract his share in it.[67] From the point of view of the Spanish court, the annual negro duty was the most profitable part of the Asiento contract, and even there the Company had availed itself of every possible pretext to avoid paying His Catholic Majesty the full amount.

The English shareholders had been ready to get rid of the Asiento in 1733. In 1744 the thirty years of the English Asiento came to an end. At the end of the War of Jenkins' Ear, the Spanish court was quite determined to get this objectionable contract finally extinguished.

§2

By the end of the war in 1748 a new spirit was abroad in Spain, more friendly to Great Britain and promising a period of amicable relations between the two powers. To extinguish the Asiento, which had been such a fruitful source of friction in the past, and had been one of the reasons for the outbreak of war in 1739, would have been a satisfactory proof of the new spirit that was directing Spanish policy. That this objective took years of hard work to reach was due to the uncompromising character of the British government under the Duke of Newcastle, rather than to the wishes of the Spanish government of Carvajal.

Don Josef de Carvajal y Lancaster [68] was proud of being able to trace his pedigree back to John of Gaunt, but he was by no means a sentimental Anglophil. He was well disposed towards Great Britain because, in his opinion, that power was the best ally for His Catholic Majesty. His policy was determined by the realisation that Spain was a great colonial power, and had also a great part to play in Europe.

The Indies, as Carvajal realised, were a potential source of great wealth that might be used to revive Spanish industry if it were not diverted into the pockets of the French, English and Dutch contrabandists. He did not think of spending part of His Catholic Majesty's very inadequate revenue to fit out more guard ships to try to prevent the illicit trade, but he was ready to wink at the contraband of one of the maritime powers, if by so doing he could turn one robber into a friend and defender. Which of the three was to be offered friendship was decided by the international position in Europe.

Carvajal hoped that, by internal reforms, Spain might be made once more a dominating force capable of preserving the balance of power between France and the Empire. To achieve this position judicious alliances would be necessary. Portugal was an obvious first choice, since friendly relations with that power would leave His Catholic Majesty with only one frontier to guard, and moreover the Portuguese fleet might be of some use for the defence of "the heart of Spanish power", the Indies. With neither France nor Austria would Carvajal consider an alliance. The emperor, having no navy, could be of no help in the colonial sphere, and being himself the frequent object of attack in Europe, must be an encumbrance to any ally. The French king had too often betrayed his Spanish cousin to be considered as a valuable ally. The Dutch republic and the Italian princes were too weak, Prussia was still a satellite of France; Russia, Carvajal did not recognise as a great power; Poland and the Scandinavian countries were in decline.

Great Britain remained to be considered. Her great naval strength might be used to protect the Spanish colonies, which in time of war were always the first objective of His Catholic Majesty's enemies. In Carvajal's opinion, the British court did not covet any of His Catholic Majesty's possessions in the New World. As for commercial privileges in the Indies, Carvajal had already decided that one expensive friend was better than three robbers. In Europe, both powers wanted to preserve the peace, and the British fleet would greatly increase His Catholic Majesty's prestige. Carvajal had no intention of allowing Spain to become another cock-boat in England's wake, he even contemplated the recovery of Gibraltar and Minorca, but he had the courage and good sense to realise that in spite of religious differences, and past colonial conflicts, Great Britain had the possibilities of making a good ally for Spain.

The death of Philip V in 1746 had brought about a change in the Spanish court, which was particularly favourable to Carvajal's designs. The melancholy Ferdinand VI had not his father's military interests, still less had the asthmatic and childless Barbara of Braganza her mother-in-law's energy and ambition. Elizabeth, herself, though she retained her old fire, had no influence on the policy of her stepson. The new monarchs were, in fact, not much interested in foreign affairs, and apart from exerting a certain influence in the direction of peace and independence, Ferdinand left the conduct of affairs largely to his ministers.

In spite, however, of the goodwill of Spain, it proved impossible to secure the extinction of the Asiento or to conclude a satisfactory Anglo-Spanish commercial treaty during the negotiations which ended after two years in the Peace of Aix-la-Chapelle in 1748. By then the Anglo-Spanish disputes over depredations in the West Indies had ceased to be of primary importance. The

Anglo-Spanish colonial war had been moribund for years, and had been kept alive only because the antagonists had become involved in the War of the Austrian Succession. During the peace negotiations, problems of the Hapsburg succession to the Empire and the French support of the Jacobite claims in England occupied the attention of the statesmen and diplomats. Even in so far as Anglo-Spanish problems received any attention, these were concerned with such political questions as an establishment for the Infant Don Philip in Italy and the restitution of Gibraltar.[69]

The extinction of the Asiento was one of the points demanded by Spanish representatives at the peace discussions at Breda and at Lisbon in 1746,[70] and in London in 1747 when Don Ricardo Wall, the cheerful Irish protégé of Carvajal, was sent to try to negotiate a separate peace. The Breda negotiation came to nothing for Macanaz, the Spanish envoy, demanded exorbitant terms and was finally disowned by his own court, while at the same time the Allies found it impossible to accept the French terms. The Lisbon negotiation did not prosper, because of Austrian and Sardinian opposition, and Don Ricardo Wall's secret negotiation to try to secure a separate peace was ruined by the collapse of Holland and the French victories in the Low Countries, which made it imperatively necessary for the Allies to make peace with France.

The Spanish diplomats were left to get the best terms they could in the negotiations for a general peace at Aix-la-Chapelle, but they were now in a stronger position. The Spanish statesmen still demanded Gibraltar, but did not consider it essential.[71] The establishment in Italy for Don Philip had been conceded by the preliminaries concluded between the Allies and France.[72] The Spanish plenipotentiary, the Duque de Sotomayor, was free to concentrate on getting rid of the Asiento. The thirty years of the contract had ended in 1744, but the privilege which had been valued by the directors and the British government was not to be lightly relinquished. The Asiento had been interrupted by war in 1739, and the British claimed that they had, therefore, at least four years more in which to enjoy the privilege. This claim had been admitted by the French preliminaries.[73] Sotomayor was disgusted: "The preliminaries show that France has left us to adjust our own difficulties with her irreconcilable enemies, the English.

St Severin wants us to treat of the Asiento in Paris, but this would be to lift the question out of Purgatory into Hell. Let us rather treat of it in London or Madrid, or Lisbon, or Vienna, or Moscow, or Constantinople."[74]

Sotomayor was faced with the problem of making the concession of the preliminaries as innocuous as possible. The duke's first move was to refuse to accede to the preliminaries: "I think that if we do not hurry the danger of our ruining the whole negotiation may make England more tractable....Our court will accede in any form, but I publish the contrary. I have begun to negotiate with Lord Sandwich, to get it stipulated that the Asiento is to be continued for four years only. If I get a favourable reply I shall accede at once, if not I shall wait a little longer."[75] By the time that the Spanish ambassador in Paris admitted that his colleague at Aix had orders to accede,[76] Sotomayor had "arranged a declaration with Lord Sandwich that an equivalent shall be arranged instead of a renewal of the Asiento privileges".[77]

In article 16 of the definitive treaty itself Sotomayor managed to get it clearly stated that the period for which the Asiento had not been enjoyed had been for four years only.[78] In this, the French plenipotentiary, St Severin, supported Spain,[79] and although the English disputed fiercely they were in no position to refuse the treaty. It had been framed to satisfy the empress queen, and she had already nearly wrecked the negotiation.[80] "The English ministers proposed an expedient for enjoying the four years without anything being said explicitly in the treaty", but this was refused as being "obviously malicious",[81] and Sotomayor remarked "in this negotiation England has behaved very stupidly for she has missed an opportunity of separating us from France. She might have voluntarily conceded what we want, now she will be forced to do so."[82]

The British ministry, under the Duke of Newcastle and John, fourth Duke of Bedford, were slow to appreciate the value of the friendship which Carvajal was ready to offer. From the Anglo-Spanish point of view the treaty of Aix-la-Chapelle had only postponed the settlement of difficulties. Gibraltar remained a thorn in the flesh of a patriotic Spanish minister; the question of freedom of navigation remained as undecided as in 1737, and the

Asiento, which had been one of the chief causes of the war in 1739, remained as the first problem with which to open a new diplomatic epoch.

The British ministry would have made more trouble over the extinction of the Asiento but for the fact that they were in an awkward position, since Lord Sandwich had omitted to get the commercial treaty of 1715 renewed in the definitive treaty of peace in 1748.[83] On paper, the treaty of 1715 had only corrected the theoretically uniform and light tariff of 1713 by re-establishing the duties in force under Charles II of Spain, and by 1749 the tariffs had changed so much that the privileges of 1715 sounded out of date. But when the trade was reopened the British merchants trading to Old Spain soon found that without the protection of the treaty of 1715 they were exposed to very irksome new duties. "English ells which were despatched in the Customs House before the war at the rate of 6,000 are now valued at 7,000, and bays which were heretofore rated at 10,000 are now valued at 12,000, and scarlet bays rated at 15,000 whereas before the war, no distinction was made in the colours,"[84] "bays, cloths, camblets, shalloons, says and in fine all English manufacturies in proportion, and must be submitted to or not despatched so that our trade is likely to be reduced to a miserable pass."[85] The treaty must be reinvalidated to protect British trade, and "Mr Pelham confessed that Mr Doddington, who has gone into the service of H.R.H. the Prince of Wales, will attack the treaty concluded at Aix-la-Chapelle unless, when Parliament opens, the ministry can show that the advantages of his commercial treaty of 1715 are firmly assured".[86]

Keene had been sent orders to renew the treaty,[87] but found Carvajal adamantly opposed to any such negotiation.[88] Carvajal strongly disliked the treaty, which, by including an English agreement with a particular Spanish town, was, in his opinion, an insult to His Catholic Majesty, and "unworthy to have been signed by a Spanish minister".[89] The Spanish plenipotentiary at Aix "had had orders to object to its reinvalidation if this had been proposed",[90] but Sandwich seemed to have neglected to mention the treaty. To repair this omission was by no means easy. By June 1749 Keene had to admit that his mission was hopeless, and advised his court to conclude a completely new treaty.[91]

In London, Wall had found it equally difficult to get the Asiento finally extinguished.[92] Keene had even been given orders to ask His Catholic Majesty for *cedulas* to allow the South Sea Company to reopen its trade. Wall asked how this was compatible with Sandwich's declaration to negotiate an equivalent, and Bedford had assured the Spanish ambassador that he knew nothing of any such agreement.[93] Even after the declaration had been accepted as valid, the British ministers persisted in making difficulties. The South Sea Company was too influential for the government to give up its privileges without a struggle. Newcastle openly censured Lord Sandwich for having persisted in his agreement to treat of an equivalent after the number of years during which the Company had not enjoyed the Asiento had been fixed at four.[94] Mr Pelham said that the South Sea Company might sacrifice its right to the annual ship for the good of the nation, but then asked if the Company might not enjoy the negro trade for four more years.[95] By August, Wall was convinced that without a new commercial treaty, or at least the lowering of the Spanish duties, Newcastle's ministry would never consent to end the Asiento,[96] and "if things are left in the air the old troubles in America will begin again".[97]

Carvajal with his schemes for Spanish recovery was reluctant to offer commercial concessions in exchange for the formal admission that the Asiento had expired, but when the proposal was made from England, he did not refuse it. Mr Pelham suggested that "as England now enjoyed most of the rights allowed her by the treaty of 1715, there could be no objection to their being granted...that Spain might renew them by a special convention...other powers might be excluded by a clause saying that these rights had been confirmed in return for the ceding by England of the claims of the South Sea Company".[98] The proposal was accepted by the Spanish court,[99] and it seemed as if the difficulty was ended when the British ministers prolonged the negotiation for nearly a year by trying to alter Pelham's proposal so as to increase the British advantages.

Newcastle wanted some new advantages, "for Parliament would be very angry if the claims of the Company were ceded solely to rectify a mistake of Lord Sandwich".[100] Bedford was anxious about the debts which the South Sea Company claimed to be still owing to it from the King of Spain, and "suggested that the Company's claims might be settled on the same terms as those of the Convention of 1739".[101] When this was refused, the British ministers tried to get "the claims of the South Sea Company for debts owing from His Catholic Majesty...passed over by Spain in silence, for the ministers do not want to face Parliament with a flat abolition of claims that interest so many people".[102] The Duke of Newcastle was ready to be accommodating,[103] but Bedford, who feared that if Parliament should be angry its censure would fall on his friend Sandwich, was unmovable[104]. Finally, the Duke of Bedford produced a counter proposition demanding that the South Sea Company's claims should be passed over in silence, or that the Asiento should be continued for twenty years, or that £200,000 should be paid in liquidation of all the claims of the Company.[105] The Spanish envoy pointed out that Spain could not give England substantial and exclusive privileges and money as well, and thereupon the two powers settled down for a seven months' wait to see who would give way first.[106]

As the time for the opening of Parliament approached, the British demands for some money compensation grew steadily more insistent. In Spain Their Catholic Majesties were in favour of accommodation, the Marquis de la Ensenada, Carvajal's most influential colleague, exerted his influence in the same direction, for until an agreement had been reached with Great Britain he could do nothing in his departments of Marine and the Indies.[107] Carvajal, himself, sincerely desired to establish friendly relations between the two courts, and finally offered to pay £100,000.[108] Newcastle had valued the South Sea Company's claims at £800,000,[109] the Duke of Bedford had estimated them at £500,000.[110] This sum, Wall said, was what the directors believed they could get in an impartial court.[111] The British ambassador had officially demanded £300,000, but was secretly ready to accept two-thirds of that sum as Ensenada knew,[112] and as Keene said, when he was forced to accept £100,000, "it is not dishonourable for the nation to receive a larger sum for a reconciliation than that which gave occasion for a rupture between the two crowns".[113]

§ 3

The commercial treaty of 1750[114] secured no new privileges for British trade, yet it was a highly successful agreement, and laid the foundation for seven years of friendly relations between Great Britain and Spain. The outstanding achievement of the treaty was that it finally ended the unfortunate Asiento. By article 1 the British right to enjoy for four more years the privilege which had been conceded by the treaty of Aix-la-Chapelle was solemnly relinquished in return for £100,000, which article 2 stipulated were to be paid in three months. All the claims of the South Sea Company were, by article 3, declared at an end, and were not to be revived at any later date. With regard to British trade with Old Spain, article 4 laid down that English merchants were to pay no higher duties than in the time of the Hapsburg King Charles II. According to article 6 subjects of His Britannic Majesty were to pay no higher duties than native Spaniards. By article 7 the most favoured nation privilege was to be reciprocal, and no nation was to pay less duties on wool or other goods exported from Spain. Article 8 laid down that innovations in commerce were to be removed both in Spain and England. The right of Englishmen to gather salt on the island of Tortugas was again confirmed by article 5. In these concessions there was nothing spectacular, but as Keene had pointed out: "I find, my Lord, the old treaties so well digested in almost every article, that there is but little room to insert any new reasonable graces. The difficulty is to have them executed according to their interest and meaning, and that must always depend upon the disposition of the two Courts." The treaty of 1750 gave a good promise for favourable relations between the two courts, for "it lays a good foundation for separating the two Houses of Bourbon",[115] and if this could be done there would be small cause for disputes between St James's and Aranjuez.

During the next seven years the new confidence and cordiality between the two courts was reflected in the thriving condition of Anglo-Spanish trade. Many petty disputes which had harassed the British envoy before 1739 did not reappear, and such difficulties as did arise were speedily adjusted. As a result of the pacific policy of the new Spanish monarch, the trade of the

Mediterranean ports was no longer disturbed by embargoes as in 1732 and 1733. In spite of the reforming energy of Carvajal and Ensenada there was no complaint over inspections by the tobacco guards, and even the old disputes over consular privileges did not reappear.

In theory, the position was the same as in the time of Patiño. No vice-consul might be appointed without His Catholic Majesty's official approval,[116] but in fact the British merchants experienced no inconvenience, and there was no dispute over any appointment. In the smaller ports, it was not usual for His Britannic Majesty to have a vice-consul. In case of any incident such as a shipwreck that required the presence of such an official "the Consul simply sent someone temporarily empowered to deal with the situation". In the larger towns, the Spanish prohibition to appoint any vice-consul without His Catholic Majesty's permission was evaded by the old trick of having the consul's assistant elected by the factory and called an agent.[117] The Spanish *Junta de Comercio* offered no serious objection to the appointment of any of the consuls nominated by His Britannic Majesty, and even accepted Consul Pringle, although he was known to have been a very successful spy.[118] In 1751 the Spanish authorities even permitted the establishment of a British consulate at Cartagena, although the English had not previously had a consul or vice-consul at that place,[119] and it was known that the Marquis de la Ensenada was determined to make "this city...the best and the strongest port in Europe".[120] British consuls felt so secure under the new regime that one of them even indulged in a bitter dispute with his factory.

It was a pity that such a precise and Protestant Englishman as Colebrook[121] should have been sent as consul to Cadiz, where the factory was predominantly Irish. Colebrook was shocked at the lazy way in which the Irish merchants had administered the national duty, which had been voluntarily imposed by the merchants in the previous century to provide a fund for the relief of any poor British subject, who might be in Cadiz by reason of shipwreck or other misfortune. Such a duty was usual in all the foreign factories at Seville, and though it was only charged by the British factory at 1 *real de plata* per ducat, or 2 *reals* per ton on bulky goods, it raised between £2,000 and £4,000 in a year. Colebrook was shocked to find that French ships had been charged double the usual duty while Irish ships had been let in free; moreover, of the money collected, much had been misappropriated and of nearly half no trace remained. In 1726 a privateer was fitted out from the national duties fund to cruise against English shipping, and in times of peace the money had been used to maintain "Irish officers in the Spanish service, and some ladies without any other merit than being agreeable to the Deputies", who administered the fund.

Consul Colebrook proposed that in future the fund should be administered either by himself or by a vice-consul appointed by him. He also wanted a certain proportion of the duty sent to England each year to be invested. But though this was only so that the duty might eventually be entirely abolished, and the consul already suggested lowering it by half, the Irish merchants opposed the suggestion furiously. Colebrook was tactless and tried to cut down the salary of the vice-consul, though the amount paid by British ships for the vice-consular duty remained unchanged. The Irish became so incensed that they appealed for help to the King of Spain, declaring that as naturalised Spanish subjects they need not pay any national duty established by British Act of Parliament.

Here was an opportunity which Patiño might have used to embarrass the English, but Carvajal and Ensenada took no share in the quarrel. The *Junta de Comercio* stated that no foreign law could have authority over Spanish subjects, but the incident never developed into a dispute between the two courts. When Holderness replaced Bedford as Secretary for the Southern Department, Colebrook was removed from Cadiz and the incident ended, but not before it had shown how much the conditions of English trade to Spain had improved under the rule of Ferdinand VI and Carvajal.

Relations between the two courts were so good that British merchants were able to carry on their trade in peace, while other traders were expelled for similar transactions. British trade with the Moors had ceased to cause friction with Spain, but their Moorish trade caused the expulsion of the Danes and Hamburgers. In 1751 all trade with the Hamburgers was forbidden by proclamation, and beat of drum, and all Hamburg merchants were ordered to leave the country because some of them had furnished warlike stores to the Algerines.[122] In 1753 the fact that the Danes had, two years before, concluded a commercial treaty with the Moors was used as a pretext for prohibiting all further trade relations between Denmark and Spain.[123] The real reason for this attack was that Carvajal's predecessor, Campillo, had concluded a disadvantageous commercial treaty with the Danes, and that on the strength of that agreement the Danish ambassador had been demanding money from Spain. It is, however, significant that trade with the Moors should have been used as the pretext for breaking off commercial relations, as it had been in the case of the Hamburg merchants, yet it caused no dispute with Great Britain.

The only outstanding commercial difficulty which worried the British ambassador, was the delay in executing the commercial treaty of 1750, and even this ended satisfactorily.[124]

This retardment... has been owing to different motives, one of which has been the opposition the treaty has met with from all the underlings employed in the Rents and Custom house... another motive of delay has been what can scarce be believed, and what they have reason to be ashamed of, I mean almost a total ignorance of what was the practice in the time of Charles II proceeding from the confusion and little order in the public offices, as well as in the ports as elsewhere, which has given a handle, that has been improved by bad intentions for wasting time.

Almost two years after the conclusion of the treaty, Keene discovered the "invisible enemy" who had delayed its execution. "Him I was the longer in finding out because I looked upon him as too low to notice. It is one, Valencia, the chief of the Directors of the Royal Rents." By then, however, Keene had obtained orders from Carvajal that in all the Customs Houses duties should be on the scale in force in the time of Charles II. No complaints came from the consuls that higher duties were being exacted, and by March 1753 Keene could say confidently that "His Catholic Majesty hath come into the great point of producing the ancient tariffs".

A new trade difficulty was the problem as to whether it was unlawful to import British linens to Spain,[125] where Chinese textiles had been prohibited since 1718. The interest in this product shows the change that was coming over the British textile industry and

European fashions, but the grievance did not become serious at this time. In fact, during the period which might be called the Seven Years' Peace, British trade to Old Spain throve so satisfactorily that it left hardly any diplomatic traces.

Between 1748 and 1756 the British statesmen showed the reality of the new friendship by being ready to overlook some irregularities on the part of Spain. Carvajal's eagerness to revive Spanish industries led to some actions entirely contrary to English economic policy. Hardly had peace been concluded when the Spanish ambassador in London was sent orders to decoy skilled British artisans to Spain.[126] This policy continued for two years, yet there was no international dispute.

An attempt to revive Spain's woollen manufactures caused the diplomat, Wall, a great deal of anxiety in 1749. A Richard Metcalf had been sent over to get machinery and skilled mechanics for the Royal Company of Granada.[127] He applied to the Spanish minister for help in carrying on a correspondence with Spain, and for money. In all, Wall advanced him £2,000, and suffered agonies of suspense when the ship in which Metcalf and his mechanics had set out was captured by the British authorities. Any one of the workmen might have turned king's evidence, and although there was little danger of His Catholic Majesty's minister being directly implicated, the situation was very uneasy.[128] It became increasingly difficult for Wall to send away other woollen manufacturers that Carvajal wanted,[129] and although he managed to send one valuable expert safely to Spain,[130] the advantages to Spanish industry were few and the risks disproportionately great.

An attempt to improve the Spanish fleet by luring British shipwrights to the Spanish yards was very well known to the British authorities. It was more successful than the attempt to secure the services of the weavers, but it caused the Spanish envoy one very serious spasm of anxiety. One of the chief advocates of the scheme was the Spanish admiral, Don Jorge Juan.[131] During the War of Jenkins' Ear,[132] he had been a prisoner in London, and in 1750 he came there again in person to collect shipwrights. The British authorities suddenly became suspicious, and "Don Jorge disguised himself as a sailor to go on board a Biscayan ship, which was opportunely dropping down the river. He went off to her pulling an oar in the Captain's boat."[133] Bedford obviously suspected something, but Wall was not implicated, and the shipwrights, thanks to a friendly Irishman, who was later to serve Wall's successor as a spy,[134] got safely to Spain.[135]

This ended the attempts of Carvajal to use Wall to debauch British workmen, but further supplies of skilled British labour were obtained privately through the Irishmen already in the service of the King of Spain. At each of the three great naval bases, Cadiz, Cartagena and Ferrol, there grew up an Irish faction. Rooth, at Ferrol, was the most important. He was "Lord Paramount" of the daily increasing Irish clan, "and his grand living, keeping an open table etc. is correspondent...he is resolved while he reigns to do the utmost in his power, in order to depreciate His Majesty's honour and authority".[136] In 1752 he was allowed £200 for his table, and the title of Captain of Ferrol,[137] and it was known that he had a connection with the city of Newcastle whence he got coals and carpenters.[138] Bryant at Cartagena and Mullins at Cadiz imitated Rooth, Mullins even going so far as to fit out a fleet to carry immigrant Irishmen as well as legitimate cargoes.[139]

The British consuls kept the Secretary for the Southern Department informed of the activities of the Irish master shipwrights, of such captains as Macnamara,[140] Stewart,[141] and Brown,[142] and of the Spanish minister's chaplain, Shaw,[143] but the question of debauching workmen never became a source of dispute between the two courts. In 1754 the evil came to a natural end with the death of Carvajal, but Newcastle, Bedford and Holderness were not to know that it would end so soon. Their patience was an indication of the new era in Anglo-Spanish relations, which had been begun by the commercial treaty of 1750.

As the Asiento treaty of 1713 had been followed by twenty-six years of uneasy relations, and the commercial treaty of 1667 by thirty-three of tolerant friendship, so the commercial treaty of 1750 ushered in the Seven Years' Peace. So long as British statesmen and merchants were prepared to satisfy their desire for Spanish-American bullion through the trade with Old Spain, relations between the two powers remained good. An attempt to obtain direct trade contact with the Spanish Indies under cover of the *Asiento de Negros* led to friction.

It does not follow, however, that trade was the decisive consideration in Anglo-Spanish relations. The Asiento did not cause the long and bitter disputes over depredations, it merely directed attention to the amount of foreign illicit trade carried on in the Spanish Indies, and embittered the relations between the two courts by providing an additional cause of dispute in the claims and counter-claims of the King of Spain and the English directors of the South Sea Company over questions of finance. In the same way the commercial treaties between Great Britain and Spain were not the cause of the peaceful epochs that followed them. They only showed that political developments had made possible a period of Anglo-Spanish friendship, which would allow the mutual interests of the profitable trade with Old Spain to weigh with politicians.

In general, Anglo-Spanish relations were determined by abstract ideas rather than by the consideration of ledger and cash-book. Even the colonial trade was highly esteemed because of its usefulness in training sailors and maintaining a merchant navy. The British trade to Old Spain was as influential in determining policy as the trade to the West Indies, but neither was the governing factor of British or Spanish policy in the first half of the eighteenth century. Religion, the true system for preserving the balance of power, national honour and dynastic interest, all had very real weight with the ministers who in the eighteenth century directed Spanish and English affairs, with their colleagues and their sovereigns. Individual affections and antipathies, personal interest, questions of parliamentary tactics, or court intrigues all contributed to the formation and execution of a policy, and in the eighteenth century the number of ministers who understood commercial problems and were free to let trade requirements influence their general policy were few. Harley, Walpole, Patiño and Carvajal, though interested in trade, were unable to allow commercial considerations to shape their policy. La Quadra was too weak to want anything but peace, and Newcastle thought it essential to try to conciliate public opinion by timid concessions. The British trade to Old Spain was as influential in determining Anglo-Spanish relations in the first half of the eighteenth century as the trade to the West Indies, but more important than either were the abstract ideals of statecraft, and the practical details of politics.

APPENDIX

PATIÑO AND THE ECONOMIC DEVELOPMENT OF THE SPANISH EMPIRE

In the case of Patiño,[1] it was not obvious early which of the able young man's qualities were later to make him famous. From the first he was obviously able, but he made several false starts before finding his true career. Having tried his young brains on Jesuit theology with some success, he suddenly left the order, and for a time devoted himself to the study of law. His essay at diplomacy in Spain was cut short by the death of Charles II, and the administrative post that he secured on his return to Italy seemed to be only a reversion to his family's connection with army finance and provisioning, if it was nothing more than a purely temporary wartime employment. However, it brought him into touch with the French, and in 1707 Philip V nominated him to a place on the *Consejo de las Ordenes Militares*. In 1708 he was made a member of the Order of Alcantara.

A cold reception nearly made Patiño desert Spain for Paris; and when he did manage to take up his place on the *Consejo de las Ordenes Militares*, he soon had to exchange it for an administrative post in the provinces. Here, however, in the *Intendencia* of Extremadura Patiño began to create a reputation. The province was naturally poor, and drained of its resources by a war with Portugal. The new intendant managed not only to restore order among the troops, but to pay them by a reform of the finances of the province. So great was his success that he was transferred to the *Intendencia* of Catalonia, in which province His Catholic Majesty's troops were besieging Barcelona. Patiño shared in the eventual triumph of King Philip's arms by the practice of a rigid economy. In this province he introduced a new and very satisfactory form of taxation, the *Catastro*; and while he was there he also began to acquire his mastery of naval problems. Bergeyck, having come to Spain to reform the finances, had observed the urgent need for new ships for the navy. As a result of his representations Admiral de Gastaneta had been asked for some designs, and it was decided that two ships were to be built near Barcelona. Patiño's energetic versatility had already been shown by his successive mastery of theology, law and administration; he now made himself an expert on the technicalities of naval construction. If Walpole was raised to power by a bursting bubble, Patiño floated into royal favour in a model ship. The legend is that he had models made for him, and not only mastered all the technicalities but actually improved on Gastaneta's designs; certainly he realised that whereas there might be other financial experts there was no minister who understood questions relating to the marine. The only rival that he feared was Tinagero, but he had already made public his theories for reviving the Spanish navy, and it was possible that the uncommunicative Patiño might have even better ones, he was certainly an able practical administrator. Alberoni appreciated Patiño's work, and he was sent in 1717 to Cadiz as military and naval intendant and President of the *Casa de Contratación* to revive the fleet.

Patiño's success in Cadiz was considerable, although it chagrined him to think that he was in fact only executing schemes designed by Tinagero. However, it was a great achievement to have created a fleet, and an arsenal [2] which actually produced ordnance, and was capable of refitting ships.

At Cadiz, too, Patiño continued his financial experience, being named by Alberoni as the head of a commission of Spanish and English merchants set up under the treaty of Utrecht to discuss tariff reforms. This was, however, interrupted by war.

Patiño, intendant at Sicily, ruined the fleet which Patiño, intendant at Cadiz, had slowly built up, and though he had only obeyed Alberoni under protest, his career nearly came to a disgraceful end. Even though he was restored to the intendancy at Cadiz, the next few years were exasperating. One story is that two successive Ministers of Marine, Don Andres de Puj and Don Antonio de Sopena, distrusted and disliked him, and though they sometimes accepted his suggestions, they never allowed him to carry them out. Even in the smallest matters both demanded exact accounts, which were the more personally insulting as the ministers were themselves wasteful and inefficient. Ripperda was hostile and had already attacked Patiño's brother Don Baltasar, and Patiño's misery was complete when he was threatened with exile to a foreign embassy.

After this slow rise and long disappointment, honours and power fell on Patiño in too great profusion. He came to Madrid to receive instructions for his embassy, but there became very conveniently indisposed. His friends used influence; Ripperda's follies and lies caused his own fall; and, since there was no one else to succeed him, Don Josef Patiño, in May 1727, became minister of the Department of Marine and the Indies. Three months afterwards Patiño tried to get His Catholic Majesty to adopt the *Catastro* system of taxation that had been so successful in Catalonia. The king only said that he would consult La Paz. However, the marquis, when confronted with the proposition, said angrily that Castelar* with the Army and his brother with the Marine seemed determined to put forward such estimates as must infallibly consume all His Majesty's revenue. Philip V took this as a resignation, and in August gave Patiño control of the Financial Department. Each of the departments, the Colonies, the Marine and the Finances, would have provided more than enough work for a political genius, yet during the crisis of 1729–32, over the introduction of Don Carlos into the Italian possessions ceded to him by the treaty of Seville, Patiño was given the additional burden of Chief Secretary of State. Their Catholic Majesties considered him more able than La Paz, and ministers were referred to him by the formula of "Give these papers to Patiño who is well informed because he has just received the latest news from America". In 1736 he died.

During the nine crowded years while he controlled Spain's finances, Patiño was more preoccupied with the political ambitions of his master and mistress than with economic theory or even financial reform. That Patiño is nevertheless remembered as the restorer of Spanish finances is only because he managed to reform them partially, so as to present no obstacle to the schemes of Elizabeth Farnese in Italy. Under the military but luxurious Bourbon and his insatiably ambitious wife, the public expenditure increased considerably because of the expeditions to satisfy the

* Baltasar, elder brother of Patiño. Created Marquis de Castelar 1693, later Spanish ambassador in Paris.

queen's maternal ambition, or to divert the king's hysterical melancholy. The public buildings undertaken in imitation of the king's illustrious grandfather were also a serious drain on the royal revenue. The best that Patiño could do was to raise the royal revenue also, but it was not till 1751 that the budget was balanced.[3]

Patiño's first office had been that of Secretary for Marine, and here his achievements were greatest. The creation and maintenance of a strong navy was essential to the gratification of Their Catholic Majesties' warlike ambitions. Though Patiño was short of money, his marine reforms were never opposed in principle. Had he had no other employment, his achievements in this department would have been greater, but even as it was they were many. He built up two Spanish navies, and though one was destroyed in 1718 and the other dared not meet an English squadron at sea when war broke out in 1739,[4] His Catholic Majesty was at least able to go to war on both occasions, to invade Sardinia and Sicily on one, send troops to Italy on the other, and to capture Oran during the intervening peace. Moreover, the sailors were paid,[5] and arsenals and dockyards were set up at Cadiz, and in Havana, which managed in some sort to supply the ships. An even more successful undertaking was the establishment of a college to train naval officers; and this flourished to such an extent that before the end of the reign it had produced two such illustrious men as Juan and Ulloa. Patiño's marine reforms have, however, been most praised because of their effect in the Spanish Indies. It is asserted that the men of war were used to suppress illicit trade, and thus reserve to His Catholic Majesty the full profits of his colonies.[6] It is even said that though the illicit trade was not entirely suppressed it was considerably diminished. The letters, however, from the South Sea Company factors, and even from the Spanish governors themselves, do not corroborate these eulogies.[7] As for the assertion that Patiño by creating a marine fostered Spanish trade to the Indies, it is only true in so far as that for fiscal reasons the minister desired regular intercourse with the colonies. In fact he enforced it without regard to the commercial results.

With regard to Colonial policy Patiño had to create one for himself. In theory, this was a vigorous enforcement of Spain's traditional theory of monopoly. His vigour served to inspire

Ensenada, but political necessity prevented Patiño from achieving any constructive reforms in this sphere. At the very outset of his ministry he had confidently decided to realise all the advantages latent in the vast American empire which, it seemed to him, the Spaniards had forgotten. His conception of the value of colonial empire was that it should supply Spain regularly with money, either in return for goods purchased from the Spanish fleets, or as duties on the goods; or as annual tribute. To achieve these aims he inspired the colonial governors with the necessity of sending a regular contribution every year. The South Sea Company factors later reported that one of the excuses offered by royal officials in the Indies for not satisfying the Company's debt was the obligation of an annual contribution to Spain.

Occasionally, however, Patiño's determination to get from the Indies as much money as possible led him to adopt expedients positively harmful to the trade of Spain. Because of the shortage of money he was driven to many shifts such as sending a worn-out warship instead of a merchantman in 1735.[8] But a more serious expedient was the constant increase of taxation on the fleets. In 1728 His Catholic Majesty, by raising the value of the coinage, was able to secure one-third of the galleons' treasure instead of the quarter which he had hitherto obtained.[9] In 1729 Patiño managed to increase the tax. Any increase in the *indulto** he realised would outrage the merchants, so he charged an additional 4 per cent for *consulado*, 2 per cent of which would certainly find its way to His Catholic Majesty. Patiño had turned to good use his intendancy at Cadiz, and "by all the little tricks that a thorough knowledge of the whole detail could suggest to him got His Catholic Majesty as great a share of these effects as he possibly could".[10]

In the autumn of 1730 the *flota* returned, and for a year the effects remained undistributed while Patiño's agents wrangled with the West Indian merchants of Cadiz in an attempt to obtain a loan for His Catholic Majesty. It was a particularly rich *flota* worth as much as 18,000,000 pieces of eight since it included many of the effects of the last *flota*;[11] Varas, the Spanish official in Cadiz charged with the chief direction of Marine and West Indies affairs, went secretly to Seville for advice,[12] and the treasurer, Dias, came

* A tax on goods imported into Spain.

later from Seville to try to obtain a loan. The English consul reported that there had been so much done to get a loan because Patiño, having promised the court of France to deliver the effects free of any extraordinary *indulto,* had found this courtesy a financial impossibility. So he had tried to get money that he could tell France had been a free loan.[13] Dias, however, used too much force, and the French merchants, in alarm, complained to their ambassador. However, in April the *consulado* agreed to a loan of 200,000 pieces of eight,[14] although this was so secretly arranged that it was first suggested to be an amount ordered to be seized for marine necessities.[15] Still the goods were not delivered, and some of His Catholic Majesty's ministers tried to secure a further loan.[16] That same year, on the return of the galleons in the autumn, Dias secured, rather unexpectedly, very favourable terms for His Catholic Majesty.[17] Not only did he get the *consulado* to agree to ask for distribution of the galleons' effects on the same terms as those of the *flota,* but he also got them to submit to a perpetual augmentation of the *indulto* from 5 to 8 per cent.

After this increase of the duties on colonial trade Patiño did not raise them again, although in 1736 the merchants feared he might find some pretext for seizing the money brought by the *Guarda Costas.*[18] Instead he pursued a policy of forcing the fleets to sail so that His Catholic Majesty might receive the duties. In 1730 Patiño urged the necessity of a *flota* for the next year although the *consulado* objected that they could not undertake further expenses till the effects of the last fleet were distributed.[19] In 1731 he continued to urge the merchants to send a *flota,* and now although the effects of the last had been delivered the *consulado* were reluctant to send goods where there was no good market. It had, however, become plain by then that Patiño did not mind whether goods sold well or ill so long as they were exchanged for bullion that His Catholic Majesty might get his *indulto.*[20] In 1735 the minister again despatched a *flota* though contrary to the earnest desire of the *consulado.* The English consul at Cadiz wrote: "as for money they seem resolved to have it from the West Indies by any means how ruinous so ever to the trade of this country."[21] In the following year Patiño was determined to despatch the galleons in order to get ready money regardless of whether the merchants lost or gained.[22] When he was forced so to ill-use his cherished colonies, it is not surprising that he was unable to effect any considerable reforms in Spain's trade.

Patiño was kept so busy supplying the immediate needs of Their Catholic Majesties that he had little time for anything but the effective execution of a hand-to-mouth policy. His economic ideas he borrowed, and even these he had little opportunity to put into practice. For his general principles he relied, like other statesmen of his age, on those practised by Colbert; and their theoretical expression he left to the able brains of his contemporary and colleague Don Gerónimo Uztariz.[23] Patiño had used Uztariz to make two reports on the Royal Factory at Guadalajara, and perhaps esteemed the work of the theorist, although in one important respect, a disregard of colonies, it differed from his own views and practice.

Uztariz's economic views are fully explained in his own book, and their significance in relation to contemporary conditions in Spain and the development of Spanish economic theory has been well explained by M. Mounier, but some examination of them here may be useful to illustrate the difference between conditions in England and Spain in the mid-eighteenth century. The very incompleteness of Uztariz's theories shows one reason why Patiño did so little to reform the existing economic system. The writings of Uztariz are free from principles derived from theology or moral philosophy, but he had been unable to substitute any purely economic principles instead. His advice to favour industry, develop a war fleet, and regulate tariffs, was sound in itself, and was illustrated by a reliable collection of facts which made him the best of the mid-eighteenth century Spanish economists, but it was not inspiring.

Patiño was immersed in a sea of detail, and Uztariz offered him no principle to which he could cling, but in so far as was possible Patiño seems to have followed his advice with regard to details. Many of the reforms advocated by Uztariz were mercantilistic in character, but he seems to have had a rather mystical conception of money, and was uncertain whether he wanted to attract money to develop production, or to develop production to attract money. He hoped that the presence of money would develop agriculture since the more money there was in circulation the more consumption there would be of provisions. He hoped too that money would stimulate industry and increase the population. Perhaps it was his assertion that if Spain could keep the bullion that came from the Indies she would become "rich, populous, powerful, and respected",[24] that made Patiño endanger the prosperity of the Cadiz trade in order that an annual supply of bullion might reach Spain.

As for the details proposed by Uztariz, they were of a sort that naturally appealed to Patiño's shrewd financial sense. To gain and retain bullion in Spain Uztariz wished to develop an "active" trade, that is a trade in which the Spaniards were to sell more than they bought. He also realised the value of the carrying trade and of Spanish merchants acting as agents, but he hoped for the best results from the development of industry. It is curious that both he and Patiño signally ignored agriculture, seemingly forgetting that before Colbert built up French trade Sully had made certain a supply of food. He suggested reforms which were to be attempted by Carvajal, but Patiño had neither time nor money to attempt to revive old industries or set up new ones. Under Philip V something was done by royal favour and example to foster industry, but this was due to the French ministers of the earlier part of the reign rather than to Patiño.

One of the chief advantages, which Uztariz had hoped would accrue if industry were revived, was the increase of exports and decrease of imports. He would also have supported the trade recovery by a wise reform of the taxes and customs. It has been said that Uztariz had no financial policy,[25] but if his advice could have been taken it would have done much to revive Spanish trade. He wanted to abolish such taxes as the *alcabalas* and *cientos* which crushed trade and consumption. He wished to reform the Customs farm so that foreigners might no longer be illegally favoured. He also wanted to replace the appalling conglomeration of taxes, that weighed heavily on Spanish export trade, by one uniform tariff favouring the export of finished goods and the import of raw materials. Patiño in his Memoir on the Royal Revenue expressed the same views,[26] but events made it impossible for him to achieve any such reform. As intendant at Cadiz he had investigated the possibility of one Book of Rates, but his work had been interrupted by the war of 1718, and although discussions were resumed after the conclusion of the treaty of Seville they led to nothing. As for the Customs farmers, when the *flota* was wrecked in 1733 just as His Catholic Majesty was about to enter the War of the Polish Succession, Patiño was forced, in order to get ready money, to farm out duties which had hitherto been in the possession of the Crown.[27] In spite, however, of his shortcomings Patiño was certainly one of the outstanding ministers of eighteenth-century Spain. What is remarkable is that in the circumstances he managed to achieve so much.

BIBLIOGRAPHY

A. BIBLIOGRAPHIES AND GUIDES TO MATERIAL

ANDREWS, C. M. *Guide to the Materials for American History to* 1783, in the Public Record Office of Great Britain. Washington, 1912–14.

ANDREWS, C. M. and DAVENPORT, F. G. *Guide to the Manuscript Materials for the History of the United States to* 1783, in the British Museum and Minor London Archives and the Libraries of Oxford and Cambridge. Washington, D.C., 1908.

BALLESTEROS Y BERETTA, DON ANTONIO. *Historia de España y su Influencia en la Historia Universal.* Vols. V and VI. Barcelona, 1929.

Cambridge History of the British Empire. Vol. I. Cambridge, 1929.

Cambridge Modern History. Vols. V and VI. Cambridge, 1908–9.

FOULCHÉ-DELBOSC, R. and BARRAU-DIHIGO, L. *Manuel de l'Hispanisant.* Vol. I. New York, 1920.

HORN, D. B. *British Diplomatic Representatives*, 1689–1789. London, 1932.

ROBERTSON, JAMES A. *List of Documents in Spanish Archives relative to the History of the United States which have been printed or of which transcripts are preserved.* (Carnegie Inst. Publications, No. 124.) Washington, D.C., 1902.

Royal Commission on Historical MSS. Report XVIII, 1917. Davenport, F. G., *Materials for Diplomatic History*, 1509–1783.

SANCHEZ, A. B. *Fuentes de la Historia Española e Hispano-Americana.* Barcelona, 1927.

B. UNPUBLISHED MATERIAL

I. DIPLOMATIC

(*a*) IN ENGLAND

P.R.O., S.P.F. Sp. 75. Correspondence of Dr Aglionby and others in Spain, 1692–1705.

P.R.O., S.P.F. Foreign Entry Books, 196. Aglionby's Mission, 1700–2.

P.R.O., S.P.F. Sp. 79–82. Correspondence of Lord Lexington, 1712–14.

P.R.O., S.P.F. Archives, 258–68. Papers relating to the Peace Negotiations at Utrecht.

P.R.O., S.P.F. Treaty Papers, 97–102. Utrecht Negotiations, 1712–15.

P.R.O., S.P.F. Foreign Entry Books, 129–42. Spain, 1711–39.

P.R.O., S.P.F. Archives, 269. Copies of Correspondence to and from Spain.

P.R.O., S.P.F. Sp. 98–171. Correspondence between the British Ambassador in Spain and the Secretary of State for the Southern Department, 1727–65, including vols. 102, 106, 114 and 117, relating to the Commission established under the Treaty of Seville, 1729.

P.R.O., S.P.F. Holland, 421–2: 1746, Aug.–Dec., Sandwich's Correspondence. 424–7: 1747, Jan.–Dec., Sandwich's Correspondence. 433–46: 1748, Correspondence of the plenipotentiaries.

P.R.O., S.P.F. Treaty Papers, 103. 1748, Aix-la-Chapelle.

B.M. Add. MSS. 32,779–32,851. The Duke of Newcastle's papers relating to diplomatic relations, 1732–54.

B.M. Add. MSS. 32,852–32,900. Newcastle's papers on general affairs, 1755–9.

B.M. Add. MSS. 43,412–43,443. Sir Benjamin Keene's papers, 1730–57. After 1748 there are some valuable originals not in the P.R.O. (These are not yet officially catalogued: access to them was made possible through the kindness of the officials of the MS. Department.)

B.M. Add. MSS. 9131. Horace Walpole the Elder's Secret Memoir on the Depredations in the West Indies before 1739.

B.M. Add. MSS. 22,205–22,207. Copies of Correspondence between the Lords Plenipotentiary for negotiating the Peace of Utrecht... and the English Secretaries of State, 1711–14.

B.M. Eg. MSS. 2170. Correspondence of George Bubb... during his residence as envoy extraordinary in Spain.

(b) IN SPAIN

Simancas, P. de E., Ing. legs. 6884–6959. The Correspondence of the Spanish Envoys in England with the Secretaries of State, 1732–65.

Madrid, Archivo Historico Nacional, Estado, Ing. leg.:

4263. Correspondence between Don Ricardo Wall and Carvajal and Ensenada, 1748–51.

4264. Correspondence between Don Ricardo Wall and the Spanish envoy at Aix-la-Chapelle, 1747.

4266. Correspondence of Wall as Secretary of State with his successor as Spanish Minister in England, Don Felix Abreu.

4267. Correspondence of Wall, Abreu and Carvajal, 1749–53.

4277. Correspondence of Don Ricardo Wall with Carvajal, 1747–53.

2. COMMERCIAL

(a) GENERAL

(i) In England

P.R.O., S.P.F. Treaty Papers, Spain, 66. The Humble Complaint of Merchants and of others His Majesty of England's subjects about 1660–9.

P.R.O., S.P.F. Sp. 212–28. Correspondence of the British Consuls in Spain with the Secretaries of State for the Southern Department, 1710–55.

P.R.O., C.O. Board of Trade Papers. (The journals of the Commissioners for Trade have been published, but there remain many valuable papers of reports, recommendations and memorials, especially vols. 127–9 for the period 1714–15.)

B.M. Add. MSS. 25,684, Nos. 1 and 2. Campillo's "Lo que hay de mas y de menos en España..." and "España despierta".

B.M. Add. MSS. 13,974. Details of Spanish register ships sailing to the Indies, 1748–53.

B.M. Add. MSS. 28,140. An Essay on the Nature and Method of Carrying on a trade to the South Sea.

B.M. Add. MSS. 22,676. For Jamaican views on the British Asiento.

(ii) In Spain

Madrid, A. H. N., Estado, Ing. legs. 606, 613, 630, 639. *Consultos* of the *Junta de Comercio*.

(b) THE SOUTH SEA COMPANY

(i) In England

B.M. Add. MSS. 25,544–9. Minutes of the General Courts.

B.M. Add. MSS. 25,494–25,543. Minutes of the Directors' Courts.

B.M. Add. MSS. 33,032. South Sea Company papers collected by the Duke of Newcastle, but his most valuable papers are scattered through his diplomatic correspondence.

B.M. Photostats of the Shelburne papers. Vols. 43 and 44. Some of the private papers of Sub-Governor Burrell.

(ii) In Spain

Simancas, Hacienda, Ing. leg. 973. Some of Don Thomas Geraldino's Correspondence concerning the financial aspect of the South Sea Company, 1732–5.

Simancas, P. de E., Ing. legs. 7006–12. Some of Geraldino's private papers concerning trade.

Seville, Archivo General de Indias, Indif. Gen. legs. 2791–3, 2851. Further letters from Geraldino to Patiño concerning the Asiento.

3. COLONIAL (SPANISH)

(a) PAPERS CONCERNING PRIZES AND ILLICIT TRADE

Seville, Archivo General de Indias:

Audiencia de Santo Domingo:

Porto Rico, legs.	2513. Prizes, 1729–71.
	2493–4. Henriquez and other privateers.
Cuba,	2167–72. Prizes, 1721–72.
	492. English prizes, 1728–38.
	498. English prizes, 1737–52.
Cumana,	625. Hostilities with the Dutch and English in the seventeenth century and after 1743.
Caracas,	759. Illicit trade, 1717–33.
	792. English and Dutch insults, 1753–6.
Española,	307. Prizes, 1700–13 and 1751–3.
Santo Domingo,	1072. English prizes, 1745–53.
	1098. Prizes, 1728–74.
	573. Henriquez.
	574. Various prizes, 1751–61.

Audiencia de Mexico:

Yucatan,	3099. Logwood and England, 1732–83.
	3162. Prizes.

Audiencia de Caracas:

891–2. Prizes, 1738–94.
193–4. Trinidad prizes, 1731–96.
924. Prizes taken by the Guipuzcoan Company.

Audiencia de Santa Fé:

953. *Guarda Costas.*
1093–5. Correspondence of the Commander of *Guarda Costas* at Cartagena.
1243. Prizes mostly, 1729–30.

Indiferente General:

1597–9. *Expedientes* concerning England, 1718–65.
1828. *Expedientes* concerning *Guarda Costas.*
1829. Illicit trade, chiefly Dutch. This bundle is supplementary to that in Audiencia de Santo Domingo, Cuba, leg. 492.

(b) CORRESPONDENCE OF SPANISH COLONIAL GOVERNORS

Seville, Archivo General de Indias:

Audiencia de Santo Domingo:

Porto Rico, legs.	2297–9.	1732–59.
Cuba,	360–74.	1729–61.
Havana,	375–403.	1731–61.
Española,	281–3.	1693–1764.

(*c*) Simancas, Marine: Expedientes, legs. 392–404. Barlovento Squadron.

Seville, A. G. de Ind., Indif. Gen. leg. 2556. Barlovento Squadron.

C. PUBLISHED SOURCES

1. DIPLOMATIC AND POLITICAL

DUMONT, J. *Corps universel diplomatique du droit des gens contenant un recueil des traités d'alliance de paix etc. faits en Europe depuis le règne de Charlemagne jusqu'à présent.* La Haye, 1726–31.

The Parliamentary History of England from the earliest period to the year 1803. Vols. IV–XV. London, printed by T. C. Hansard, 1808–13.

Historical MSS. Commission Publications, especially No. 23, the *Cowper Papers*, London, 1838–9, and No. 29, the *Portland Papers*, London, 1891–1931.

Journals of the House of Commons, 1700–89. Vols. 13–28.

Journals of the House of Lords, 1700–59. Vols. 16–29.

Recueil des Instructions données aux Ambassadeurs de la France:

En Angleterre. Introd. and notes by J. J. Jusserand. Paris, 1929.
En Espagne. Introd. and notes by A. P. V. Morel-Fatio in collaboration with M. H. Leonardon. Paris, 1894–9.
En Hollande. Introd. and notes by Louis André and Émile Bourgeois. Paris, 1922–4.

SOMERS, JOHN (Baron). *A Collection of scarce and valuable tracts.* 2nd ed. London, 1809–15.

State Trials. Cobbett's complete collection of. London, 1809.

Statutes at Large. Vols. 3–6. London, 1763–4.

2. COMMERCIAL AND COLONIAL

The Acts of the Privy Council, Colonial. Vols. II–IV. Hereford, 1910; London, 1911.

Calendar of State Papers, Colonial. London, 1910–36.

CANTILLO, A. DEL. *Tratados, convenios y declaraciones de Paz y de Comercio.* Madrid, 1843.

HERTSLET, L. *A complete collection of the Treaties, Conventions, and reciprocal regulations at present subsisting between Great Britain and foreign Powers and of the laws, decrees and orders concerning the same...so far as they relate to commerce and navigation.* London, 1827.

Hist. MSS. Comm. Publications, No. 67. *Polwarth MSS.* London, 1911–31.

JENKINSON, CHARLES, Earl of Liverpool. *A Collection of all the Treaties of Peace, Alliance and Commerce between Great Britain and other Powers from...1648 to...1783.* 3 vols. London, 1785.

Journals of the Assembly of Jamaica from Jan. 20, 1663–4, *etc.* Jamaica, 1811–29.

Journal of the Commissioners for Trade and Plantations, especially volumes relating to 1704–15. London, 1920–5.

D. CONTEMPORARY MATERIAL

1. DIPLOMATIC

Admiral Hosier's Ghost. 1758.

Admiral Vernon's Ghost. 1740.

ARGENSON, RENÉ LOUIS VOYER DE PAULMY, Marquis d'. *Mémoires du Marquis d'Argenson.* France, 1846.

BEDFORD, Duke of. *Correspondence of John, fourth Duke of Bedford.* London, 1842–6.

BOLINGBROKE. *Letters and Correspondence, public and private, by the... Lord Viscount Bolingbroke during the time he was Secretary of State.* London, 1798.

COXE, WM. *Memoirs of the Administration of the Rt. Hon. Henry Pelham.* 2 vols. London, 1829.

—— *Memoirs of Horatio, Lord Walpole*, selected from his correspondence and papers from 1678–1752. London, 1802 and 1808.

—— *Memoirs of the Life and Administration of Sir Robert Walpole, Earl of Orford.* London, 1798.

GRENVILLE, RICHARD. *The Grenville Papers.* Correspondence between R. Grenville and the Rt. Hon. George. London, 1852–3.

GRAFTON, Duke of. *Autobiography and Political Correspondence of Augustus Henry, third Duke of Grafton, K.G.*, ed. Sir W. R. Anson. London, 1898.

HERVEY, JOHN (Baron). *Memoirs of the Reign of George II from his accession to the death of Queen Caroline.* London, 1848.

NOAILLES, ADRIAN MAURICE, Duc de. *Mémoires politiques et militaires...* composés sur les pièces originales recueillies par A. M. de Noailles. Paris, 1776.

PERCIVAL, M. O. *Political Ballads*, illustrating the administration of Sir Robert Walpole. Oxford, 1916.

RICHELIEU, LOUIS FRANÇOIS ARMAND DU PLESSIS, Maréchal et duc de. *Mémoires du Maréchal duc de Richelieu.* Paris, 1790–3.

WALPOLE, HORACE, Earl of Orford. *Reminiscences.* Written in 1788. London, 1819.

WILLIAMS, Sir CHARLES HANBURY. *Works*, with notes by H. Walpole. London, 1822.

WILLIAMS, W. W. *Political Ballads of the Seventeenth and Eighteenth Centuries.* London, 1860.

Pamphlets

(i) Opposition

Britain's mistake in the commencement and conduct of the present war. By a merchant and citizen of London, 1740.

Considerations upon the present state of our affairs at home and abroad.

The English Cotejo, or the Cruelties, Depredations and Illicit trade charged upon the English in a Spanish libel recently published.

An Enquiry into the Conduct of our Domestic Affairs from the year 1721 *to the Present time...*, being a sequel to *Politicks on both sides*, by W. Pulteney, Earl of Bath. London, 1734.

An Essay on the management of the present War with Spain... on the part of Great Britain. London, 1740.

Further Considerations upon the present state of our affairs. See the Works of George, Lord Lyttleton. 2nd ed. 1775.

Hireling Artifice detected: or the profit and loss of Great Britain in the Present War with Spain.

Ministerial Prejudices in favour of the Convention.

The National Dispute. Collected by Francklin.

Observations on the Present Convention with Spain. 1739.

The Politicks on both sides with regard to foreign affairs.... By W. Pulteney, Earl of Bath. London, 1734.

Political State of Great Britain. 1739.

Remarks on a letter to the Craftsman.... 1734.

A Review of all that hath passed between the Courts of Great Britain and Spain relating to our trade and navigation from the year 1721 *to the present Convention*; with some particular observations upon it. By W. Pulteney, Earl of Bath. 1739.

A Short View of the State of affairs with relation to Great Britain for four years past; with some remarks on the treaty lately published in a pamphlet entitled: *Observations upon it.* London, 1730.

Spanish Insolence corrected by English Bravery.

A State of the Rise and Progress of our disputes with Spain, and the conduct of our Ministers relating thereto. London, 1739.

A View of the Depredations and Revenges Committed on the British Trade and Navigation. 1731.

(ii) Ministerial

An Address to the merchants of Great Britain. By a merchant, retired.

An Appeal to the unprejudiced concerning the present discontents occasioned by the late Convention with Spain.

The Conduct of the late Administration with regard to foreign affairs. 1742.

Considerations on the war. 1742.

The Convention vindicated from the misrepresentations of the enemies of our peace. 1739.

The Grand Question whether war or no war with Spain impartially considered. . . .

Great Britain's Complaints against Spain impartially examined, and the conduct of each nation from the Treaty of Utrecht to the late declarations of war compared. 1740.

A letter to the Craftsman upon the change of affairs in Europe. By H. Walpole. 1734.

A Letter to a Member of Parliament concerning the present state of affairs at home and abroad. 1740.

Miscellaneous thoughts on the present posture both of our foreign and domestic affairs. By Hervey.

Observations upon the Treaty between the Crowns of Great Britain, France and Spain concluded at Seville on the ninth of November. 1729.

A Series of wisdom and policy manifested in a review of our foreign negotiations. 1734.

Periodical

The Gentleman's Magazine.

2. COMMERCIAL

(i) BRITISH IN GENERAL

A New Account of the Inhabitants, Trade and Government of Spain. London, 1762.

ANDERSON, A. *An historical and chronological deduction of the origin of Commerce from the earliest accounts to the present time.* . . . 2 vols. London, 1764. Revised by W. Combe. 4 vols. 1787–9.

Application to Parliament by the merchants upon the neglect of trade. 1742.

Britain's mistakes in the Commencement and Conduct of the present war. London, 1740.

The British Merchant. (Published by Chas. King.) 1743.

BURKE, EDMUND. *The Speeches of the Rt. Hon. Edmund Burke in the House of Commons and in the Westminster Hall.* 4 vols. London, 1816.

CAMPBELL, JOHN, LL.D. *Candid and Impartial Considerations on the Nature of the Sugar Trade, the comparative importance of the British and French islands in the West Indies, etc.* London, 1763.

—— *A View of the Dangers to which the Trade of Great Britain to Turkey and Italy will be exposed if Naples and Sicily fall into the hands of the Spaniards.* London, 1734.

CARY, J. *A Discourse on Trade and other matters relative to it.* . . . 2nd ed. London, 1745.

—— *An Essay towards regulating the trade, and Employing the Poor of this Kingdom.* London, 1717.

DAVENANT, CHAS. *Considerations upon the present state of affairs at home and abroad.* 1739.

—— *The Political and Commercial works of Charles D'Avenant.* Collected and revised by Sir Charles Whitworth. 5 vols. London, 1771.

DECKER, Sir M. *An Essay on the causes of the Decline of the Foreign Trade....* 2nd ed. Dublin, 1749.

DEFOE, D. *The Trade with France, Italy, Spain and Portugal considered, with some observations on the Treaty of Commerce between Great Britain and France.* London, 1713.

GEE, JOSHUA. *The Trade and Navigation of Great Britain considered.* London, 1729.

GODOLPHIN, Sir WILLIAM. *Hispania Illustrata*: or the maxims of the Spanish Court and memorable affairs, from...1667 to...1678 laid open in Letters to the Lord Arlington from the Earl of Sandwich, the Earl of Sunderland and Sir Wm. Godolphin during their Embassies in Spain...also a treatise by my Lord Sandwich, concerning the advantages of a nearer union with that Crown, and another by Sir Wm. Godolphin about the Woolls of Spain.... England, 1703.

I.R. *The Trade's Increase.* England, 1615.

MACPHERSON, D. *Annals of Commerce, Manufactures, Fisheries and Navigation....* 4 vols. London and Edinburgh, 1805.

PETTY, Sir W. *The Petty Papers....* Edited from the Bowood Papers by the Marquis of Lansdowne. 2 vols. London, Boston and New York, 1927.

—— *Political Arithmetic, or a discourse concerning the value of lands, people, etc.* London, 1690.

POSTLETHWAYT, MALACHY. *Britain's Commercial Interest Explained and Improved....* 2 vols. London, 1757.

—— *Considerations on the Revival of the Royal British Asiento between His Catholic Majesty and the South Sea Company.* London, 1749.

—— *Great Britain's True System.* London, 1757.

—— *In Honour to the Administration. The Importance of the African Expedition considered.* London, 1758.

—— *The Universal Dictionary of Trade.* Translated with large additions from the work of G. Savary des Bruslons. London, 1751.

A Proposal for Humbling Spain. Written in 1711. London, 1740.

SAVARY, J. *Le Parfait Négociant....* 2nd ed. Revue et corigie par P. L. Savary. Paris, 1749.

Short Essay upon Trade in general but more enlarged on that branch relating to the woollen manufactures of Great Britain and Ireland. London, 1741.

Spain, a new account of the inhabitants, trade and government. 1762.

164 BIBLIOGRAPHY

A SUSSEX FARMER. *The Advantages and Disadvantages which will attend the prohibition of the merchandise of Spain impartially examined.* London, 1740.

TUCKER, JOSIAH (Dean of Gloucester). *A brief essay on the advantages and disadvantages which respectively attend France and Great Britain with regard to trade.* 2nd ed. London, 1750.

—— *Four tracts on political and commercial subjects.* Glos. 1776.

—— *The true interest of Britain set forth in regard to the Colonies.* Philadelphia, U.S.A., 1776.

The Grand Question of whether war or no war with Spain impartially considered, about 1739.

WHITWORTH, Sir CHARLES. *State of the Trade of Great Britain in its Imports and Exports progressively from the year 1697.* London, 1776.

WOOD, WM. *A Survey of Trade... together with considerations on our money and Bullion.* London, 1718.

(ii) SOUTH SEA COMPANY

An Address to the Proprietors of the South Sea Capital containing a discovery of the illicit trade carried on in the West Indies.... London, 1732.

"Affidavits about the South Sea Private trade relating to the *Prince William's* illicit trade." *The Gentleman's Magazine,* p. 582. London, 1732.

A Defence of the Observations on the Asiento trade.... London, 1728.

Some Observations on the Asiento Trade. London, 1728.

TEMPLEMAN, D. *The Secret History of the late Directors of the South Sea Company.* London, 1735.

TOLAND, JOHN. *The Secret History of the South Sea Scheme.* 1726.

A True and Impartial Account of the Rise and Progress of the South Sea Company. 1743.

(iii) SPANISH

CAMPILLO, J. *Nuevo sistema de Gobierno economico para America.* Madrid, 1789.

CLARKE, E. *Letters concerning the Spanish Nation.* Written in 1761 and 1762. London, 1763.

PATIÑO, JOSEF. *Memoir on Taxation.* Published in Canga de Arguelles, *Diccionario de Hacienda,* vol. II, pp. 121–5. Madrid, 1833–4.

ULLOA, BERNARDO DE. *Rétablissement de Manufactures et du Commerce d'Espagne.* 1753.

UZTARIZ, G. DE. *Teorica y Practica de Comercio y de Marina.* Madrid, 1742.*

ZABALA Y AUNON, M. *Representación.* Madrid, 1732.

* An English translation is Uztariz, G. de. *The Theory and Practice of Commerce and Maritime Affairs,* translated from the original by John Kippax. 1751.

3. British Colonies

(i) GEORGIA

An account showing the progress of the Colony of Georgia.... London, 1741.

A brief account of the causes that have retarded the progress of the Colony of Georgia.... London, 1743.

History of the rise, progress and present state of the Colony of Georgia. 1744.

An Impartial Inquiry into the state and utility of the Province of Georgia. London, 1741.

A new and accurate account of the Provinces of South Carolina and Georgia. London, 1733.

Reasons for establishing the Colony of Georgia with regard to the trade of Great Britain. London, 1733.

A true account of the Colonies of Nova Scotia and Georgia. Newcastle, 1780.

(ii) JAMAICA

The laws of Jamaica,...to...1684 to which is added a state of Jamaica as it is now.... London, 1684–98.

LESLIE, C. A new history of Jamaica, from the earliest accounts to the taking of Porto Bello by Vice-Admiral Vernon. London, 1740.

E. LATER WORKS

1. Diplomatic

ARANDA, J. M. DE. El Marques de la Enseñada. Madrid, 1898.

ARMSTRONG, E. Elizabeth Farnese "the Termagant of Spain". London, 1892.

BAUDRILLART, A. Philippe V et la Cour de France.... Paris, 1890–1900.

BOURGEOIS, É. La Diplomatie secrète au 18ème siècle. Paris, 1909–10.

BROGLIE, J. V. A., Duc de. La Paix d'Aix-la-Chapelle. Paris, 1892.

COXE, W. Memoirs of the Kings of Spain of the House of Bourbon.... London, 1813.

DANVILA Y BURGUERO, A. Estudios españoles del siglo XVIII: Fernando VI y Doña Barbara de Braganza, 1713–48. Madrid, 1905.

—— Estudios españoles del siglo XVIII: Luisa Isabel de Orleans y Luis I. Madrid, 1902.

FEILING, K. A History of the Tory Party, 1640–1714. Oxford, 1924.

FERNANDEZ, OLBES L. La Paz de Aquisgran. Pontevedra, 1926.

FERRANDIS TORRES, M. "Don Josef de Carvajal." Revista Histórica. Organo de la Facultad de Historia de Valladolid, Oct.–Dec. 1924.

FITZMAURICE, E. G. PETTY, Baron. Life of William, Earl of Shelburne. London, 1912.

FORTESCUE, J. W. *History of the British Army.* 2nd ed. Vols. I and II. London, 1910.

GARCIA, RINES A. *Fernando VI y Doña Barbara de Braganza.* Madrid, 1917.

GROVESTINS, C. F. S. VAN. *Histoire des luttes et rivalités politiques entre les puissances maritimes et la France durant la seconde moitié du 17ème siècle.* Paris, 1851–4.

HARRIS, F. R. *The Life of Edward Montagu, First Earl of Sandwich,* 1625–72. London, 1912.

HARROP, R. *Bolingbroke.* A political study and criticism. London, 1884.

HORSFALL, F. L. *British Relations with the Spanish Colonies in the Caribbean,* 1713–39. Unpublished thesis in the University of London.

HOTBLACK, KATE. *Chatham's Colonial Policy....* London, 1917.

ILCHESTER, G. S. H. F. STRANGWAYS, Earl of. *Henry Fox, first Lord Holland, his family and relations.* London, 1920.

LEADAM, I. S. *The History of England....* 1702–60. Vol. IX of W. Hunt and L. R. Poole's *The Political History of England.* London, 1909.

LECKY, W. E. H. *A History of England in the Eighteenth Century.* London, 1892.

LEGRELLE, A. *La Diplomatie française et la Succession d'Espagne.* Paris, 1888–92.

LODGE, Sir R. *The History of England,* 1660–1702. Vol. VIII of Hunt and Poole's *The Political History of England.* London, 1910.

—— *The Private Correspondence of Sir Benjamin Keene, K.B.* Cambridge, 1933.

—— *Studies in Eighteenth-Century Diplomacy,* 1740–48. London, 1930.

MACKNIGHT, T. *The Life of H. St John, Viscount Bolingbroke.* London, 1863.

MAHAN, A. T. *The Influence of Sea Power upon History.* London and Cambridge, U.S.A., 1890.

MICHAEL, W. *Englische Geschichte im 18en Jahrhundert.* Vols. I–IV. Hamburg and Leipzig, 1896, 1920, 1934, 1937.

PARES, R. *War and Trade in the West Indies,* 1739–63. Oxford, 1936.

Recueil des Instructions données aux Ambassadeurs de la France:

En Angleterre. Ed. by J. J. Jusserand. Paris, 1929.

En Espagne. Ed. by A. P. V. Morel-Fatio. Paris, 1894, 1898–9.

En Hollande. Ed. by Louis André and Émile Bourgeois. Paris, 1922–4.

REYNALD, H. *Succession d'Espagne. Louis XIV et Guillaume III....* 2 vols. Paris, 1883.

RICHMOND, Sir H. *The Navy in the War of* 1739–48. London, 1920.

RODRIGUEZ, VILLA A. *Don C. de Somodevilla, Marques de la Enseñada....* Madrid, 1878.

—— *Patiño y Campillo.* Madrid, 1882.

SANDERS, LLOYD CHARLES. *Patron and Place Hunter,* a study of George Bubb Dodington, Lord Melcombe. London and New York, 1919.

SEELEY, Sir JOHN R. *The Expansion of England.* London, 1883.

SICHEL, W. *Bolingbroke and his Times. Selected Correspondence.* London, 1901.

—— *Bolingbroke and his Times: the Sequel.* London, 1902.

SOTOMAYOR, A. VALLADARES DE. *Fragmentos historicos para la vida del excelentisimo Señor Josef Patiño.* Madrid, 1790.

SOULANGE-BODIN, A. *La Diplomatie de Louis XV et le Pacte de Famille.* Paris, 1894.

—— *Le Pacte de Famille, Louis XV et Ferdinand VI.* Paris, 1894.

STANHOPE, PHILIP H., fifth Earl of. *History of England from the Peace of Utrecht (to the Peace of Versailles)....* London, 1839–54.

STEPHEN, Sir LESLIE. *History of English Thought in the Eighteenth Century.* 3rd ed. London, 1927.

TEMPERLEY, H. W. V. "The Causes of the War of Jenkins' Ear." *T.R.H.S.* 3rd Series, vol. III, pp. 197–236.

VAUCHER, P. *Robert Walpole et la politique de Fleury,* 1731–42. Paris, 1924.

WEBER, O. *Der Friede von Utrecht. Verhandlungen zwischen England, Frankreich und den Generalstaaten,* 1710–13. Gotha, 1891.

2. COMMERCIAL

(*a*) BRITISH TRADE IN GENERAL

ALTON, H. and HOLLAND, H. *The King's Customs.* London, 1908.

ASHLEY, Sir W. J. *Surveys, Historic and Economic.* London, 1900.

BEER, G. L. *British Colonial Policy,* 1754–65. New York, 1907.

—— *The Commercial Policy of England towards the American Colonies.* New York, 1893.

—— *The old Colonial System,* 1660–1754. 2 vols. New York, 1912.

BONNASSIEUX, PIERRE. *Les Grandes compagnies de Commerce.* Paris, 1892.

BROOKE, T. H. *A History of the Island of Saint Helena, from its discovery to the year* 1823.... London, 1824.

BROWN, V. L. *Studies in the History of Spain in the second half of the Eighteenth Century.* Smith College Studies, vol. XV, Nos. 1 and 2. Northampton, U.S.A., 1929–30.

CLARK, G. N. "War Trade and Trade War, 1710–13." *Econ. Hist. Review.* 1928.

CUNNINGHAM, WM. (Archdeacon of Ely). *The Growth of English Industry and Commerce in Modern Times.* 2 vols. Cambridge, 1925.

DAHLGREN, ERIK WILHELM. *Les relations commerciales et maritimes entre la France et les côtes de l'Océan Pacifique—commencement du 18ème siècle.* Paris, 1909.

EDWARDS, BRYAN. *The History, civil and commercial, of the British Colonies in the West Indies.* 3 vols. London, 1793–1801.

FORTESCUE, J. W. *Military History.* Cambridge Manuals of Science and Literature. 1914.

GIRARD, A. *Le Commerce français à Séville et Cadix aux temps des Hapsbourgs.* Paris, 1932.

—— *La rivalité commerciale et maritime entre Séville et Cadix jusqu'à la fin du 18ème siècle.* Paris, 1932.

HANNAY, D. *The Great Chartered Companies.* London, 1926.

JANISCH, H. R. *Extracts from the St Helena Records.* St Helena, 1885.

LIPSON, E. *The History of the English Wool and Worsted Industries.* London, 1921.

LONG, EDWARD (Judge of Admiralty Court in Jamaica). *The History of Jamaica....* 3 vols. London, 1774.

MARTIN, F. *The History of Lloyd's and of Marine Insurance in Great Britain.* London, 1876.

MURRAY, A. E. *A History of the Commercial and Financial Relations between England and Ireland from the Period of the Restoration.* Studies in Economics and Political Science, London School of Economics. London, 1903.

NETTLES, CURTIS. "England and the Spanish American Trade, 1680–1715." *The Journal of Modern History,* vol. III, pp. 1–32.

OPPENHEIM, M. *History of the Administration of the Royal Navy, and of Merchant Shipping in relation to the Navy, 1509–1660.* London, 1896.

ROBERTSON, J. M. *Bolingbroke and Walpole.* London, 1919.

SAXBY, H. *The British Customs....* London, 1757.

SCOTT, WM. ROBERT. *The Constitution and Finance of English, Scottish and Irish Joint-Stock Companies to 1720.* 3 vols. Cambridge, 1910–12.

SUMNER, W. G. "The Spanish Dollar and the Colonial Shilling." *American Historical Review,* vol. III, pp. 607–19.

SUVIRANTA, BR. *The Theory of the Balance of Trade in England.* Helsingfors, 1923.

UNWIN, GEO. *Industrial Organisation in the Sixteenth and Seventeenth Centuries.* Oxford, 1904.

WEEDON, W. B. *Economic and Social History of New England, 1620–1789.* 2 vols. Boston and New York, 1890.

(*b*) SOUTH SEA COMPANY

BATCHELOR, L. E. M. *The South Sea Company and the Assiento.* Unpublished thesis in the Institute of Historical Research, London.

BROWN, V. L. "Contraband Trade as a factor in the Decline of Spain's Empire in America." *Hisp. Am. Hist. Rev.* vol. VIII, pp. 178–89.

—— "The South Sea Company and Contraband Trade." *A.H.R.* vol. XXXI, pp. 662–78.

SCELLE, GEO. *La traite négrière aux Indes de Castille.* 2 vols. Paris, 1906.

WAGSTAFF, E. *The political aspect of the South Sea Bubble.* Unpublished thesis in the Institute of Historical Research, London.

3. COLONIAL

(a) BRITISH

Cambridge History of the British Empire. 1929.

EDWARDS, BRYAN. *The History, civil and commercial, of the British Colonies in the West Indies.* 3 vols. London, 1793–1801.

ETTINGER, A. O. *James Edward Oglethorpe, Imperial Idealist.* Oxford, 1936.

HERTZ, Sir GERALD BERKELEY (later Hurst). *British Imperialism in the Eighteenth Century.* London, 1908.

HOTBLACK, KATE. *Chatham's Colonial Policy—a study in fiscal and economic implications.* London, 1917.

—— "The Peace of 1763." *T.R.H.S.* 3rd Series, vol. II, pp. 235–64.

LONG, EDW. *The History of Jamaica.* 3 vols. London, 1774.

LUCAS, Sir CHAS. PRESTWOOD, K.C.B. *A Historical Geography of the British Colonies of the British Empire.* Oxford, 1888.

—— *Introduction to a Historical Geography of the British Colonies.* Clarendon Press, Oxford, 1887.

NEWTON, ARTHUR P. *The European Nations in the West Indies, 1493–1688.* London, 1933.

PENSON, LILLIAN M. *The Colonial Agents of the British West Indies.* London, 1924.

—— *The Colonial Background of British Foreign Policy.* London, 1930.

PITMAN, FRANK WESLEY. *The Development of the British West Indies, 1700–1763.* Yale Hist. Publications, vol. IV. New Haven, U.S.A., 1917.

PITT, WM., Earl of Chatham. *Correspondence of William Pitt when Secretary of State with Colonial Governors and Military and Naval Commissioners in America.* Ed. by Gertrude S. Kimball. New York and London, 1906.

STEVENS, W. B. *A History of Georgia from its first discovery by Europeans to the adoption of its present constitution in 1798.* 2 vols. New York, 1847–59.

(b) (i) SPANISH

AITON, ARTHUR SCOTT. "The Real Hacienda in New Spain under the first Viceroy." *Hisp. Am. Hist. Rev.* vol. VI, pp. 232–45.

BALLESTEROS Y BERETTA, A. *Historia de España....* Vols. V and VI. Barcelona, 1929, 1932.

BANCROFT, HUBERT HOWE. *A Popular History of the Mexican People.* San Francisco, 1888.

BASTERRA, RAMON. *Una Empresa del Siglo 18. Los Navios de la Ilustración. Gran Compania Guipuzcoana de Caracas y su influencia en los destinos de América.* Caracas, 1925.

BROWN, V. L. "Anglo-Spanish Relations in America in the closing years of the Colonial Era." *Hisp. Am. Hist. Rev.* vol. V, pp. 333–483.

—— "Contraband Trade as a Factor in the decline of Spain's Empire in America." *Hisp. Am. Hist. Rev.* vol. VIII.

CAMPBELL, JOHN. *A Concise History of Spanish America...collected chiefly from Spanish writers.* London, 1741.

CASTAÑADA, C. E. "The Corregidor in Spanish Colonial Administration." *Hisp. Am. Hist. Rev.* vol. IX, pp. 446–70.

CUNNINGHAM, C. H. *The Audiencia in the Spanish Colonies*, as illustrated by the Audiencia of Manila, 1583–1800. Berkeley, U.S.A., 1919.

—— "Institutional Background of Spanish American History." *Hisp. Am. Hist. Rev.* vol. I, pp. 24–39.

DANVILA, MANUEL. *Significación que tuvieron en el gobierno de América la Casa de la Contratación de Sevilla y el Consejo Supremo de las Indias.* Madrid, 1892.

FISHER, LILLIAN ESTELLE. *The Intendant System in Spanish America.* Berkeley, U.S.A., 1929.

—— *Viceregal Administration in the Spanish American Colonies* (with a Bibliography). Univ. of California Publications in History, vol. XV. Berkeley, U.S.A., 1926.

HARING, CLARENCE HENRY. *Trade and Navigation between Spain and the Indies in the time of the Hapsburgs.* Harv. Econ. Studies, vol. XIX. Cambridge, U.S.A., 1918.

MERRIMAN, ROGER BIGELOW. *The Rise of the Spanish Empire in the Old World and in the New.* 4 vols. New York, 1918–34.

MOSES, BERNARD. *Spain's Declining Power in South America, 1730–1806.* Berkeley, U.S.A., 1919.

—— *The Spanish Dependencies in South America....* 2 vols. London, 1914.

PEZUELA, J. DE LA. *Historia de la Isla de Cuba.* Madrid, 1868–78.

PIERNAS Y HURTADO, J. M. *La Casa de Contratación de las Indias.* Madrid, 1907.

SCHURZ, W. L. "Mexico, Peru and the Manila Galleon." *Hisp. Am. Hist. Rev.* vol. I, pp. 389–402.

—— "The Royal Philippine Company." *Hisp. Am. Hist. Rev.* vol. III, pp. 491–508.

(ii) SPANISH (ECONOMIC)

CANGA ARGUELLES, AUGUSTIN. *Diccionario de Hacienda....* 2nd ed. 2 vols. Madrid, 1833–4.

DESDEVISES DU DEZERT, GEORGES. *L'Espagne de l'ancien régime.* 3 vols. Paris, 1897–1904.

MOUNIER, ANDRÉ. *Les faits et la doctrine économiques en Espagne sous Philippe V. Gerónimo de Uztariz, 1670–1732.* Bordeaux, 1919.

NOTES

In general no reference is given when a fact or conclusion has appeared in an article by the author, but some further details on topics treated in this book may be found in "Documents illustrating Anglo-Spanish trade between...1667 and...1713" in the *Cambridge Historical Journal*, vol. IV, no. 3; "The Uneasy Neutrality, a study in Anglo-Spanish disputes...1756–59" in the *Cambridge Historical Journal*, 1938; and "The Seven Years' Peace" in the *English Historical Review*, 1938.

DATES: Most of the dates given in the text are New Style, as this was the form used by the British diplomats in Spain and the Spanish diplomats in England. The dates of Parliamentary proceedings, and those of the Commissioners for Trade and despatches from the English Secretary of State, have usually been corrected to New Style by the addition of 11 days. Other dates given from a secondary authority have generally been left in the form used in the book quoted. When both dates are given, this is done in the form June 4/15 or June 28/July 9. The year is always taken as beginning on January 1.

CHAPTER I

1 The best example of this is the period 1748–54 when the chief minister was Don Josef de Carvajal, a sincere Anglophil. (Ferrandis, "Don Josef de Carvajal", *Revista Histórica*. Organo de la Facultad de Historia de Valladolid, Oct.–Dec. 1924.)

But even during the reign of Philip V and Elizabeth Farnese, relations between Spain and France were not always cordial. When they were bad the Spanish court was correspondingly friendly towards Great Britain, as for example in 1735, when the French king abandoned his Spanish ally and concluded a separate peace with the emperor. (See Keene to Newcastle, 1735, Nov. 28: P.R.O., S.P.F., Sp. 123.)

Another period of friendliness was after the British court had prevailed upon the emperor to agree in the second treaty of Vienna to the peaceful succession of Don Carlos to the Italian duchies. (Keene to the Duke of Newcastle, 1731, March 2: P.R.O., S.P.F., Sp. 107; Keene to Newcastle, 1731, Nov. 24: P.R.O., S.P.F., Sp. 108.)

Spain was friendly and courteous towards Great Britain between 1733 and 1735, because Patiño, the able chief minister of Philip V, feared that unless Great Britain were handled with care His Britannic Majesty might go to war in support of the emperor. The Spanish court even went so far as to negotiate with the British court in an attempt to secure a separate peace with the emperor. (Keene to Newcastle, 1734, Nov. 27: P.R.O., S.P.F., Sp. 120.)

From 1735 to 1737 the Spanish court treated Great Britain with consideration because Patiño hoped, as he had hoped before 1735, to secure favourable terms of peace as the result of British mediation. (Keene to Delafaye, 1734, March 14: P.R.O., S.P.F., Sp. 119; Keene to Newcastle, 1733, Dec. 14: P.R.O., S.P.F., Sp. 117.)

2 *Products of British Colonies.* C. Whitworth, *State of the Trade of Great Britain in its Imports and Exports progressively from the year* 1697 (London, 1776), Introduction, pp. xli–lxix; C. M. Andrews, "Anglo-French Commercial Rivalry", *A(merican) H(istorical) R(eview)*, vol. XX, pp. 539–56, 761–80.

3 K. Hotblack, *Chatham's Colonial Policy* (London, 1917), pp. 68–9.
4 C. Whitworth, *State of Trade*, Introduction, pp. xix–xxi, xxxii–iv, xxxvi–vii.
5 *Levant Trade.* C. Whitworth, *State of Trade*, Introduction, pp. xxxviii–ix;
M. Decker, *An Essay on the Causes of the Decline of Foreign Trade* (1749), pp. 43–7,
on the monopoly of the Turkish Company; J. Gee, *The Trade and Navigation of
Great Britain Considered* (1729), p. 9.
6 *East India trade.* C. Whitworth, *State of Trade*, Introduction, pp. xxi–ii;
W. Cunningham, *The Growth of English Industry and Commerce in Modern Times*
(1925 edition), vol. II, pp. 255–71.
7 *Dangers of French trade.* C. Whitworth, *State of Trade*, Introduction, pp.
xxiii–iv; D. Defoe, *The Trade with France, Italy, Spain and Portugal considered, with
some observations on the Treaty of Commerce between Great Britain and France* (1713),
pp. 6–12; C. M. Andrews, "Anglo-French Commercial Rivalry", *A.H.R.*
vol. xx, pp. 539–56, 761–81.
8 C. Whitworth, *State of Trade*, Introduction, pp. xxiv–vi.
9 *Dutch trade.* C. Whitworth, *State of Trade*, Introduction, pp. xxvi–vii;
M. Postlethwayt, *Great Britain's True System* (1757), Introduction, pp. xxi–ii.
"The Dutch, by their large stock in trade, by their interest of money being lower
than ours, and by their having little or no duties upon the goods imported into
Holland, are by such policy enabled to make their country a general magazine
of merchandise, and therewith to carry on a general traffic throughout the world.
And if the Dutch did not purchase great quantities of our produce and manufactures our plantation and West Indies goods we could not depend on any
other such parsimonious people to introduce our commodities so cheap into so
many parts of the world."
10 *Italian trade.* C. Whitworth, *State of Trade*, Introduction, pp. xxviii–ix;
D. Defoe, *The Trade with France, Italy, Spain and Portugal considered*, pp.·4–5;
J. Gee, *Trade and Navigation. . .considered*, p. 10.
11 *Spanish and Portuguese trades.* C. Whitworth, *State of Trade*, Introduction,
pp. xxxi–ii, xxxiv–vi; J. Gee, *Trade and Navigation. . .considered*, pp. 11–12;
A. B. W. Chapman, "The Commercial Relations of England and Portugal,
1487–1807", *Transactions of the Royal Historical Society*, 3rd Series, vol. I, pp. 157–79.
12 *The British Merchant* (1743), published by Charles King, vol. III, p. 198;
A Proposal for Humbling Spain, written 1711, reprinted 1739–40, p. 24.
13 J. Cary, *A Discourse on Trade and other matters relative to it. . .* (1745), p. 42.
14 *Mediterranean market for English woollens.* J. Gee, *Trade and Navigation. . .
considered*, p. 67. Under Queen Elizabeth English woollens "gained the reputation of being the best in Europe, and a market was opened for them not only in
Spain, France, Italy. . .". *Heavy cloths.* V. L. Brown, *Studies in the History of
Spain in the second half of the Eighteenth Century.* Smith College Studies, Northampton, Mass., vol. xv, nos. 1 and 2, p. 44.
15 J. Cary, *Discourse on Trade*, p. 64.
16 J. Gee, *Trade and Navigation. . .considered*, p. 55.
17 J. Gee, *Trade and Navigation. . .considered*, pp. 53–7. I.R., *The Trade's
Increase* (1615), showed that there was a considerable trade to Malaga in Irish
timber for pipe staves.
18 J. Cary, *Discourse on Trade*, p. 84.
19 J. Cary, *Discourse on Trade*, p. 64.
20 D. Defoe, *The Trade with France, Italy, Spain and Portugal considered*, p. 5.
"By Act of Parliament such ships as carry out our manufactures are to have
16 guns and 32 men, of which there is now a much greater number than there

were 16 or 20 years ago. But small ships with an easy charge of men can fetch wines from France."

21 J. Cary, *Discourse on Trade*, p. 64.

22 *The British Merchant*, published by Charles King, vol. III, p. 81.

23 For the characteristic trades carried on from the various ports of Old Spain see *A New Account of the Inhabitants, Trade and Government of Spain* (1762).

24 A Sussex Farmer, *The Advantages and Disadvantages which will attend the prohibition of the merchandise of Spain impartially examined* (1740), p. 15.

25 *Wools of Spain*. In 1667, at the time of the commercial treaty, Sir William Godolphin was sent to Segovia to inspect the wool trade. The following report appears in "A Discourse by Sir William Godolphin touching the Wools of Spain" published in *Hispania Illustrata* (1703), pp. 107–8: "The wools of Spain are commonly known by the names of Segovia, Soria and Andalusia; Segovia is the finest, and is sold (neither sorted nor washed, but just as it comes off the sheep's back) at 70 *reals de vellon* the *arroba*, an *arroba* is 25 lbs. weight. Soria wools are next in fineness, and in like manner sold at 50 *reals de vellon* the *arroba*. Andalusian wools are the worst and the coarsest, and are in like manner sold at 20 *reals de vellon* the *arroba*. The wools washed and sorted are put in bags of 8 arrobas which are sold from 1,350 to 1,400 *reals de vellon* being Segovia cloth wools; it is said cloth wools in distinction from Segovia lambs wool wherewith they make not cloth but hats...when the buyer will have the best of these sorts, there is an increase of 20 % upon the weights. Viz. for 100 lbs. weight of wool, he pays the price of 120 lbs. weight in regard the best sort being taken away the second and third sell for much less. It is calculated that there is yearly exported out of Spain, from 36,000 to 40,000 bags of all sorts of wool; and that usually from the port of Bilbao are shipped off 20,000 bags of wool in a year. It is judged that these wools are taken off in this manner:

Holland, Hamburg and the adjacent countries, 22,000,
England, from 2,000 to 7,000,
France, from 6,000 to 7,000,
Venice and the other parts of Italy, 3,000,
Africa, 1,000.

This exportation is of all sorts of wool, and of this perhaps 27,000 bags may be Segovia or Soria wools; what are spent in Spain are usually of the third sort of Soria and Segovia wools."

26 *For a discussion of the value of Spanish wool, soap and dyes see* A Sussex Farmer, *Advantages and Disadvantages*, pp. 10–12, 14–15, 28–9.

27 J. Cary, *Discourse on Trade*, p. 65.

28 A. Mounier, *Les faits et la doctrine économiques en Espagne sous Philippe V, Gerónimo de Uztariz*, 1670–1732 (1919), p. 136.

29 V. L. Brown, "Anglo-Spanish Relations in America in the closing Years of the Colonial Era", *H.A.H.R.* vol. v, p. 336.

30 J. Campbell, *A Concise History of Spanish America* (1741), p. 300.

31 For details of the Spanish exports to the Indies during the years 1748–53 see in the British Museum the Kingsborough Collection of Spanish MSS., Brit. Mus. Add. MSS. 13,974, ff. 504–6.

32 J. Savary, *Le Parfait Négociant* (1742), vol. I, book 2, chap. v, p. 163 and following. Cloth is the best merchandise to export in the Fleets.

33 *The Spanish colonial trade*. For a full study of the complicated system of annual fleets see C. H. Haring, *Trade and Navigation between Spain and the Indies*

in the time of the Hapsburgs (1918), *passim*; J. Campbell, *Spanish America*, pp. 279–320. For the history of the rivalry of Seville and Cadiz for the Indies trade see C. H. Haring, *Trade and Navigation between Spain and the Indies*, part I, pp. 7–15. See also A. Girard, *Commerce français à Séville et Cadix aux temps des Hapsbourgs* (1932), *passim*, and A. Girard, *La rivalité commerciale et maritime entre Séville et Cadix jusqu'à la fin du 18ème siècle* (1932).

34 *A New Account of the Inhabitants, Trade and Government of Spain*, p. 48.

35 J. Campbell, *Spanish America*, pp. 300–1.

36 See the details of the goods sent to the Indies in register ships, 1748–53, Brit. Mus. Add. MSS. 13,974, ff. 504–6.

37 Consul Cayley from Cadiz to the Duke of Newcastle, 1738, Sept. 23. P.R.O., S.P.F., Sp. 223.

38 Consul Parker at Corunna to the Duke of Newcastle, 1730, May 8. P.R.O., S.P.F., Sp. 216.

39 For the full text of a treaty of Peace and Friendship between Great Britain and Spain of 1667, May 12/23, see Hertslet, *Commercial Treaties* (1827), vol. II, pp. 140–95.

40 J. Savary, *Le Parfait Négociant*, vol. I, book 2, chap. v, pp. 155–66.

41 A Sussex Farmer, *Advantages and Disadvantages*, pp. 30–1.

42 J. Gee, *Trade and Navigation...considered*, p. 11.

43 Horace Walpole's Secret Memoir on the Depredations in the West Indies and the threat of war, 1738–9. Brit. Mus. Add. MSS. 9131, f. 238.

44 *Chief export trades of Spain*. Canga Arguelles, *Diccionario de Hacienda*. See under the alphabetical heading for each country, especially vol. I, p. 28 for Germany, vol. I, pp. 479–80 for France, vol. I, p. 625 for Great Britain.

45 *Wine trade in the eighteenth century. A New Account of the Inhabitants, Trade and Government of Spain*, p. 2. For some interesting details of the history of wine drinking in England see A. Simon, *Wines and Spirits* (1919); C. Whitworth, *State of Trade*, Introduction, p. xxvi.

46 *Products of Spanish ports. A New Account of the Inhabitants, Trade and Government of Spain*, p. 53, gives a list of the towns of Spain and the goods they exported, these included: Alicante, wine, mostly red; Almeira, fruits and oil; Ayamonte, excellent kind of wine, but strong; Bilbao, iron, wool, saffron and chestnuts; Cadiz, all those who carry on a traffic by sea have also their agents, correspondents, and factors here, the best wine in Spain; Cartagena, salt fishes, especially tunnies; Malaga, wool, olives, oil, raisins, sack and other wines; San Sebastian, a very considerable trade, especially in iron, steel and wool; St Ander, fine fruits and wine, fish; Salobugna, sugar, fish; Santogna, iron cannon; Tarragona, corn, oil, flax, very good wine; Tortosa, corn, fruits, silk, oil and pretty kinds of earthenware; Valencia, almonds.

47 *The Grand Question of whether war or no war with Spain impartially considered* (1739), p. 8.

48 *The British Merchant*, 1743 edition, vol. III, p. 88.

49 *A Proposal for Humbling Spain*, written 1711, reprinted 1739–40, p. 24; *The Grand Question of whether war or no war with Spain*, p. 8.

50 *Official English figures of Customs Returns*. Some very suggestive figures were published by Sir Charles Whitworth in his *State of Trade*, 1776. They purport to be the figures for the total amount of goods exported from England and imported by British merchants from the other countries of the world for the period 1697–1776. They cannot be taken as being very accurate, as has been shown by Professor G. N. Clark in his *Guide to English Commercial Statistics*,

1696–1782, but they do give some means of checking the lamentations and boasts of eighteenth-century writers on the conditions of the various branches of British trade.

51 Godolphin in the House of Commons, 1712. *Hansard, House of Commons Debates*, vol. VI, col. 1147.

52 For a lugubrious picture of this failure see I.R., *The Trade's Increase* (1615).

53 An illuminating statement of the Elizabethan attitude towards the Spanish empire, rich in gold and silver, is given in A. P. Newton, *The European Nations in the West Indies*, 1493–1688 (1933), p. 96: "The traditional story leaves an impression of the almost unchequered success of English bravery against Spanish apathy and cowardice, but this is an illustration of the persistent influence of patriotic propaganda on the verdict of history."

54 W. R. Scott, *The Constitution and Finance of English, Scottish and Irish Joint-Stock Companies to 1720*, vol. I (1910), p. 262.

55 F. R. Harris, *Life of Edward Montagu, First Earl of Sandwich* (1912), vol. II, p. 100.

56 "The Humble Complaint of Merchants and others His Majesty of England's subjects of...losses under which they have lain by the King of Spain's breach of Articles, together with some proposals in order to the future. P.R.O., S.P.F., Treaty Papers, Spain, vol. 66, f. 98. For an abstract of this document see J. McLachlan, "Documents illustrating Anglo-Spanish Trade between the Commercial Treaty of 1667 and the Commercial Treaty and the Asiento Contract of 1713" in the *Cambridge Historical Journal*, vol. IV, no. 3, pp. 299–304. This also contains a further examination of the Treaty of 1667.

57 *Trading conditions in seventeenth-century Spain.* "Merchants' Complaint", Articles 12, 38, 74. P.R.O., S.P.F., Treaty Papers, Spain, vol. 66.

58 E. Clarke, *Letters Concerning the Spanish Nation* (1763), p. 268.

59 Sir W. Godolphin, "Discourse on the Wools of Spain", *Hispania Illustrata*, pp. 106–9.

60 A. Mounier, *Les faits et la doctrine économiques en Espagne sous Philippe V*, pp. 32–47.

61 "Merchants' Complaint", Articles 7, 8, 9. P.R.O., S.P.F., Treaty Papers, Spain, vol. 66.

62 *Relations of English Merchants and Spanish Tax Farmers.* Details as to the working of this system are given in *The British Merchant*, vol. III, pp. 165–73, 183–91, 195–7, 208–14, 229–40.

63 The principle of electing and paying a *Juez Conservador* which had been enjoyed by merchants trading in Andalusia was made general by article 9 of the Treaty of 1667: Hertslet, *Commercial Treaties* (1827), vol. II, p. 144. Article 27 allowed the establishment of British consuls: Hertslet, *Commercial Treaties*, vol. II, p. 152.

64 *Necessity of trading in partnership to Spain.* J. Savary, *Le Parfait Négociant*, vol. I, book 2, chap. V, p. 157. The Spanish consular papers contain several references to such firms, e.g. Merrett & Son: see Merrett to Merrett, 1716, Jan. 26, P.R.O., S.P.F., Sp. 213 and Hammond, Revelly & Barker: see Barker (Alicante) to Newcastle, 1727, Aug. 17, P.R.O., S.P.F., Sp. 215. "Merchants' Complaint", Article 13 against seizures by Court of *Cruzada*. P.R.O., S.P.F., Treaty Papers, Spain, vol. 66.

65 When the shareholders of the South Sea Company wanted permission to exchange the Asiento for a money equivalent in 1732, His Britannic Majesty failed to encourage the desire, apparently on Walpole's advice. See Brit. Mus.

Add. MSS. 25,545, South Sea Company, General Court Records, 1735, March 20.

66 W. Cunningham, *Growth of English Industry and Commerce* (1925), vol. II, p. 274, note.

67 According to the South Sea Company Accounts preserved in the Spanish archives the annual ships involved smaller expenditure and profits than did the negro trade. Madrid, Archivo Historico Nacional Estado, leg. 4267.

68 "Tratado declaratorio de algunos articulos del Asiento de Negros que se pacto el 26 de Marzo de 1713, concluido en Madrid el 26 de Mayo de 1716" (Bubb's Asiento Treaty, Article 8). A. del Cantillo, *Tratados...de Paz y de Comercio* (1843), p. 174.

69 *List of Annual Ships* (compiled from Brit. Mus. Shel(burne) Photostats, I, ff. 4–5):

1714   Two permission ships sent: H.M.S. *Elizabeth* to Vera Cruz; H.M.S. *Bedford* to Cartagena and Portobello.

1716   Bubb's Treaty.

1717   *Royal Prince* to Vera Cruz.

1718–20   War.

1721   *Royal George* to Cartagena.

1722   His Catholic Majesty did not find it convenient to grant a *cedula*.

1723   Two *cedulas* granted. *Royal Prince's* second voyage to Vera Cruz.

1724   *Royal George's* second voyage to Cartagena. As protest against flagrant illicit trade of last two ships, *cedula* delayed till December.

1725   *Prince Frederick* to Vera Cruz.

1727–9   War.

1730   *Prince William* to Portobello.

1732   *Royal Caroline* to Vera Cruz.

70 Add. MSS. 32,819, ff. 189–90, Annual Ships never created permanent market: "As some must be had to answer the present want, the people are found in such exigencies to...supply themselves...with those of other nations which, though of different specie, & neither so intrinsically good, nor so much liked are thus first of all taken through necessity, and afterwards worn till they are preferred and the other by degrees laid aside & forgot agreable to a received principle of commerce, that where the supply of a commodity is uncertain the consumption of it will be so too."

71 *List of the Silver Fleets and Galleons* that sailed to Vera Cruz and Portobello from 1713 to 1739 (Seville, Archivo General de Indias, Inventorio de Contratación (vols. III and IV):

Flotas to Nueva Espana		Galleons to Tierra Firma
	1713	Echevero y Zubiza
	1714	
Pintado	1715	
Medina y Salazar	1716	
Serrano	1717	
Baltazar y Gurburre	1718	
Medina y Salazar	{ 1719	
	{ 1720	
	1721	Baltazar Gurburre
Serrano	1722	

Flotas to Nueva Espana		Galleons to Tierra Firma
(Azoques)	1723⎱ 1724⎰	Grillo
Serrano	1725	
	1728	Pintado
Mari	1729	
Torres (Azoques)	1730	Pintado
Alderete (Azoques)	1731	
Morales	1732	
(Azoques)	1733	
	1734	
Pintado	1735	
(Azoques)	1736	
(Azoques)	1737	(Guarda Costa Galleons)
	1738	
	1739	

72 See G. Scelle, *La traite négrière aux Indes de Castille* (1906), vol. II, p. 553.

73 Don Thomas Geraldino (Spanish Minister in London) to Don Josef Patiño (Chief Minister in Spain), 1735, March 31. Seville, A. G. de Ind., Indiferente General, leg. 2791.

74 The British consul at Cadiz was always indifferent to the fate of the silver fleet and galleons, as for example in his letters of 1727, April 1, when there was a serious delay, 1727, Sept. 28 and 1729, Aug. 25, when many *indultos* were imposed. P.R.O., S.P.F., Sp. 218–19.

75 See F. Horsfall, unpublished thesis on *British Relations with the Spanish Colonies in the Caribbean*, 1713–39, p. 90, in the Library of the Institute of Historical Research, University of London.

76 J. Campbell, *Spanish America*, pp. 301–2.

77 *Spanish favour to French merchants during war*, 1701–13. The Representation of Charles Russell and other Seville Merchants, 1715, July 14. P.R.O., S.P.F., Spanish Consular Papers, 212.

78 *British exports to Old Spain and the Spanish West Indies*. In 1722 British exports to the Spanish West Indies amounted to about £200,000; those to Old Spain to £600,000. In 1725 to the Spanish West Indies, £240,000; to Old Spain, £630,000. In 1730 to the Spanish West Indies, £240,000; to Old Spain, £770,000. In 1732 to the Spanish West Indies, £230,000; to Old Spain, £820,000. Thereafter the exports to the Spanish West Indies were worth about £20,000 until they stopped altogether in 1739. C. Whitworth, *State of Trade*, pp. 31–2, 79–80.

79 "A letter to a member of Parliament on the Resolution of the House to settle a trade from Great Britain to the South Seas of America." *Somers Tracts* (1814), vol. XIII, p. 117.

80 Shortage of coin was one of the reasons given for the number of bad debts owing to the Company. For details of these see Brit. Mus. Shel. Photostats, I, ii, ff. 291–9.

81 Decision of the Directors' Court, 1732, April 28. Brit. Mus. Add. MSS. 25,494–25,543, vol. XII, Directors' Court Minutes.

82 "Some Considerations humbly offered to prevent the farming out of the factories on the island of Cuba." Brit. Mus. Shel. Photostats, I, ii, ff. 279–81.

178 NOTES TO CHAPTER I

83 Factor Butcher from Caracas to Sub-Governor Burrell, 1738, June 9. Brit. Mus. Shel. Photostats, II, iii, f. 617.

84 Butcher (Caracas) to Burrell, 1738, Jan. 13. "It is impossible to sell negroes between crops, for the inhabitants have no money." Brit. Mus. Shel. Photostats, II, iii, f. 629.

85 The views of some of the Jamaican merchants are expressed in "Reasons against any additional duty on negroes exported from Jamaica", Brit. Mus. Add. MSS. 22,676, f. 75: An objection to the Jamaican negro duties was that they "will be an inducement to the South Sea Company to remove the Asiento ...the consequence whereof to this island...will be in a very short time a return of that deplorable scarcity which we as fully experienced before their settlement here as we have the great relief which the establishment of that trade has brought to this country". Add. MSS. 22,676, f. 79: "To the honourable the members of His Majesty's Council of this island. The humble petition of the underwritten Merchants of this island in behalf of themselves and others, 1727." Negro duties "will plunge us again into the like miserable condition for want of currency from which we are but lately recovered by the Spanish trade & Asiento".

86 *South Sea Company's Agents.* The South Sea Company's agent in Amsterdam was Messrs Muilman & Sons. See resolution of the Directors' Court, 1732, June 9 and 1734, Aug. 2. Brit. Mus. Add. MSS. 25,502 and 25,507, Directors' Court Minutes. The South Sea Company's agent in Hamburg was Mr Hasley. See resolution of the Directors' Court, 1725, July 8/19 and 1734, Sept. 27/Oct. 8. Brit. Mus. Add. MSS. 25,502 and 25,507, Directors' Court Minutes.

87 By 1738 one of the Spanish authorities admitted that "he found matters were much altered since the signing of the Treaty of 1670" and that "neither the Spanish coin nor the fruits of their countries could pass as proofs for condemning an English vessel of having been guilty of illicit commerce" (Minister Keene to the Duke of Newcastle, 1738, Feb. 3. P.R.O., S.P.F., Sp. 130). Yet the presence of cocoa, mules or Mexican money was still accepted by Spanish Colonial Prize Courts as proof of illicit trade and was adduced by the Spanish diplomats as proof of this (Complaints, La Quadra to Keene, 1738, Feb. 21. P.R.O., S.P.F., Sp. 130).

88 For details of the earlier Asientos see G. Scelle, *La traite négrière aux Indes de Castille, passim.*

89 *Illicit trade with the Spanish Colonies* (see also Chapter IV). The governors of the great Spanish Islands in the Caribbean sent many bitter complaints of illicit trade carried on by English, Dutch and French colonists. From Cuba Don Dionisio Martinez de la Vega wrote to the Chief Minister Patiño complaining that English illicit trade was rife at Puerto del Principe, and that the local justices themselves were its directors (De la Vega to Patiño, 1728, Sept. 28. Seville, A. G. de Ind., Audiencia de Santo Domingo, leg. 360). Governor Ximenes reported that the island was too poor to defend its coasts against the numerous foreign illicit traders (Ximenes to Patiño, 1730, May 19. Seville, A. G. de Ind., Aud. S. Dom. leg. 362). Governor Horcasitas urged the need of at least one guard ship to check the illicit trade that passed through the Bahama Channel (Horcasitas to Torrenueva (the Secretary for Marine and the Indies after Patiño), 1737, Aug. 23. Seville, A. G. de Ind., Aud. S. Dom. leg. 498). Governor Abadia of Porto Rico reported that "since about June of last year our foreign neighbours have been very aggressive" (Abadia to Patiño, 1735, June 6. Seville, A. G. de Ind., Aud. S. Dom. leg. 2513).

Chapter II

1 The Commons' slowness with regard to foreign affairs "had given general disgust to the nation, and particularly the City of London", the merchants inspired the Kentish and Legion Petitions of May 1701. *The Parliamentary History of England from the earliest period to the year* 1803, printed by T. C. Hansard, vol. v, col. 1250. "The town would have forced us into it last winter", J. Brydges to T. Coke, 1701, Nov. 8/19. Hist. MSS. Comm. *Cowper Papers* (1888), vol. II, p. 438.

2 "In the first war of the series (1689–97, 1702–13, 1739–48, 1756–63, 1775–83, 1793–1802, 1803–15), however, though it stands marked in histories of North America as the 'first intercolonial war', the colonial question is not very prominent. But it is prominent in the second, which has been called the War of the Spanish Succession.... The Spanish Succession touched us because France threatened by establishing her influence in Spain to enter into the Spanish monopoly of the New World, and to shut us irrevocably out of it. Accordingly the great practical results of this war to England were colonial, namely, the conquest of Acadie and the Asiento contract, which for the first time made England on the great scale a slave trading power." See J. Seeley, *The Expansion of England* (1883), pp. 32–3.

See also Lord Somers' letter to William III, 1698, Aug. 28/Sept. 8, urging the importance of the trade with Spanish America. *Parliamentary History*, vol. v, cols. 1247–8.

3 The Partition Treaty of 1700 had been unpopular "more particularly with the large mercantile class trading to the Mediterranean". Keith Feiling, *A History of the Tory Party*, 1640–1714 (1924), p. 346.

That the importance of trade considerations was kept steadily before the notice of the Secretary of State for the Southern Department is shown by frequent references to it in the despatches of Dr Aglionby, see P.R.O., S.P.F., Sp. 95.

4 "It grieves me to the heart to find that now that the affair becomes public here nearly everyone rejoices that France prefers the will to the Treaty." William III to Heinsius, 1700, Nov. 8. H. Reynald, *Succession d'Espagne, Louis XIV et Guillaume III* (1883), vol. II, p. 325.

"The whole nation appears to agree to accept the execution of the will." French Ambassador Tallard to Torcy, 1700, Dec. 18. H. Reynald, *Succession d'Espagne, Louis XIV et Guillaume III*, vol. II, p. 334.

5 "Our intention in sending you thither is to represent to the Agents and such others of the ministers and principal men of the Court as you can have proper opportunities to discuss with that it has always been our inclination and desire to maintain and cultivate a sincere friendship with the Crown of Spain, and that we have not been wanting to give the best proofs thereof on all occasions in our power, as has been manifest by a series of many years, and if of late we have been induced to enter into some measures that may be thought less agreeable to the interests of Spain, we can't have done it with any other intention, than only to make use of the most profitable means, as affairs then stood, to preserve a general tranquillity in Europe.... But the late King and his ministers having found out another way for the preservation of their monarchy, we shall be very well satisfied with it, if it has the effects they propose to themselves; and especially if by this means they shall be able to preserve their liberty and independency entire, to which we shall ever be ready to contribute to the

utmost of our power." Aglionby was then instructed to express readiness to renew or enlarge the existing treaties between England and Spain or conclude new ones. Finally, he was to press the Spanish authorities to notify his court as soon as possible of the accession of the Prince that England might send her compliments quickly as a proof of her inclination to preserve the good friendship with Spain. P.R.O., S.P.F., Foreign Entry Books, 1700, Dec. 8.

6 See Sir Wm. Trumball to Harley, 1700, June 18/29. Hist. MSS. Comm. *Portland MSS.* (1891), vol. III, p. 621.

7 See Keith Feiling, *A History of the Tory Party* (1924), p. 346.

8 Keith Feiling, *A History of the Tory Party* (1924), p. 347.

9 William III to Heinsius, 1700, Nov. 8. H. Reynald, *Succession d'Espagne, Louis XIV et Guillaume III*, vol. II, p. 325.

10 On November 19 and 29, 1700, the States General of the United Provinces discussed the Spanish question. The friends of William III insisted that Louis XIV would rob Holland of the barrier which it had taken her so long to obtain, that he would open the Scheldt to trade, and that the Dutch trade with Spain and the Spanish colonies would be ruined, but the majority believed that there would be no danger in allowing Philip V to accede to the Spanish throne. H. Reynald, *Louis XIV et Guillaume III*, vol. II, pp. 344-5.

11 "For my greatest object is to prevent the Spanish Netherlands from falling into the hands of France." William III to Heinsius, 1700, Nov. 8. H. Reynald, *Succession d'Espagne, Louis XIV et Guillaume III*, vol. II, p. 326.

12 Tallard, the French Ambassador in London, to Torcy, 1700, Dec. 18. H. Reynald, *Succession d'Espagne, Louis XIV et Guillaume III*, vol. II, p. 334.

13 Tallard to Louis XIV, 1700, Dec. 21. H. Reynald, *Succession d'Espagne, Louis XIV et Guillaume III*, vol. II, p. 337.

14 R. Lodge, *The History of England*, 1660–1702 (1910), pp. 438–9.

15 Louis XIV to Tallard, 1700, Dec. 30. H. Reynald, *Succession d'Espagne, Louis XIV et Guillaume III*, vol. II, pp. 339, 341.

16 G. Scelle, *La traite négrière aux Indes de Castille* (1906), vol. II, pp. 3–68.

17 For a study of the French trade to the Spanish Indies see E. W. Dahlgren, *Les relations commerciales et maritimes entre la France et les côtes de l'Océan Pacifique* (1909), pp. 76–103.

18 Lord Somers to William III, 1698, Aug. 28/Sept. 8. *Parliamentary History*, vol. v, col. 1248.

19 R. Lodge, *Political History of England*, 1660–1702, p. 445.

20 G. Scelle, *La traite négrière aux Indes de Castille*, vol. II, p. 112.

21 "An Essay on the Nature and Methods of Carrying on a Trade to the South Sea." Brit. Mus. Add. MSS. 28,140, f. 20.

22 Charles Russell to Lord Polworth, 1718, Nov. 7/18. Hist. MSS. Comm. *Polworth MSS.* (1911), vol. I, 637.

23 *French negotiation for an Asiento*, 1701. G. Scelle, *La traite négrière aux Indes de Castille*, vol. II, pp. 122, 124, 129, 131, 133.

24 *French Companies trading to the South Seas.* E. W. Dahlgren, *Les relations commerciales et maritimes entre la France et les côtes de l'Océan Pacifique*, pp. 108, 120, 153, 271.

25 F. Schonenberg (the Dutch minister at Madrid who had been given English credentials, 1699) to Secretary Vernon, 1701, Aug. 10. P.R.O., S.P.F., Sp. 75.

26 *Danger of French ships policing Spanish American Seas*, 1701. Schonenberg to Vernon, 1701, March ? and 23, Sept. 22. P.R.O., S.P.F., Sp. 75.

27 Aglionby to Vernon, 1701, June 15. P.R.O., S.P.F., Sp. 75.

28 *Menace to English tobacco trade.* Vernon to Aglionby, 1701, May 20, enclosing a Memorial of Richard March and Edward Haistwell of London— merchants trading in Virginia tobacco to Spain. P.R.O., S.P.F., Foreign Entry Books, 196. Schonenberg to Vernon, 1701, July 13, Aug. 24. P.R.O., S.P.F., Sp. 75.

29 Aglionby to Vernon, 1701, June 15. P.R.O., S.P.F., Sp. 75.

30 *Wine trade threatened.* Schonenberg to Vernon, 1701, Sept. 21. P.R.O., S.P.F., Sp. 75.

31 Schonenberg to Vernon, 1701, Oct. 5. P.R.O., S.P.F., Sp. 75.

32 Schonenberg to Vernon, 1701, Nov. 2. P.R.O., S.P.F., Sp. 75.

33 Schonenberg to Vernon, 1701, Nov. 30. P.R.O., S.P.F., Sp. 75.

34 Aglionby to Vernon, 1701, April 6. P.R.O., S.P.F., Sp. 75.

35 Schonenberg to Vernon, 1701, Aug. 24. P.R.O., S.P.F., Sp. 75.

36 *Danger of French influence in Madrid.* Schonenberg to Vernon, 1701, Sept. 7 and 22. P.R.O., S.P.F., Sp. 75.

37 H. Reynald, *Succession d'Espagne, Louis XIV et Guillaume III*, vol. II, p. 347.

38 S. van Grovestins, *Histoire des...rivalités politiques...* (1851–4), vol. VII, p. 440.

39 Aglionby to Vernon, 1701, June 29. P.R.O., S.P.F., Sp. 75.

40 Keith Feiling, *A History of the Tory Party* (1924), p. 347.

41 H. Reynald, *Succession d'Espagne, Louis XIV et Guillaume III*, vol. II, p. 348.

42 *Parliamentary History*, vol. V, col. 1250.

43 *William III's foreign policy supported by his last Parliament.* R. Lodge, *The History of England*, 1660–1702, pp. 442, 446–8; *Parliamentary History*, vol. V, cols. 1329–30, 1333–4.

44 J. Brydges to T. Coke, 1701, Nov. 8/19. Hist. MSS. Comm. *Cowper Papers* (1888), vol. II, p. 438.

45 Instructions to Paul Methuen, 1714/15, Jan. 15/26. P.R.O., S.P.F., Foreign Entry Books, 135.

CHAPTER III

1 G. Scelle, *La traite négrière aux Indes de Castille*, vol. II, p. 113.

2 For some details of the creation of the South Sea Company see *Hansard*, vol. VI, cols. 1019–23.

3 Keith Feiling, *A History of the Tory Party* (1924), p. 431.

4 "A letter to a member of Parliament on the Resolution of the House to settle a trade from Great Britain to the South Seas to America." *Somers' Tracts* (1814), vol. XIII, p. 117.

5 Bolingbroke, *Sketch of the History of Europe*, quoted in W. E. Lecky, *A History of England in the Eighteenth Century* (1892), vol. I, p. 124.

6 Gaultier to Torcy, 1710, Dec. 28. See I. S. Leadam, *The History of England*, 1702–60 (1921), p. 106.

7 Hist. MSS. Comm. *MSS. of the Duke of Portland at Welbeck*, vol. V, p. 35.

8 *Conclusion of Peace Preliminaries*, 1711. I. S. Leadam, *The History of England*, 1702–60, p. 187.

9 See P.R.O., S.P.F., Archives, 269. Copies of correspondence to and from Spain 1711–14.

10 G. Scelle, *La traite négrière aux Indes de Castille*, vol. II, pp. 524–7.

11 Lexington's Instructions, 1712, Sept. 1. P.R.O., S.P.F., Foreign Entry Books, 133.

12 For details of Lexington's negotiations and a penetrating analysis of the Asiento Contract see G. Scelle, *La traite négrière aux Indes de Castille*, vol. II, pp. 523–76.

13 *Manual Manasses Gilligan*. See G. Scelle, *La traite négrière aux Indes de Castille*, vol. II, p. 122, note. For details of the pension granted to Gilligan out of the Asiento duties, see Geraldino to Patiño, 1734, Nov. 18, which mentions that Gilligan had been granted a pension for the term of the Asiento because he had done so much to secure its adjustment; he had left England in July 1725, and had died in Barbadoes on Sept. 29, 1728. His heir had arrived to claim the pension due from 1725–8. Seville, Archivo General de Indias, Indiferente General, leg. 2790. For his relations with Oxford see *Parliamentary History*, vol. VII, Appendix, cols. lxxi–ii.

14 G. Scelle, *La traite négrière aux Indes de Castille*, vol. II, p. 541.

15 For a text of the Asiento Treaty of March 26, 1713, see M. Postlethwayt's *Dictionary of Commerce* (1774), vol. I, under Asiento. Preliminary Treaty of Peace and Friendship between the Crowns of England and Spain signed on March 27, 1713. Cantillo, *Tratados...de Paz*, p. 70 onwards.

16 Treaty of Peace and Friendship signed July 2/13, 1713. Cantillo, *Tratados...de Paz*, p. 75.

17 Preliminary Treaty of Commerce, July 13, 1713. Cantillo, *Tratados...de Paz*, p. 115.

18 Proposition of the factory of Cadiz, articles 5 and 6: P.R.O., S.P.F., Sp. 79. Freedom and Security for the English Trading to and in the Spanish Dominions: P.R.O., S.P.F., Sp. 105, 269. See also F. Horsfall, *British Relations with the Spanish Colonies in the Caribbean*, 1713–39, p. 39.

19 Bolingbroke to Shrewsbury, 1713, Feb. 18. Bolingbroke, *Letters and Correspondence, public and private* (1798), vol. III, p. 445.

20 Articles of Commerce presented by Lord Lexington, 1713, July 13. P.R.O., S.P.F., Archives, Spain, 269.

21 Bolingbroke to Strafford, 1713, July 13. Brit. Mus. Add. MSS. 22,206, f. 102.

22 Bolingbroke to Lexington, 1712/13, Jan. 7/18; Bolingbroke to Gilligan, 1712/13, Jan. 25/Feb. 5. Bolingbroke, *Correspondence*, vol. III, pp. 291, 347.

23 Lexington to Oxford, 1713, March 28. Hist. MSS. Comm. *Portland MSS.* vol. III, p. 272; Lexington to Dartmouth, 1713, April 17. P.R.O., S.P.F., Sp. 80.

24 Lexington to Bolingbroke, 1713, Sept. 4. P.R.O., S.P.F., Sp. 81.

25 For arguments in favour of the *Juez Conservador* see *The British Merchant*, vol. III, pp. 158–65, 174–83, 201–8.

26 "...Arthur Moore, who was then a Commissioner of Trade and had originally been a footman. On commercial questions, Bolingbroke's knowledge was scarcely more profound than that of the country gentlemen who supported him, and Arthur Moore had on these subjects been his constant advisor.... He was supposed to be a great authority on matters relating to the trade with Spain, and professed to know how England could enrich herself by this traffic more than by all her continental alliances and privileges extorted from her partners in the war. But this great idea did not prevent him, when relying on his knowledge Bolingbroke allowed him to superintend the negotiations of the Spanish commercial treaty, from accepting an enormous bribe from the Spanish Minister to acquiesce in some unjust stipulations which excited the utmost indignation of the House of Commons: T. Macknight, *The Life of H. St. John*

Viscount Bolingbroke (1863), p. 336. See also W. Sichel, *Bolingbroke and his Times* (1901), vol. I, p. 391; R. Harrop, *Bolingbroke* (1884), pp. 149–50.

27 *Parliamentary History*, vol. VI, col. 1361.

28 *Parliamentary History*, vol. VI, col. 1362.

29 *Failure of English trade to Spain to recover after* 1713. *The British Merchant*: A Collection of Papers relating to the Trade and Commerce of Great Britain and Ireland (2nd edition, 1743), published by Mr Charles King, vol. III, pp. 81, 84, 95, 227.

30 *Spanish tariff as regulated by Commercial Treaty of* 1713. *The British Merchant*, vol. III, p. 171.

31 A. Mounier, *Les faits et la doctrine économiques en Espagne sous Philippe V*, pp. 40–1.

32 *Spanish duties increased by the Commercial Treaty of* 1713. *The British Merchant*, vol. III, p. 209; cf. pp. 171–2, 231–2.

33 Memorial of the Turkey Company, 1714, July 15. P.R.O., C.O. 389, 24.

34 *Opinions of British merchants on evils of the Commercial Treaty of* 1713. *Journal of the Commissioners for Trade and Plantations*, 1708/9–1714/15; 1713, Aug. 13/24 and 20/31, Oct. 2/13, pp. 464, 468, 473. The merchants estimated that the duties in Andalusia were about 10 per cent after the king's abatement, but that English merchants paid 11 per cent where the Dutch paid 5 per cent and the French 7 per cent or 8 per cent. In Catalonia the duties were 7 to 10 per cent, and Valencia and Aragon 7 to 8 per cent. In the Canaries duties had been at 6 per cent. At Alicante duties had been raised to 20 per cent, but Biscay and Guipuzcoa were almost free ports with duties at 1 per cent.

35 *The value of having a Juez Conservador.* For the view that such an official was unnecessary see *Journal of the Commissioners for Trade and Plantations*, 1708/9–1714/15: 1713, Aug. 12/23, 13/24, p. 463; comments on clause 18, p. 465. For the view that he was urgently needed see *The British Merchant*, vol. III, pp. 159–60, 161, 162, 164, 204. For orders to recover this protector for British trade see *Journal of the Commissioners for Trade and Plantations*, 1708/9–1714/15, 1714, May 27, p. 538.

36 *Parliamentary discussion of the Commercial Treaty of* 1713. *Parliamentary History*, vol. VI, cols. 1256–9, 1343–5, 1348, 1361.

37 For an examination of the relative importance of the Annual Ship and the exemption from the 15 per cent duty at Cadiz see G. Scelle, *La traite négrière aux Indes de Castille*, vol. II, pp. 532, 552–4.

38 "A Plan for preventing a trade being carried on from France to the South Seas"; "For preserving our trade with the Spanish West Indies": P.R.O., C.O. 388, 17. See also F. Horsfall, *British Relations with the Spanish Colonies*, p. 72.

39 Harris to the Commissioners for Trade, 1714/15, Jan. 7. P.R.O., C.O. 388, 17.

40 Bolingbroke to the envoys at Utrecht, 1713, Aug. 29. P.R.O., S.P.F., Foreign Archives, Holland, Utrecht, 1713, vol. 269.

41 Lt.-Governor Pulleine of Bermuda to the Commissioners for Trade and Plantations, 1714, Jan. 9: "The Spaniards, from several of the ports, here in the North Seas, arm out sloops with commissions to seize all English vessels in which they find any Spanish money (even to the value of ten pieces of eight), any salt, cacao, or hides for which reasons any vessels that trade in those parts, from port to port, are certainly prizes." *Cal. St. Pap. Col.* July 1712–July 1714, p. 285.

42 Address of the Council and Assembly of Jamaica to Her Britannic Majesty, 1713 Dec., sent by Bolingbroke to the Commissioners for Trade and Plantations, 1714, March 18. *Cal. St. Pap. Col.* July 1712–July 1714, pp. 315–17.

43 Instructions to Lord Bingley, 1714, May 8, and additional instructions, June 2. See *Journal of the Commissioners for Trade and Plantations*, 1708/9–1714/15, pp. 529, 535–40, 548–9, 552–4.

44 *Parliamentary investigation into the Commercial Treaty of 1713 and the Asiento of 1715*. *Parliamentary History*, vol. VII, cols. 53, 66, 74; Appendix, col. viii, ix, lxx-lxxii.

45 *State Trials* (1809), xv, 1179.

46 See Townshend to the Commissioners for Trade and Plantations, 1714, Dec. 22, enclosing Instructions for Mr Paul Methuen: P.R.O., C.O. 388, 17; Methuen's Instructions of 1715, Jan. 15/26, and additional instructions Feb. 2/13: P.R.O., S.P.F., Foreign Entry Papers, 135. Also mentioned in F. Horsfall, *British Relations with the Spanish Colonies*, p. 64.

47 See *Cambridge Modern History*, vol. v (1908), p. 378.

48 Memorial of the Spanish Merchants, 1714/15, Jan. 10: P.R.O., C.O. 388, 17. See also F. Horsfall, *British Relations with the Spanish Colonies*, p. 58.

49 F. Horsfall, *British Relations with the Spanish Colonies*, p. 62.

50 Townshend to the Commissioners for Trade and Plantations, 1714, Oct. 28, enclosing Pontchartrain to d'Iberville, 1714, Oct. 17: *Cal. St. Pap. Col.* Aug. 1714–Dec. 1715, pp. 35-6.

51 Memorial of the Spanish Merchants, 1714/15, Jan. 10: P.R.O., C.O., Board of Trade Commercial Original Correspondence, 1710–40, vol. 17. See also F. Horsfall, *British Relations with the Spanish Colonies*, p. 58.

52 T. Bannister to the Commissioners for Trade and Plantations, 1715, July 7: *Cal. St. Pap. Col.* Aug. 1714–Dec. 1715, pp. 222-5. See also F. Horsfall, *British Relations with the Spanish Colonies*, p. 61.

53 *Journal of the Assembly of Jamaica* (1811–29), II, 176, 1715, Dec. 28.

54 Instructions to Paul Methuen, 1714/15, Feb. 2/13: Brit. Mus. Egerton MSS. 2170, f. 11. See also F. Horsfall, *British Relations with the Spanish Colonies*, p. 64.

55 Stanhope to Methuen, 1715, April 26. P.R.O., S.P.F., Foreign Entry Books, 135.

56 *Methuen's attempt to improve conditions of English trade in Spain.* W. Michael, *Englische Geschichte im 18en Jahrhundert* (1896), vol. I, pp. 687, 689.

57 Orford to Bubb. Brit. Mus. Egerton MSS. 2170, f. 23.

58 *Bubb's negotiation of a Commercial Treaty*, 1715. Lloyd C. Sanders, *Patron and Place Hunter* (1919), p. 26.

59 Methuen had presented a Memorial of English trade complaints, 1715, April 22. P.R.O., S.P.F., Sp. 83.

60 Brit. Mus. Egerton MSS. 2170, ff. 195-8.

61 Stanhope to Bubb, 1715, Oct. 19. Lloyd C. Sanders, *Patron and Place Hunter*, p. 28.

62 Lloyd C. Sanders, *Patron and Place Hunter*, pp. 28–9.

63 *Bubb's successful negotiation of the Commercial Treaty of 1715.* W. Michael, *Englische Geschichte im 18en Jahrhundert*, vol. I, pp. 698–701.

64 Treaty explanatory of those of peace and commerce confirmed between England and Spain in 1713, 1715, Dec. 3/14. Hertslet, *Commercial Treaties*, vol. II, p. 221.

65 1715, Dec. 20, the Treaty was laid before the Board, on Dec. 21 it was approved. *Journal of the Commissioners for Trade and Plantations*, 1714–18, p. 100.

66 Lloyd C. Sanders, *Patron and Place Hunter*, p. 29.

67 W. Michael, *Englische Geschichte im 18en Jahrhundert*, vol. I, p. 701.

68 *Agitation over English right to take salt at Tortudos.* Dummer, agent of Massachusetts, several times appeared before the Commissioners for Trade and

Plantations with complaints of ships seized at Tortudos. *Journal of Commissioners for Trade and Plantations*, 1708–14; 1713, Sept. 25/Oct. 6, Oct. 6/17, Dec. 1/12, 4/15, pp. 471, 474, 486, 488. Bolingbroke to the Commissioners for Trade enclosing the Memorial, 1713, Sept. 25. *Journal of Commissioners for Trade and Plantations*, 1708–14, p. 471.

69 Bubb to Stanhope, 1715, Dec. 15, quoted by W. Michael, *Englische Geschichte im 18en Jahrhundert*, vol. I, p. 700.

70 *Possibility of Anglo-Spanish alliance*, 1716. Bubb to Stanhope, 1716, Feb. 19, quoted by W. Michael, *Englische Geschichte im 18en Jahrhundert*, vol. I, p. 704. For Stanhope's reply see *ibid.* vol. I, p. 705.

71 *Bubb's negotiation of a new Asiento Treaty*, 1716. See W. Michael, *Englische Geschichte im 18en Jahrhundert*, vol. I, p. 706, and Lloyd C. Sanders, *Patron and Place Hunter*, pp. 30–2.

72 Declaratory Treaty making clear some of the articles in the *Asiento de Negros*, 1716, May 26. Cantillo, *Tratados...de Paz*, pp. 173–4.

73 Methuen to Bubb, 1716, Aug. 14, quoted by W. Michael, *Englische Geschichte im 18en Jahrhundert*, vol. I, p. 706.

74 Consul Herne to Stanhope, 1716, March 16: "I informed the Envoy that the late treaty as yet is not taken notice of or put in practice." P.R.O., S.P.F., Sp. Consular, 213.

75 Reynolds and Hervey (Bilbao) to Stanhope, 1716, March 13. P.R.O., S.P.F., Sp. Consular, 213.

76 Consul Russell (Cadiz) to Craggs, 1718, April 30. P.R.O., S.P.F., Sp. Consular, 213.

77 Consul Russell (Cadiz) to Methuen, 1717, March 8: "The imposition of 2 p. 100 in Sevilla and 1½ p. 100 upon the Customs of all goods imported and exported which was laid on in the war and ought to have bin taken off with the Peace still continued to bee levied and paid which is a grievance to the trade and commerce and the Ministers in the respective ports excuse themselves with saying they have noe orders fro Court to suspend the recovery and in the meane while the Merch^ts suffer." P.R.O., S.P.F., Sp. Consular, 213.

78 Herne (Alicante) to Addison, 1717, Dec. 26. P.R.O., S.P.F., Sp. Consular, 212.

79 Russell (Cadiz) to Addison, 1717, July 28. P.R.O., S.P.F., Sp. Consular, 213.

80 For details of Patiño's career see Appendix.

81 Russell (Cadiz) to Addison, 1717, Sept. 27. P.R.O., S.P.F., Sp. Consular, 213.

82 Blakeley (Alicante) to Undersecretary Craggs, 1718, July 3. P.R.O., S.P.F., Sp. Consular, 213.

83 *Woollen and fish trades menaced*. Blakeley (Alicante) to Craggs, 1718, July 3. P.R.O., S.P.F., Sp. Consular, 213.

84 *Dispute over privileges of foreign Consuls*: see also notes Chap. IV, nn. 80, 89; Chap. V, n. 117. Minister Keene to Newcastle, 1728, June 21; Consul Cayley to Keene, 1728, June 22; Consul Russell to Addison, 1717, Sept. 27; Consul Wescombe to Bolingbroke, 1714, Sept. 23; Consul Holloway to Stanhope, 1716, March 24, June 30. P.R.O., S.P.F., Sp. 99, 212, 213, 218.

85 *Exactions at Cadiz and Alicante*. Consul Wescombe (Cadiz) to Bolingbroke, 1714, July 15; Solomon Merrett Jnr. (Alicante) to Solomon Merrett & Sons, 1716, Jan. 26; Consul Herne (Alicante) to Addison, 1716, Dec. 26. P.R.O., S.P.F., Sp. Consular, 212, 213.

86 Merrett to Merrett, 1716, April 5. P.R.O., S.P.F., Sp. Consular, 213.
87 Herne (Alicante) to Addison, 1717, Aug. 16. P.R.O., S.P.F., Sp. Consular, 213.
88 Herne (Alicante) to Addison, 1718, Jan. 3. P.R.O., S.P.F., Sp. Consular, 213.

CHAPTER IV

1 *The British Merchant*, 1743 edition, vol. III, p. 104.

2 The Company's servant Plowes, in a sworn statement made to the Spanish plenipotentiary at the Congress of Soissons, stated that the Chevalier d'Eon had received £1000 and £800 a year for conniving at the fraud. V. L. Brown, "The South Sea Company and Contraband Trade", *Am. Hist. Rev.* vol. XXXI, p. 666.

3 The Jamaican agents reported a new spirit among the Spanish authorities. Of one captain of a negro sloop who was punished for smuggling it was said: "He suffers more from the rigour of the times than for his crimes." Merewether (Jamaica) to Sub-Governor Burrell, 1737, Sept. 6: Brit. Mus. Shel. Photostats, II, iv, f. 875.

In an undated letter bound among those written at this time the South Sea Company agent mentions: "The new and severe regulations of the Spaniards." Merewether to Burrell, undated: Brit. Mus. Shel. Photostats, II, iv, f. 901.

4 Merewether to Burrell, 1737, Sept. 5: "It would be for the Company's service that the same Captain did not always go to the same port." Brit. Mus. Shel. Photostats, II, iv, f. 831.

5 Reported in Merewether to Burrell, 1736, Sept. 6. Brit. Mus. Shel. Photostats, II, iv, f. 875.

6 Factor Nicholson (Havana) to Burrell, 1732, Jan. 24, contained details of the difficulties of the captain of the *Belmont* who had tried to smuggle unknown to the factors. Brit. Mus. Shel. Photostats, II, iv, f. 964.

7 Merewether to Burrell, 1736, June 5. Brit. Mus. Shel. Photostats, II, iv, f. 893.
8 Merewether to Burrell, 1736, Jan. 26. Brit. Mus. Shel. Photostats, II, iv, f. 863.
9 Merewether to Burrell, 1737, Sept. 30. Brit. Mus. Shel. Photostats, II, iv, f. 826.

10 D. Templeman, *The Secret History of the late Directors of the South Sea Company* (1735), p. 40.

11 *Illicit trade of South Sea Company Agents in Jamaica.* Merewether to Burrell, 1736, Jan. 25. Brit. Mus. Shel. Photostats, II, iv, ff. 861–2.

12 Merewether to Burrell, 1736, June 5. Brit. Mus. Shel. Photostats, II, iv, f. 892.

13 Merewether to Burrell, 1736, Sept. 6. Brit. Mus. Shel. Photostats, II, iv, f. 875.
14 Merewether to Burrell, 1736, June 5. Brit. Mus. Shel. Photostats, II, iv, f. 893.

15 In V. L. Brown, "The South Sea Company and Contraband Trade", *Am. Hist. Rev.* vol. XXXI, pp. 666, 668.

16 *Connivance of Governor of Buenos Ayres in illicit trade.* Faure (Buenos Ayres) to Burrell, 1738, Aug. 25. Brit. Mus. Shel. Photostats, II, ii, ff. 359, 361.

17 Hutchinson (Panama) to Burrell, 1731, Dec. 4. Brit. Mus. Shel. Photostats, II, iii, f. 539.

18 V. L. Brown, "The South Sea Company and Contraband Trade", *Am. Hist. Rev.* vol. XXXI, p. 668.

19 *An address to the Proprietors of the South Sea Company Capital* (1732), pp. 6–9.

20 D. Templeman, *The Secret History of the late Directors of the South Sea Company*, pp. 14–24.

21 V. L. Brown, "The South Sea Company and Contraband Trade", *Am. Hist. Rev.* vol. xxxi, pp. 666 onwards.

22 Patiño to Geraldino, 1735, March 7; cited in Geraldino to Patiño, 1735, March 24. Seville, A. G. de Ind., Indif. Gen. leg. 2791.

23 Because of the illicit trade of the two previous ships the licence for the *Royal George's* second voyage in 1724 was not granted till December. Memoir sent by M. van der Meer to Sir Robert Walpole, 1727, Aug. 30: P.R.O., S.P.F., Sp. 98.

24 Horace Walpole's secret Memoir for the instruction of the Duke of Bedford. Brit. Mus. Add. MSS. 9131, ff. 232–3.

25 Don Francisco Antonio de Ayala y Castillo to Don Miguel de Santisteban, 1739, March 2. Seville, A. G. de Ind., Aud. S. Dom. leg. 498.

26 *English trade with Spanish Colonies,* 1702–13. Curtis Nettles, "England and the Spanish American Trade, 1680–1715", *The Journal of Modern History,* vol. iii, p. 19.

27 *A New History of Jamaica* (1740), pp. 272–3.

28 Merewether (Jamaica) to Burrell, 1737, Sept. 5. Brit. Mus. Shel. Photostats, ii, iv, f. 831.

29 Merewether to Burrell, 1736, Sept. 6. Brit. Mus. Shel. Photostats, ii, iv, f. 876.

30 Merewether to Burrell, 1736, Jan. 6. Brit. Mus. Shel. Photostats, ii, iv, ff. 867–8.

31 Merewether to Burrell, undated. Brit. Mus. Shel. Photostats, ii, iv, f. 901.

32 V. L. Brown, "Contraband Trade as a factor in the Decline of Spain's Empire in America", *Hisp. Am. Hist. Rev.* vol. viii, p. 178.

33 For details of the Carerra de Indias see C. H. Haring, *Trade and Navigation between Spain and the Indies in the time of the Hapsburgs* (1918); A. P. Newton, *The European Nations in the West Indies,* 1493–1688 (1933); John Campbell, *A Concise History of Spanish America* (1741).

34 For details of the working of the Barlovento Squadron see in Simancas, Marine Papers, Expediciones, legs. 392–404; and in Seville, A. G. de Ind., Indif. Gen. leg. 2556.

35 For a very interesting explanation of the trade routes in the West Indies and the influence on them of winds and currents see F. Horsfall, *British Relations with the Spanish Colonies in the Caribbean,* 1713–39, pp. 3–14, based on a general description of the Spanish West Indies written in the year 1718 by Captain Domingo Gonzalez Carranza, principal pilot to the King of Spain for the *Flotas,* "faithfully translated from the original Spanish manuscript into English and humbly presented by Your Grace's most devoted and obedient servant, James Shaftoe", 1740: P.R.O., C.O. 319, 2; and "An account of the several Sea Ports belonging to the Spaniards in America, which John Fengess has been in a trading with a description of their fortifications to the best of his knowledge" delivered to the Council of Trade, 1705, Sept. P.R.O., C.O., Jamaica, 51.

36 Lt.-Gov. Pulleine (Bermuda) to the Commissioners for Trade and Plantations, 1714, Jan. 9. *Cal. St. Pap. Col.* July 1712–July 1714, p. 285.

37 F. Horsfall, *British Relations with the Spanish Colonies in the Caribbean,* 1713–39, pp. 52–3.

38 Van der Meer to Stanhope, 1727, May 26; to Walpole, 1727, July 8; to La Paz, 1727, Aug. 19; to La Paz, 1727, Sept. 23. P.R.O., S.P.F., Sp. 98.

39 Keene (Madrid) to Newcastle, 1728, Aug. 21. P.R.O., S.P.F., Sp. 99.

40 Petition of the Jamaican Merchants, 1730, May 28. P.R.O., S.P.F., Sp. 101.

41 Hayman and Haynes to Bonham (owner of the *Anne*), 1730, July 24. P.R.O., S.P.F., Sp. 101.

42 Keene to Delafaye, 1730, Sept. 28. P.R.O., S.P.F., Sp. 104.

43 Newcastle to the Admiralty, 1730, Sept. 25/Oct. 6. P.R.O., S.P.F., Sp. 101.

44 Admiral Stewart to Burchett at the Admiralty, 1731, March 9. P.R.O., S.P.F., Sp. 101.

45 J. Dennis (Cuba) to Burrell, 1731, Nov. 2. Brit. Mus. Shel. Photostats, II, ii, f. 346.

46 That the ex-slave really had such high-sounding titles is proved by official documents in the Spanish archives, e.g. an Auto drawn up at Porto Rico, 1730, Dec. 15, Seville, A. G. de Ind., Aud. S. Dom. leg. 573.

See also The South Sea Company factor (Cuba) to the Governor of Jamaica, 1731, Aug. 18: "Though we fear it is not in Your Excellency's power to remedy these mischiefs those vermin called *Guarda Costas* are daily committing on the British nation, yet we can't avoid informing you that we hear at this time, as we learn from the best information, there are twelve or fourteen of these sloops at Sea, most of which carry a hundred men and upwards, cruizing on the English under pretence of guarding their own coasts, out of Porto Rico belonging to one man, a mulatto, named Miguel Henriquez, are the following:

1. Diego de Morales (a little man as to size), born in Port St Mary's in Spain, and married to a negro woman in Porto Rico, sails in a sloop called the *Esperanza* with guns and 12 swivels and upwards of 100 men.

2. Gaspar Lerrudo, born in the Canary Islands, married in Cumana.

3. Pedro Juan, born Port St Mary's, married in Canaries.

4. Cyprian Zemenes de la Cruz, born in Havana.

5. Bernado Figueroa, born Galicia, married in Porto Rico.

6. Josef Ortez—commands a low galley.

7. Melcher Berrera, married in Santiago de Cuba; he now sails out of this last place in the merchant service, having for the present left off pirating.

8. Louis de la Londer.

9. Pedro—known by no other name...now cruising among the Bahama Isles.

"By this list your Excellency will see what a pretty armada of pirates belong to the above Island of Porto Rico where the owner of them, Miguel Enriquez, is in a manner absolute Lord, and by virtue of several cedulas from His Catholic Majesty is exempt from the jurisdiction of the Governor there." P.R.O., S.P.F., Sp. 101.

47 Dennis to Burrell, 1731, Nov. 2. P.R.O., S.P.F., Sp. 101; Brit. Mus. Shel. Photostats, II, iii, ff. 346–7.

48 Don Josef de Pozo y Onesto to His Catholic Majesty, 1728, Oct. 9. Seville, A. G. de Ind., Aud. S. Dom. leg. 2513.

49 Dennis (Cuba) to Burrell, 1731, Nov. 2. Brit. Mus. Shel. Photostats, II, ii, f. 345.

50 Keene to Newcastle, 1731, Feb. 18. "M. Patiño told me that if the report of His Majesty's having made a Treaty with the Emperor proved true, and that the security of Don Carlos' succession was fully provided for, and that it contained

nothing to prejudice Spain they would immediately accede to it and enter into a guaranty of the Emperor's succession...we should be made easy in our commerce and though he (Patiño) would not expressly say that their works at Gibraltar...should be demolished, he assured me that in proportion to the friendship Their Catholick Majesties should receive from the King they would do what would be agreeable to His Majesty and the nation...." P.R.O., S.P.F., Sp. 107.

51   Keene to Newcastle, 1731, Oct. 20, with news that the Spanish fleet had joined Admiral Wager at Barcelona; Keene to Newcastle, 1731, Oct. 26, Admiral Wager sailing with the Spanish fleet: P.R.O., S.P.F., Sp. 108. Keene to Newcastle, 1731, Oct. 31, Nov. 24, Wager sends news of Don Carlos's safe arrival and is rewarded with a portrait of Philip V set in diamonds: P.R.O., S.P.F., Sp. 108.

52   Keene to Newcastle, 1731, April 13. P.R.O., S.P.F., Sp. 107.

53   Stewart to Newcastle, 1732, April 28. P.R.O., S.P.F., Sp. 115.

54   La Paz to Keene, 1731, May 13, enclosed in Keene to Newcastle, 1731, May 22, informing him that orders to stop depredations had been sent to the Governors of Havana, Cuba, Porto Rico, Santo Domingo and Trinidad, and that in future not even illicit trade was to be an excuse for prizing British ships. P.R.O., S.P.F., Sp. 107.

55   Keene to Newcastle, 1731, July 26. P.R.O., S.P.F., Sp. 101.

56   Carta Orden enclosed in Keene to Newcastle, 1732, Feb. 9. P.R.O., S.P.F., Sp. 111.

57   Privateering regulations, 1733, July 20. Seville, A. G. de. Ind., Indif. Gen. leg. 1597.

58   The Seville Commission, 1732. Keene to Newcastle, 1731, Aug. 3, "The Spanish Commissioners are named": P.R.O., S.P.F., Sp. 108; do. 1731, Sept. 21, "Work is to begin soon": P.R.O., S.P.F., Sp. 108; Keene to Delafaye, 1732, Feb. 23, "The Commission has opened": P.R.O., S.P.F., Sp. 111.

59   Keene to Delafaye, 1732, April 11. P.R.O., S.P.F., Sp. 111.

60   After long discussions on the restoration of prizes, and the future regulations for trade, the Commission reached the end of the time laid down by the Treaty of Seville for its existence, and the Commissioners came home. Stert to Delafaye, 1733, July 31: "I think so long as this Court remains at San Ildefonso our conferences cannot be renewed to any purpose, for Mr Keene will always be obliged to attend wherever His Catholic Majesty is, and two of the Spanish Commissioners tell me that they must constantly be within call of M. Patiño...." P.R.O., S.P.F., Sp. 117.

61   Horace Walpole's Secret Memoir. Brit. Mus. Add. MSS. 9131, f. 238.

62   English ships prized by Guarda Costas.

1733. Oct. 27. Keene to Patiño, reclaiming the Robert of Liverpool and Mary of Liverpool. P.R.O., S.P.F., Sp. 117.

1734. Sept. 18. Keene to Patiño, Eagle, and four ships already reclaimed on July 27, 1733. P.R.O., S.P.F., Sp. 123.
       Sept. 22. Keene to Patiño, Levret. P.R.O., S.P.F., Sp. 120.
       Dec. 9. Keene to Patiño, Friends' Adventure. P.R.O., S.P.F., Sp. 120.

1735. April 4. Keene to Newcastle, mentioning the Friendship. P.R.O., S.P.F., Sp. 122.
       July 8. Keene to Patiño reclaiming the Gibraltar and Dispatch. P.R.O., S.P.F., Sp. 123.

1735. July 26. Keene to Patiño reclaiming the *Jamaica, Endeavour* and five others. P.R.O., S.P.F., Sp. 123.

Sept. 7. Keene to Patiño, *Blessing*. P.R.O., S.P.F., Sp. 123.

63 Quoted in Keene to Patiño, 1735, July 26. P.R.O., S.P.F., Sp. 123.

64 Abadia (Porto Rico) to Patiño, 1736, July 18. Seville, A. G. de Ind., Aud. S. Dom. leg. 2297.

65 *Spanish privateering instructions*. A series of privateering regulations is preserved in Seville, A. G. de Ind., 1674, Aud. S. Dom. leg. 2513; 1718, Nov. 17, Indif. Gen. leg. 1828; 1732, Jan. 28, Aud. S. Dom. leg. 2171; 1733, July 20, Indif. Gen. leg. 1597; 1734, May 30, Aud. S. Dom. leg. 492; 1738, July 20, Indif. Gen. leg. 1828.

66 Horace Walpole's Secret Memoir. Brit. Mus. Add. MSS. 9131, ff. 221–2.

67 Keene to Newcastle, 1738, Feb. 3. P.R.O., S.P.F., Sp. 130.

68 De la Vega (Cuba) to Patiño, 1728, Sept. 28. Seville, A. G. de Ind., Aud. S. Dom. leg. 360.

69 Don Juan de Hoyo to His Catholic Majesty, 1728, Aug. 12. Seville, A. G. de Ind., Aud. S. Dom. leg. 360.

70 Abadia (Porto Rico) to Patiño, 1734, April 10. Seville, A. G. de Ind., Aud. S. Dom. leg. 2513.

71 Ximenes (Cuba) to Patiño, 1730, May 19. Seville, A. G. de Ind., Aud. S. Dom. leg. 362.

72 Horcasitas (Cuba) to Torrenueva, 1737, Aug. 23. Seville, A. G. de Ind., Aud. S. Dom. leg. 498.

73 Abadia (Porto Rico) to Patiño, 1736, July 18. Seville, A. G. de Ind., Aud. S. Dom. leg. 2297.

74 Abadia (Porto Rico) to Patiño, 1735, June 6. Seville, A. G. de Ind., Aud. S. Dom. leg. 2513.

75 Abadia (Porto Rico) to Patiño, 1737, March 10. Seville, A. G. de Ind., Aud. S. Dom. leg. 2513.

76 Abadia (Porto Rico) to Patiño, 1736, July 18. Seville, A. G. de Ind., Aud. S. Dom. leg. 2297.

77 Don Francisco Cornejo to Don Benito Tigueroa y Prado, 1734, Jan. 25, enclosed by Consul Parker (Corunna) to Newcastle, 1734, Sept. 26: "...for tho' I have a modern Hydrographical plan of the Coasts in Yucatan, yet it is not sufficient for me to explain myself with satisfaction. To which I add, that I am unacquainted with the circumstances of the present condition of the English there, as to the men themselves; whether they have built any Fort, on what sort of ground, and how, or with what defences, or the numbers existing there, &c....

"...at the end of the year 1716, happening to be at Vera Cruz, I joined in making of an Armament which went over to that Lake, where we were likewise met by some men of Campeche, and, in that Lake 24 sail, half of them ships, were taken, and the English driven away from thence; and to prevent their returning for the future, a small Fort called Carmel was raised upon the entrance, with Fascines, Earth and Stakes, together with some Guns of 24 pound Ball, which I got transported thither, and likewise a Company of 70 Foot and a good Commander, Major Jerome de Andrade; Notwithstanding which, in a short time afterwards, three English Brigantines went to that place, and landed three hundred men, who advanced with such resolution quite uncovered, that they entered the Fort, and killed the Commander and others, but the rest of the Spaniards behaved themselves with so great valour as to drive the English out of the Fort. Who having left many of their companions dead, retired, and after that time never returned to that Lake." P.R.O., S.P.F., Sp. 217.

78 Abadia (Porto Rico) to Patiño, 1737, March 10. Seville, A. G. de Ind., Aud. S. Dom. leg. 2513.

79 Tucker (Alicante) to Newcastle, 1730, April 26. P.R.O., S.P.F., Sp. 216. Cf. Cayley (Cadiz) to Newcastle, 1730, May 9. From Cadiz Cayley wrote that ever since his arrival in 1728 "our trade has been subject to very great and frequent oppressions. Every article almost of the treaties have been infringed, and privileges of all kinds broke through" (P.R.O., S.P.F., Sp. 219). Keene to Newcastle, 1730, Dec. 15. Even the ambassador himself had to admit that "it is not only in the Indies that His Majesty's subjects suffer by these manifest violations of our treaties and public faith, the ports of Spain furnish but too many examples of this kind" (P.R.O., S.P.F., Sp. 104).

80 *Dispute over rights of foreign Consuls continued*: see also notes Chap. III, n. 84; Chap. IV, n. 89; Chap. V, n. 117. The question of consular privileges was once again the chief source of complaints, and continued to be so until early in 1731. No new point was raised, but the desire of the Spanish ministers to have the Consul's powers limited in their *cedula* of approbation, and the refusal of the Consuls to accept such *cedulas*, resulted in the British merchants being without their legal protectors for nearly four years. Parker at Corunna was the first to run foul of the new reforming spirit in the Spanish administration, but although the Governor at first refused to admit him because the question of consular rights had not been settled, he was peacefully exercising his duties before the end of 1727 (Parker (Corunna) to Delafaye, 1727, Sept. 1: P.R.O., S.P.F., Sp. 215). Early in 1728 new Patents were issued to all the British Consuls, since Keene had hoped that at last His Catholic Majesty might accede to their claim to nominate Vice-Consuls (Stanyan to Holloway, 1728, Feb. 19: P.R.O., S.P.F., Sp. 104, 140). It was found, however, that the diplomat had misjudged the situation, for when in June His Catholic Majesty approved the appointments he did so in terms which strictly limited the Consular powers (Keene to Newcastle, 1728, June 21: P.R.O., S.P.F., Sp. 99). For six months Keene struggled to get permission for Vice-Consuls to work in the same port as their principals, and for Spaniards to be allowed to serve in this capacity, but La Paz was firm in his refusal, "for these as well as the rest which you call restrictions are nothing else but points of formality, which, without being contrary to the treaties, were established for a general rule to restrain the too great latitude the Consuls had given themselves through the carelessness of the Royal Ministers during the reign of King Charles II" (La Paz to Keene, 1728, Dec. 28: P.R.O., S.P.F., Sp. 99). Keene remarked "it is inconceivable with what *opiniâtreté* our consuls' patents are refused approbation in the usual form. Had they their lictors like their elder brethren in Rome they could not be more dreaded by M. de la Paz, and the *Junta de Extranjeros* established at Madrid, which I wish heartily I could get abolished" (Keene to Delafaye, 1730, July 21: P.R.O., S.P.F., Sp. 103). But not till late in 1730 was a compromise reached. Persons other than Englishmen were to be eligible to serve as Vice-Consuls, and Consuls might be helped in their duties by secretaries or agents so long as these were not called Vice-Consuls (Keene to Newcastle, 1731, Nov. 3: P.R.O., S.P.F., Sp. 104). Consul Cayley objected to accepting his limited *cedula*, but on Keene's advice he did so (Cayley to Newcastle, 1731, Jan. 16: P.R.O., S.P.F., Sp. 219); the other Consuls had made no objections, and although the principle remained undetermined, after 1731 the fact gave no further trouble.

81   *Molestation of English trade in Spain*, 1727–32. Barker (Alicante) to Newcastle, 1727, Aug. 17: "A judge...was sent hither some time since by Don Josef Patiño, President of the Royal Council of the *Hacienda* to inspect into some abuses which he suspected to have been committed by the principal officers of the Customs House, and in order to make a discovery of that affair, said Judge has entered the dwelling houses of several merchants of other nations, has demanded their books, and on their refusing to exhibit them, has laid a mulct of 500 ducats upon them, confining them to their houses for a prison under the penalty of a thousand ducats, and taken an inventory of their effects, and on the 12th current he proceeded against the house of Masset Hall & Co. English merchants residing here...and on the 16 day against the house of Hammond, Barker and Revelly English merchants also, in the which I am concerned." P.R.O., S.P.F., Sp. 215. Holloway (Malaga) to Newcastle, 1732, April 20: "I have also to acquaint your Grace that the Mayor of Malaga, attended by the administrator of the Customs House with three scriveners, and divers other officers did on the 26th March, enter and search the Houses of all the merchants there, of all nations, with the pretext, that they looked for printed linens and calicoes, which were some time ago prohibited to be imported, because they could not be distinguished from such as were made in Turkey and Barbary, which were absolutely prohibited to be introduced and though they did not find any, the merchants were much alarmed at this novelty. The Consuls of all nations have complained against it and demanded a testimony in form of what had been transacted, in order to remit to their respective Ministers at Seville, but they were not able to obtain any so were obliged to be content with sending to each minister a duplicate of the Representation they had made upon this affair to which they had not been able to procure any answer, from the Spanish Officers, and magistrates." P.R.O., S.P.F., Sp. 216.

82   *Health regulations used to oppress English trade.* Cayley (Cadiz) to Newcastle, 1728, July 20: "...The two or three ships that arrived here since the publications of that Edict, having performed their quarantaines, are now to undergo the *Fondeo* or examination thereby directed before their cargoes can be brought ashore; and they began upon the first yesterday in the following manner. Four Officers named for that purpose by the Governour go on board the ship and cause her whole lading to be taken out and put into boats, when having deliberately examined it, they suffer it to be landed; or that part of it, which is not designed for this port but for some other, to be put into her hold again.

"Besides the great inconveniency and loss that must accrue to the merchant from having his goods thus opened and removed backwards and forwards, he is obliged to pay these officers for doing it about six pieces of eight a day, besides their victuals; which is an excessive hardship and imposition, and the more so, as it is not only in contradiction to the very Edict itself, which said, that the several regulations therein made shall be executed with as little expense and burden to trade as possible, but no doubt will be likewise a temptation to these fellows to keep each ship under their examination as long a time as ever they can, in order to get the more by her. And what is very extraordinary, the Governor will not consent to have any more than one set of these officers to examine all the ships that arrive; so that being two, three, four or five days in clearing one ship, as they must be and sometimes longer according to their slow way of going about it, they will hardly ever be able to get through them all; at least it will be after a very considerable detention; whereas if he would appoint a set of officers for each nation and fix a certain sum to be paid to them by each ship, how long or short a time so ever they might be at work upon her, the imposition would be in some degree less grievous. But the truth is, the Governour who is miserably covetous finds his Court very much inclined to treat us ill, and is as ready to make his Advantage of it." P.R.O., S.P.F., Sp. 218.

Cf. Cayley (Cadiz) to Newcastle, 1728, July 6. P.R.O., S.P.F., Sp. 218.

83 *English trade interrupted by embargoes.* Holloway (Malaga) to Newcastle, 1730, March 14: "...An Order is come from Court, for the embargoeing all the joysts of timber and all the boards there are in this place for the King's service, as also for buying up 500 empty buts and 1500 empty hogsheads but 'tis not yet said upon what account." P.R.O., S.P.F., Sp. 216.

Tucker (Alicante) to Newcastle, 1730, July 5: Added on to copy of letter of May 24, 1730, to Newcastle: "...The expedition here is now going on in earnest, vessells of all nations embargoed—their pay is but 2½ Pes. of 8/8 per ton p. mth. and 5 % for ye master, with 2 mos advances, tho as yet have pd. nothing...." P.R.O., S.P.F., Sp. 216.

Tucker (Alicante) to Newcastle, 1730, Aug. 16: "The loaden ships have still their goods aboard, many are disabled by a Span. man of war the *Victory* coming hither from Barcelona who returned thither with sevll. Engl. to whom they gave 2 mos. pay advance, the men were not forced but entered voluntarily, I made my complaints to the V.G. but believe the men of war's want of hands was so great 'twas impossible to do without them and the V.G. connived thereat, & if more of their men of war come hither our ships cannot put to sea...." P.R.O., S.P.F., Sp. 216.

84 *The Philippine Company.* Early in 1732 a project first made its appearance with regard to the reorganisation of the trade to the Philippines (Keene (Seville) to Newcastle, 1732, March 14: P.R.O., S.P.F., Sp. 111). Don Isidro de Messay wanted permission to make one voyage to these islands. He was very poor and his only hope of success was to go to England and solicit the support of the merchants of London; however, the idea proved attractive. In May ten other Spaniards "of no greater note than the former" had solicited Patiño to make them into a Company to trade to the Philippines. The minister was not the man to discourage any scheme however wild. A Philippine Company if it succeeded would develop a valuable part of the Spanish Empire, and be a useful nursery for sailors. It would increase the value of the royal revenue drawn from the export and import duties at Cadiz, and it would divert to Spain the 3,000,000 piastres which under the existing system were kept in America by the Acapulco galleon (Keene to Newcastle, 1732, May 23: P.R.O., S.P.F., Sp. 111, and Enclosure A, "Copie d'une Lettre écrite à M. van der Meer de Cadiz le 18 de May, 1732"; Enclosure B, "Account of the Commerce and Trade of the Philippine Islands". Patiño was rumoured to be redrafting the proposed charter, and to be inducing more respectable persons to join in the scheme (Keene to Newcastle, 1732, July 18: P.R.O., S.P.F., Sp. 112). Consul Cayley was seriously disturbed to learn that overtures had been made to the leading Roman Catholic Irish merchants residing in Spain, to get them to support the Company (Cayley (Cadiz) to Newcastle, 1732, Aug. 26: P.R.O., S.P.F., Sp. 220), and when he had recalled Butler to his allegiance he felt that he had helped to defeat a project which might have done much to ruin English trade (Cayley (Cadiz) to Newcastle, 1732, Sept. 2: P.R.O., S.P.F., Sp. 220). Newcastle's attitude was the same as that of the Consul. He feared that he might be accused of having failed to project British trade, and he ordered Keene to make a formal

representation against the Company (Newcastle to Keene, 1732, July 6/17 and 14/25: P.R.O., S.P.F., Sp. 113). Some attempt was made to get the French and Dutch Governments to join in this project (Keene to Newcastle, 1732, Aug. 1: P.R.O., S.P.F., Sp. 112), but the French refused, and the Dutch, who were busy trying to get the Treaty of Seville once more made valid, would only agree to allow van der Meer to sign Keene's Memorial (Keene to Newcastle, 1732, Aug. 19: P.R.O., S.P.F., Sp. 112). As might have been expected, the only answer was that His Catholic Majesty's subjects had a perfect right to trade to any of the Spanish dominions, and that if necessary His Catholic Majesty was prepared to support them by force (La Paz to Keene and van der Meer, 1732, Sept. 4: P.R.O., S.P.F., Sp. 112). Patiño was genuinely amused at the disturbance the Philippine Company had caused, and "smiled at our having any jealousies of a Company in Spain where there is so little skill and credit" (Keene to Newcastle, 1732, Aug. 19: P.R.O., S.P.F., Sp. 112). In spite of his enthusiastic support he shared the opinion of the French and British diplomats that want of faith and credit would do more to make the scheme miscarry than all the objections of foreign powers (Keene to Delafaye, 1732, Aug. 19: P.R.O., S.P.F., Sp. 112). The French ambassador had said that the scheme could only take root by opposition, and Keene suspected that the court of France was so certain that the project must fail that she had encouraged it in order to be able to exasperate Their Catholic Majesties against those who had opposed it. If on the contrary England had passed over the scheme in silence it would have been French policy to pique Patiño at the contemptuous indifference (Keene to Newcastle, 1732, Aug. 19: P.R.O., S.P.F., Sp. 112). By the end of 1732 it was clear that the Company could not flourish, but by then it had helped to make the Spanish court more friendly towards France just when a new diplomatic crisis had arisen during the course of which Their Catholic Majesties had to choose between St James's and Versailles.

85 Keene to Delafaye, 1732, Aug. 19. P.R.O., S.P.F., Sp. 112.

86 *Dispute over Tobacco Duties.* Keene to Newcastle, 1736, April 6. P.R.O., S.P.F., Sp. 125.

Herne (Alicante) to the Earl of Dartmouth, 1713, Feb. 6: "I find a new plan of Government occasioned by the making this Kingdom of Valencia a province of Castile and consequently governed by their laws and customes which alters entirely the commerce of this place from what formerly in King Charles the Second's time used to be.

"Particularly they have introduced and fixed a Farm on Tobacco under such severe penalties, that that particular branch of trade will be entirely lost to us. This place dispatching above fifteen hundred to two thousand hogsheads of tobacco yearly & by it favoured the dispatch of many other commodities." P.R.O., S.P.F., Sp. 212.

The Tobacco Customs were regulated by a *cedula* of July 31, 1735. How this was carried out is shown in a report called "An Account of the beginning and present state of the dispute with regard to the visiting of the small embarcations in the ports of Spain", enclosed in Keene's letter to Newcastle, 1737, April 15: P.R.O., S.P.F., Sp. 127.

Parminter's Petition, 1730, Feb. 10: "To the King's Most Excellent Majesty, the humble petition of Messrs. Parminter & Tristam of Barnstaple Merchants." P.R.O., S.P.F., Sp. 101.

Tucker (Alicante) to Newcastle, 1730, March 1: "The most deplorable condition happened to a Mahon Boat Patron Sebastian Baulo who after having suffered very much in a storm & putting in upon this coast above a year ago was seized & brought hither, kept prisoner aboard & all the crew insulted most vilely without any regard for His Majesty's Colours for only having tobacco aboard for Gibraltar, a few days ago they were brought ashore & flung into a dungeon, denied any subsistence & must inevitably have perished if not relieved by me who still subsist them... & have obtained getting them out of the dungeon into the common gaol, what the poor creatures have & do still suffer is inexpressible." P.R.O., S.P.F., Sp. 216.

Tucker (Alicante) to Newcastle, 1730, May 24: "Although nothing is proved against them, (they) are condemned to pay all the charges, which will be very considerable & much more than the goods amount to." P.R.O., S.P.F., Sp. 216.

Parker (Corunna) to Newcastle, 1730, May 17: "I acquainted your Grace with the transactions relating to the packets having waiters put on board, since which an order hath been notified to me by the Governor to receive on board all ships the Guards of the Rent of the Tobacco.

"This new Pretension of the Tobacco Rent is expressly opposite to the tenor of all the articles of peace we ever had with Spain, particularly excepting admission of any offices of the contraband, which is the tobacco, which if permitted will doubtless ruin the just freedom of the Commerce." P.R.O., S.P.F., Sp. 216.

Parker (Corunna) to Newcastle, 1732, Jan. 8: "About two months past, a Newfoundland ship, called the *Margaret*...coming into the harbour to seek for a market, the Guards of the Tobacco—pretended to put 3 officers on board her, and likewise to search her and the cargo, threatening the same should be practised by every ship not excepting the packets...the next day the Master landing at the Customs House was seized...& had been carried to prison had he not found means to get into my house for refuge." P.R.O., S.P.F., Sp. 216.

Keene to Newcastle, 1737, April 15: Enclosed Castres' Paper. "The Count de Ilia, Deputy Governor of the Province of Galicia, having on the 15th December 1731 signified to His Majesty's Consul at Corunna, that he had received orders from his Court to acquaint him, for preventing the running of tobacco in His Catholick Majesty's Dominions, all large vessels, which are called *de Bugue mayor*, should upon their arrival admit those tobacco Guards on board, and that the small craft, or *Embarcaciones minores* such as *saitras, tartanes*, and other vessels without a Deck should be instantly after their arrival examined and visited, and if any contraband Goods were found on board...they should be liable to a confiscation." P.R.O., S.P.F., Sp. 127.

Patiño to Keene, 1734, Oct. 22: "On Dec. 6th, 1733, at night a covered boat tried to moor in the Bay of Cadiz. The Tobacco Guards bade her retire, which she did, but Muskerry in the *Romney* thinking that the boat had been seized fired on the Tobacco Guard ship and chased her. The Guard ship was seized, and another coming to her assistance 2 men were killed." P.R.O., S.P.F., Sp. 120.

Parker (Corunna) to Newcastle, 1736, March 7. P.R.O., S.P.F., Sp. 217.

87 Cayley (Cadiz) to Newcastle, 1737, Sept. 10: "The Governor expressed a good deal of resentment at the ill success of our application (for the release of a Spanish *tartan* taken by the Moors)...&...positively declared that when any English merchant ships hence-forward arrived in this port with Moors on board, as they frequently do, he would take every Moor out of them by way of reprisal." P.R.O., S.P.F., Sp. 222.

88 Keene to Newcastle, 1736, April 6. P.R.O., S.P.F., Sp. 125.

89 *Dispute over rights of foreign Consuls*: see also notes Chap. III, n. 84; Chap. IV, n. 80; Chap. V, n. 117. Parker (Corunna) to Newcastle, 1737, Dec. 11: "I have been privately informed he (Count d'Ytre)... is commanded to deprive them (the foreign Consuls) of all jurisdiction, not to allow them to have deputys in the ports of their residence, nor in any other place, unless they be Subjects of the nation they act for... and not suffer them to have any Arms over their doors; he hath not signified this yet to any of the Consuls.... I therefore request Your Grace to lay the account hereof before His Majesty...." P.R.O., S.P.F., Sp. 224.
Parker (Corunna) to Newcastle, 1738, May 3. P.R.O., S.P.F., Sp. 224.

90 *Export of Bullion investigated.* Cayley (Cadiz) to Newcastle, 1738, Sept. 30. P.R.O., S.P.F., Sp. 223.

91 *New duty imposed on English trade.* Cayley (Cadiz) to Newcastle, 1737, Dec. 17; Cayley (Cadiz) to Newcastle, 1738, Feb. 25. P.R.O., S.P.F., Sp. 222.

92 *Dispositions of the King and Queen of Spain.* Keene to Newcastle, 1737, Dec. 13; Keene to Newcastle, 1737, July 1. P.R.O., S.P.F., Sp. 128.
Keene to Newcastle, 1737, May 27: "I have nothing further to trouble you with except that everything here is in perfect inaction, the least air imaginable keeping Their Catholic Majesties from stirring out of their apartments, little or no business is done, and what I never imagined I should see, the King hearing music with patience." P.R.O., S.P.F., Sp. 127.
Keene to Courand, 1737, Oct. 6 and 7: P.R.O., S.P.F., Sp. 128; Keene to Newcastle, 1737, May 27: P.R.O., S.P.F., Sp. 127.

93 *Characters of the Spanish favourites.* Keene to Newcastle, 1737, Dec. 13, Most private and particular. P.R.O., S.P.F., Sp. 128.

94 For details of Patiño's achievements see Appendix.

95 *Characters of La Quadra and Torrenueva.* Keene to Newcastle, 1737, Dec. 13, Most private and particular. P.R.O., S.P.F., Sp. 128.

96 Keene to Newcastle, 1739, March 9. P.R.O., S.P.F., Sp. 133.

97 Keene to Newcastle, 1737, Dec. 13, Most private and particular. P.R.O., S.P.F., Sp. 128.

98 *Character of Montijo.* Keene to Newcastle, 1737, Dec. 13, Most private and particular. P.R.O., S.P.F., Sp. 128.
Montijo had early formed a very poor opinion of England. Montijo to La Paz, 1732, Dec. 1: "Each day I am confirmed in what I told the Marquis de Castelar in case it might prove useful to him more than 15 days ago, that from these people there is nothing either to fear or hope, and I may now add that I think them much embarrassed, fearing everyone without feeling friendly towards any power, and thinking only how to avoid any possible rupture." Simancas, P. de E., Ing. leg. 6884.
Montijo to Patiño, 1733, July 6: "...They are resolved to do nothing but pass offices...since they know themselves feeble, and incapacitated from all action for want of credit in the country." Simancas, P. de E., Ing. leg. 6885.
During Montijo's embassy he was known to suggest repeatedly that England intended to make war on Spain (see Keene to Newcastle, 1734, May 3: P.R.O., S.P.F., Sp. 119; Sept. 6 and Nov. 8: P.R.O., S.P.F., Sp. 120; 1735, March 7: P.R.O., S.P.F., Sp. 122), so that Keene had to be at hand to pour water on his squibs (Keene to Delafaye, 1734, May 3: P.R.O., S.P.F., Sp. 119). Only after he had left England did Montijo suspend his noise against that country (Keene to Newcastle, 1735, Dec. 19 and 21: P.R.O., S.P.F., Sp. 123).
The pompous self-important Montijo was eager for office; while he had been ambassador in England he had continually laid down the law to La Paz. On the

death of Patiño he had offered to take over the whole business of Government (see Keene to Walpole, 1736, Dec. 4, Duplicate, most private: P.R.O., S.P.F., Sp. 126). When this came to nothing he busied himself trying to become President of the *Consejo de Indias* (Keene to Newcastle, 1737, March 11: P.R.O., S.P.F., Sp. 127), and though for a time he was unsuccessful (see Keene to Newcastle, 1737, March 25: P.R.O., S.P.F., Sp. 127) in June he was given the post (see Keene to Newcastle, 1737, June 17: P.R.O., S.P.F., Sp. 127).

For Keene's favourable opinion of Montijo see H. W. V. Temperley, "The Causes of the War of Jenkins' Ear", *Transactions of the Royal Historical Society*, 3rd Series, vol. III, p. 199.

99 Keene to Newcastle, 1737, Dec. 13, Most private and particular. P.R.O., S.P.F., Sp. 128.

100 *English Memorials reclaiming prizes.* Keene to La Quadra, 1737, Oct. 30, Nov. 8, Dec. 10: P.R.O., S.P.F., Sp. 128; Keene to La Quadra, 1738, Feb. 28, March 1: P.R.O., S.P.F., Sp. 130.

101 Keene to Newcastle, 1737, Dec. 23. P.R.O., S.P.F., Sp. 128.

102 La Quadra to Keene, 1738, May 26. P.R.O., S.P.F., Sp. 130.

103 The *Hopewell*, and a Bristol ship, reclaimed by Keene to La Quadra, 1737, Oct. 30: P.R.O., S.P.F., Sp. 128. The *Fanny*, a Philadelphia ship, and a Nevis ship. See Abadia to Torrenueva, 1738, Feb. 8: Seville, A. G. de Ind., Indif. Gen. leg. 1597.

104 General Matthews to the Commissioners for Trade and Plantations, 1737, July 14. P.R.O., S.P.F., Sp. 129.

105 List of offices passed 1735–7 enclosed in Keene to Newcastle, 1737, Nov. 11. P.R.O., S.P.F., Sp. 128.

106 Abadia (Porto Rico) to Torrenueva, 1738, Feb. 8. Seville, A. G. de Ind., Indif. Gen. leg. 1597.

107 *Spanish Answers to English Memorials reclaiming prizes.* La Quadra to Keene, 1737, Dec. 19: P.R.O., S.P.F., Sp. 128; La Quadra to Keene, 1738, Feb. 21, May 26: P.R.O., S.P.F., Sp. 130; Consulta, 1738, May 6: Seville, A. G. de Ind., Indif. Gen. leg. 1597; Cedula to the Governor of Porto Rico, 1738, Oct. 22: Seville, A. G. de Ind., Aud. S. Dom. leg. 498.

108 *Consulta*, 1738, May 6. Seville, A. G. de Ind., Indif. Gen. leg. 1597.

109 *The Case of the "Rebecca", Captain Jenkins.* Jenkins' Deposition, 1731, June 17; Keene to La Paz, 1731, July 19; La Paz to Keene, 1731, Nov. 20; Keene to Newcastle, 1731, July 26: P.R.O., S.P.F., Sp. 101; Demands of the English Commissioners, 1732, June 19: P.R.O., S.P.F., Sp. 106; *Parliamentary History*, vol. x, col. 638. Jenkins later entered the service of the East India Company, was sent out to St Helena to investigate charges against the Governor and from 1741–2 ruled the island. See T. H. Brooke, *A History of the Island of St Helena* (1824), pp. 228–9 and H. R. Janisch, *Extracts from the St Helena Records* (1885), pp. 182–3.

110 Depositions by the Owners and Surgeon of the *Robert*, 1731, May 15. P.R.O., S.P.F., Sp. 101.

111 Newcastle to Keene, 1731, Nov. 18. P.R.O., S.P.F., Sp. 101.

112 *Condition of thirty-one English sailors, prisoners in Cadiz.* Geraldino (the Spanish envoy) to La Quadra, 1738, March 10, 14. Simancas, P. de E., Ing. leg. 7623. Torrenueva to the *Consejo de Indias*, concerning the treatment of twenty Dutch prisoners taken by the Guipuzcoan Company filed as part of correspondence beginning with a letter to Torrenueva dated 1738, Jan. 15. Seville, A. G. de Ind., Aud. S. Dom. leg. 498; Cayley (Cadiz) to Newcastle, 1738, May 13.

P.R.O., S.P.F., Sp. 222; Geraldino to La Quadra, 1738, April 3. Simancas, P. de E., Ing. leg. 7621.

113 Translation of a Draft of a Memorial to be presented by Mr Keene to the King of Spain, sent to Mr Keene 1737, Nov. 4/15. P.R.O., S.P.F., Sp. 129.

114 Keene to Newcastle, 1738, Feb. 23. P.R.O., S.P.F., Sp. 130.

115 Newcastle to Keene, 1738, March 28. P.R.O., S.P.F., Sp. 132.

116 Undated rough draft. P.R.O., S.P.F., Sp. 128.

117 Lillian M. Penson, *The Colonial Agents of the British West Indies* (1924).

118 One copy of the Merchants' Petition of February 1737 is in Brit. Mus. Shel. Photostats, i, iii, ff. 381–4.

119 Geraldino to La Quadra, 1738, March 14: To the effect that, "Yesterday the Merchants' Memorials were laid before Parliament...special stress was laid on the case of the *Anne Galley*. The value of the *Anne* deposited in the Indies had been 60,000 *pesos*. A *cedula* for restitution had been granted but had only had the effect of recovering for the Captain 2000 *pesos* and 2 negroes. The owners had presented 7 memorials to the Ministry, and 4 to the Privy Council." Simancas, P. de E., Ing. leg. 7623.

120 Geraldino to La Quadra, 1738, March 14. Simancas, P. de E., Ing. leg. 7623.

121 Geraldino to La Quadra, 1738, March 20: "The Opposition proposed that His Britannic Majesty be asked to show Parliament what had been negotiated with Spain since 1732 especially with regard to the Permission Ship, but because these papers were very voluminous I supposed that the examination would be postponed, as had happened on other occasions, but now much enthusiasm is shown to execute this work....This is because it is thought that the ill-founded claims of the Company, and the weak attempts made by the Ministry to check them, have caused the vexations which the ships of this nation have experienced in their navigation." Simancas, P. de E., Ing. leg. 7624.

122 Geraldino to La Quadra, 1738, March 24. Simancas, P. de E., Ing. leg. 7624.

123 Geraldino to La Quadra, 1738, March 27. Simancas, P. de E., Ing. leg. 7624.

124 Geraldino to La Quadra, 1738, April 12: To the effect that, "On the 10th Parliament resolved to Memorialise His Britannic Majesty, which is only done on rare occasions." Simancas, P. de E., Ing. leg. 7621.

125 Geraldino to La Quadra, 1738, April 23: "The Parliamentary Memorials are usually printed but this one has not been,...I am told that it was worded in more moderate terms than the House had desired." Simancas, P. de E., Ing. leg. 7622.

126 Geraldino to La Quadra, 1738, April 23: "On April 18th Parliament voted an extra 10,000 sailors, and on the 21st the House agreed to allow £500,000 for their pay. Two ships, that were ready to convoy the Annual cod fishing fleet to Newfoundland, have been ordered to go to Port Mahon. These measures make people believe that the ministry has been forced into making war." Simancas, P. de E., Ing. leg. 7622. Cf. *Journals of House of Commons*, vol. XXIII, pp. 138 and 141.

127 Geraldino to La Quadra, 1738, April 23. Simancas, P. de E., Ing. leg. 7622.

128 The Spanish claims were chiefly for men of war destroyed off Sicily in 1718. See paper "On the Amounts Claimed by both parties" bound after Keene to Newcastle, 1738, June 2. P.R.O., S.P.F., Sp. 131.

129 For a detailed treatment of the dispute over the Florida limits see A. O. Ettinger, *James Edward Oglethorpe, Imperial Idealist* (1936).

130 Geraldino to La Quadra, 1738, April 23. Simancas, P. de E., Ing. leg. 7622.

131 *Don Thomas Geraldino on British politics.* Geraldino to La Quadra, 1738, April 23, Private: "You know that the Ministry has to act against its judgment to satisfy the popular demands, which have been industriously fomented. It might, therefore, be well to accept Mr Stert's plan." Simancas, P. de E., Ing. leg. 7622.

A week later he urged his Government to accept the Plan in Geraldino to La Quadra, 1738, May 1, Private: "It is impossible to restore good relations between our two Courts without first settling this question of the depredations. In other questions which depend solely from the ministry we may be able to get a better treatment, but this depends on Parliament, which is in this country a terrible monster, and is ruled by private interests under the plausible name oı the Public Good.... Mr Stert's Plan is advantageous to Spain for several reasons. It preserves His Catholic Majesty's dignity by preventing the necessity of examining all the merchants' claims in detail. It wipes out all the English claims which are of great value, and could never otherwise be totally extinguished. It provides that the sum remaining to be paid by Spain shall be paid through the South Sea Company." Simancas, P. de E., Ing. leg. 7622.

In his official despatch of the same date he wrote: "...I really think that the English Government will try to avoid a breach, but this is impossible, unless some satisfaction is given for the depredations."

Geraldino to La Quadra, 1738, June 19: To the effect that, "I think that it is my duty to lay before His Majesty some considerations which concern the composition and situation of this Government, and may incline his royal mind to show some condescension for the love of peace, which according to your letter His Majesty appears to desire in so far as it is in conformity with his royal dignity.

"I shall, therefore, try to answer your objections. The nature of this Government and the crisis caused by the incidents of the last session of Parliament make it impossible for the administration to enter into a negotiation which must actually be long and delicate for when Parliament meets again the Ministry will be asked to show results. This is the reason why the Plan makes no attempt to prevent contraband in the future, but this may be negotiated separately later, once the popular outcry has been stilled.

"You say that the Plan provides for the satisfaction of England but does nothing to satisfy the Spanish complaints concerning the English claim to freedom of navigation, so that ships cannot be apprehended for contraband unless caught in the act, the English usurpations in Georgia, and finally the frauds and delays in paying the negro duties. To this I would reply that the Plan provides that some of the payment to His Catholic Majesty shall be made by the South Sea Company and it is to be believed that the Ministry will see that these payments are made regularly...the Georgian disputes are to be settled by Commissioners;...and the principle of no search on the High Seas is only the same as that which is observed with regard to the smugglers off the coast of England itself.

"You also object that the whole £200,000 is to appear to have been paid by His Catholic Majesty...but this is only to preserve the Ministry." Simancas, P. de E., Ing. leg. 7623.

132 Geraldino to La Quadra, 1738, May 1, Private. Simancas, P. de E., Ing. leg. 7622.

133 Geraldino to La Quadra, 1738, May 2. Simancas, P. de E., Ing. leg. 7622.

134 Geraldino to La Quadra, 1738, May 9. Simancas, P. de E., Ing. leg. 7622.

135 Geraldino to. La Quadra, 1738, May 29. Simancas, P. de E., Ing. leg. 7621.

136 La Quadra to Keene, 1738, May 26. P.R.O., S.P.F., Sp. 130.

137 Geraldino to La Quadra, 1738, June 19. Simancas, P. de E., Ing. leg. 7622.

138 Geraldino to La Quadra, 1738, July 3. Simancas, P. de E., Ing. leg. 7622.

139 Newcastle to Keene, 1738, June 21, July 2. P.R.O., S.P.F., Sp. 132.

140 Keene to Newcastle, 1738, July 7. P.R.O., S.P.F., Sp. 131.

141 Keene to Newcastle, 1738, July 14, Private and particular. La Mina has been sent orders to propose a new treaty with France. P.R.O., S.P.F., Sp. 131.

142 Newcastle to Keene, 1738, June 1. P.R.O., S.P.F., Sp. 132.

143 Keene to Newcastle, 1738, June 30. P.R.O., S.P.F., Sp. 131. Cf. Keene to Newcastle, 1738, Aug. 2, Private: "His Majesty's orders of the 1st of June relating to the withdrawing and securing the effects and shipping of the British subjects residing in Spain, and for preventing as far as possible any other English vessels from coming into the Spanish ports were immediately executed...it is certain at present that our trade with this country is entirely at a stand": P.R.O., S.P.F., Sp. 131; and Geraldino to La Quadra, 1738, July 31: "On the arrival of the French ordinary the English merchants divulged the fact that their correspondents in Cadiz report that the English Consul, on a hint from Keene, warned them to remove their shipping. I asked the Duke of Newcastle why he had sent such orders, without so much as hinting them to me. He said that he had never sent such orders, and couldn't tell me what Keene's motive might have been since he had had no letters later than July 7. This did not seem regular to me in the present crisis, and I am very suspicious of the orders sent to Mr Keene through the disunion between the two Ministers, for this step is contrary to the desires of Sir Robert Walpole." Simancas, P. de E., Ing. leg. 7621.

144 Keene to Newcastle, 1738, Aug. 2. La Quadra said that he had told Geraldino at once that the Plan was inadmissible, and that if the envoy had not understood this letter it was not La Quadra's fault. P.R.O., S.P.F., Sp. 131.

Keene to Newcastle, 1738, Aug. 2, apart. Montijo and La Quadra are angry enough with Geraldino to upset the whole negotiation. P.R.O., S.P.F., Sp. 131.

145 Keene to Newcastle, 1738, Aug. 2, enclosing Keene's explanation of Stert's Plan. P.R.O., S.P.F., Sp. 131.

146 Geraldino to La Quadra, 1738, July 31: "The said Minister (Walpole) awaits with anxiety the result of the negotiation, and he had charged his brother to inform him at once should the Spanish reply arrive while he is away in Norfolk." Simancas, P. de E., Ing. leg. 7621.

147 Geraldino to La Quadra, 1738, Aug. 7. Simancas, P. de E., Ing. leg. 7621.

148 Geraldino to La Quadra, 1738, Aug. 14. Simancas, P. de E., Ing. leg. 7621.

149 Geraldino to La Quadra, 1738, Aug. 21. Simancas, P. de E., Ing. leg. 7624.

150 Geraldino to La Quadra, 1738, Aug. 21: "On August 16 I saw Sir Robert Walpole on the pretext of telling him that I was empowered to pay the money if an agreement was reached and Plenipotentiaries were named. Sir Robert said that he could not discuss this because the Privy Council had reached no decision on the previous night, and must meet again...the next day a dependent of Walpole's told me that the Privy Council had decided to accept the Counter Project, by which His Catholic Majesty was to pay £95,000." Simancas, P. de E., Ing. leg. 7624.

151 A list of some of the Spanish officials paid through the South Sea Company in 1734 is to be found in Simancas, P. de E., Ing. leg. 7009.

152 An undated paper headed "Abstract of two papers presented by the British Minister, Mr Keene, with observations on its various heads, and the reply that befits the Minister's representation": Seville, A. G. de Ind., Indif. Gen. leg. 2792.

153 The details of this negotiation are in Geraldino's papers at Simancas, Hacienda, leg. 973; P. de E., Ing. leg. 7006–12; and Seville, A. G. de Ind., Indif. Gen. legs. 2790–3, 2851.

154 The last Annual Ship to sail was the *Royal Caroline* in 1732. Brit. Mus. Shel. Photostats, 1, i, ff. 4–5.

155 Geraldino to Patiño, 1733, Aug. 20. Simancas, Hacienda, leg. 973. Geraldino to Patiño, 1734, Nov. 4: "The South Sea Company said that the point had never been raised before of my arrival." Simancas, Hacienda, leg. 973.

156 Geraldino to Patiño, 1733, Aug. 20: To the effect that, "The Treaty of Utrecht, Article 2, stipulates that the duty on each negro should be 33⅓ *reales de plata*. This was before the rise of money in Spain—which did not affect the Indies; so I think that the Company ought to pay at the rate of 10 *reales de plata*; or 18 of *vellon* and not 15 of *vellon* as the Company maintains." Simancas, Hacienda, leg. 973.

157 Geraldino to Patiño, 1734, Nov. 4. Simancas, Hacienda, leg. 973.

158 Burrell to Keene, 1736, May 27/June 7: "We are now in earnest trying to accommodate this affair likewise fixing the value of the dollars." Brit. Mus. Add. MSS. 32,791, f. 194.

159 Geraldino to La Quadra, 1737, July 11, enclosing the South Sea Company's Plan. Seville, A. G. de Ind., Indif. Gen. leg. 2793.

160 Geraldino to La Quadra, 1738, Aug. 21. Simancas, P. de E., Ing. leg. 7624.

161 Geraldino to La Quadra, 1738, Aug. 28. Simancas, P. de E., Ing. leg. 7624.

162 Geraldino to La Quadra, 1738, Aug. 28. Simancas, P. de E., Ing. leg. 7624.

163 Geraldino to La Quadra, 1738, Sept. 10, by extraordinary. Simancas, P. de E., Ing. leg. 7624.

164 Keene to Newcastle, 1738, Oct. 13. P.R.O., S.P.F., Sp. 131.

165 Keene to Newcastle, 1738, Sept. 29. P.R.O., S.P.F., Sp. 131.

166 Keene to Newcastle, 1738, Sept. 15. P.R.O., S.P.F., Sp. 131. Spain would prefer to pay by an order on the South Sea Company; she thinks sending actual money will be too like buying a peace.

167 Keene to Newcastle, 1738, Oct. 13, Most private. P.R.O., S.P.F., Sp. 131.

168 Castres to Courand (Newcastle's Secretary), 1738, Oct. 13. P.R.O., S.P.F., Sp. 131.

202 NOTES TO CHAPTER IV

169 *South Sea Company's objections to Cedulas,* 1738. Geraldino to La Quadra, 1738, Nov. 6: "On October 31 the Governors of the South Sea Company visited Sir Robert Walpole. He said that he could not advise them, but that they should bear in mind that on the result of their deliberations depended the restoration of a good harmony between the two countries. If the negotiation, to achieve this end, were ruined by the Company the Governors must consider the consequences, particularly when the nation...should learn the reason for that failure." Simancas, P. de E., Ing. leg. 7624.

Geraldino to La Quadra, 1738, Oct. 30: "To-day the Governors of the South Sea Company waited upon me. I let them see plainly that in this political crisis it was necessary for the Company to accommodate its differences with the King of Spain; and I gave them sufficient reasons for deliberating the question very seriously." Simancas, P. de E., Ing. leg. 7624.

Geraldino to La Quadra, 1738, Nov. 13: "One of the Directors came to see me...and I, doubting whether the Ministry had made it quite clear to the Directors what was the real gravity of the situation, answered him, and said that the only formal answer which I hoped to hear was that the Company had decided to pay the sum His Majesty had assigned on them, and that if they refused the Asiento would be suspended." Simancas, P. de E., Ing. leg. 7623.

170 Geraldino to La Quadra, 1738, Nov. 24 (Simancas, P. de E., Ing. leg. 7623), returned to La Quadra:

1. The Spanish Ratifications.

2. 8 *cedulas* which he was to have given to the Company had it agreed to pay the £95,000.

3. La Quadra's letter authorising Geraldino to borrow £95,000 had the Company refused to pay, but the Ratifications been exchanged.

171 Geraldino to La Quadra, 1738, Oct. 30: "Your extraordinary of Oct. 13 arrived here on 26th with the *Cedulas* for the restoration of the South Sea Company's effects, the Ratification, and the explanation of the separate articles 1 and 2....I saw Sir Robert Walpole and told him that if the Company refused to pay the £95,000 I had orders to do so, but that in such a case the Asiento would be immediately suspended." Simancas, P. de E., Ing. leg. 7624.

172 *Expedient for evading annulling of Asiento by negotiation of new Convention.* Geraldino to La Quadra, 1738, Nov. 24. Simancas, P. de E., Ing. leg. 6904.

173 See for example Keene to Newcastle, 1739, Jan. 13, enclosing correspondence with La Quadra; Dec. 22–Jan. 2, about the South Sea Company, Keene to La Quadra, 1739, April 17. P.R.O., S.P.F., Sp. 133.

174 Keene to Newcastle, 1739, Jan. 14, enclosing the Convention. P.R.O., S.P.F., Sp. 133.

175 Declaration attached to Convention, 1739, Jan. 13. P.R.O., S.P.F., Sp. 133. See also La Quadra to Keene, 1739, Jan. 11. P.R.O., S.P.F., Sp. 133.

176 Geraldino to La Quadra, 1739, Jan. 29. Simancas, P. de E., Ing. leg. 7626.

177 Geraldino to La Quadra, 1739, Feb. 6. Simancas, P. de E., Ing. leg. 7626.

178 *Opinion in England after conclusion of Convention of the Pardo.* Geraldino to La Quadra, 1739, Feb. 26, March 5, 12 and 26. Simancas, P. de E., Ing. legs. 6904, 7626, 7628.

179 Geraldino to La Quadra, 1739, March 5: "The Ministry opposed the proposition that the South Sea Company Directors should be examined as to the

Declaration. This surprised everyone, and me too, but I learnt that the motive was to avoid the delays which an enquiry would have occasioned.... The Commons want papers concerning the Company's negotiations with Spain from December 24, 1737...." Simancas, P. de E., Ing. leg. 7626.

180 H. W. V. Temperley, "The Causes of the War of Jenkins' Ear", *T.R.H.S.* 3rd Series, vol. III, p. 228.

181 *Walpole's reasons for countermanding Haddock's return.* Geraldino to La Quadra, 1739, March 26. Simancas, P. de E., Ing. leg. 7628.

182 H. W. V. Temperley, "The Causes of the War of Jenkins' Ear", *T.R.H.S.* 3rd Series, vol. III, pp. 216, 228–30.

183 Keene to Newcastle, 1739, March 9. P.R.O., S.P.F., Sp. 133.

CHAPTER V

1 Lea's Calculation of profits that might be got from trade to Guatemala. Proposal for establishing the factory at Portobello. Calculations in favour of setting up a factory at Santo Domingo. Brit. Mus. Shel. Photostats, I, ii, ff. 210–11, 233–9 and 258–9.

2 An anonymous paper stated that the considerable and profitable illicit trade at Buenos Ayres could only be carried on with the connivance of the chief factor, who had been chosen by Mr Jackson's influence, and the considerable illicit trade at Caracas was managed by Mr Pratter, who had been chosen entirely by Mr Bristow's interest. Unless the trade was reorganised Messrs Bristow, Jackson and their friend might openly show great zeal for the Company, yet privately reap great profits. Brit. Mus. Shel. Photostats, II, ii, f. 449.

3 1732, June 16: Sir John Eyles laid the first mention of an equivalent before the Court of Directors: Brit. Mus. Add. MSS. 25,545, Gen. Court Minutes. 1732, Nov. 22: Don Thomas Geraldino made the first formal offer of an equivalent: Brit. Mus. Add. MSS. 25,544, Gen. Court Minutes.

4 *Parliamentary History*, vol. VII, cols. 685–911.

5 Geraldino's Memorial to the South Sea Company Directors, 1734, April 8. Seville, A. G. de Ind., Indif. Gen. leg. 2790.

6 1732, June 16: A mysterious letter was left at the Sub-Governor's asking what equivalent the Company would take for the Annual Ship. Brit. Mus. Add. MSS. 25,544, Gen. Court Minutes.

7 1732, June 16: Sir John Eyles answered that the Directors had never even thought of such a thing (as the equivalent suggested by Tyrry). Brit. Mus. Add. MSS. 25,544, Gen. Court Minutes.

8 1732, Nov. 22: Geraldino laid the proposal for an equivalent before the Board. Brit. Mus. Add. MSS. 25,544, Gen. Court Minutes.

9 1733, March 22: It was decided to ask the Attorney-General whether the Company might treat with Spain for an equivalent. Brit. Mus. Add. MSS. 25,545, Gen. Court Minutes.

10 1734, Jan. 25: The consideration of Geraldino's proposal was further adjourned. Brit. Mus. Add. MSS. 25,545, Gen. Court Minutes.

11 1734, April 8: Geraldino to the Directors, enclosed in Geraldino to Patiño, 1734, April 8. Seville, A. G. de Ind., Indif. Gen. leg. 2790.

12 Geraldino to Patiño, 1734, April 8. Seville, A. G. de Ind., Indif. Gen. leg. 2790.

13 Geraldino to Patiño, 1734, April 9. Seville, A. G. de Ind., Indif. Gen. leg. 2790.

14 Geraldino to Patiño, 1734, April 22. Seville, A. G. de Ind., Indif. Gen. leg. 2790.

15 The South Sea Company Memorial to His Britannic Majesty, 1734, July 4/15. Simancas, P. de E., Ing. leg. 7009.

16 Geraldino to Patiño, 1734, April 22. Seville, A. G. de Ind., Indif. Gen. leg. 2790.

17 Geraldino to Patiño, 1734, Aug. 2. Seville, A. G. de Ind., Indif. Gen. leg. 2790.

18 Directors to Keene, 1734, Dec. 5/16. Brit. Mus. Add. MSS. 32,786, f. 344.

19 Geraldino to Patiño, 1735, Feb. 10. Seville, A. G. de Ind., Indif. Gen. leg. 2791.

20 Geraldino to Patiño, 1735, March 31. Seville, A. G. de Ind., Indif. Gen. leg. 2791.

21 Geraldino to Patiño, 1735, April 14. Seville, A. G. de Ind., Indif. Gen. leg. 2791.

22 Geraldino to Patiño, 1735, April 28: "More shareholders met than I have ever seen before...for the last three days articles have been appearing in the Press about this affair...then followed great debates...." Seville, A. G. de Ind., Indif. Gen. leg. 2791.

23 Carvajal to Wall, 1748, May 18: "The damage done by the Asiento is far greater than that of the Annual Ship. The ship is of little harm to Spain, for nearly all the registers and Fleets carry foreign goods, and whether the Cadiz trade flourishes or not is not of primary importance to His Catholic Majesty. On the contrary the negro trade is dangerous. It allows an able English factor, with money in his hands, to be established in the chief ports of the Indies...they know the ports, the armaments, the strength and weakness of each place, and can transmit this information with complete safety since the letters all go in their own ships. In short, he is a powerful and dangerous enemy within the house.

"As to the contraband, there is no limit to it...it is a muffled file which is wearing away the trade of Spain." Madrid, A.H.N., Estado, Ing. leg. 4277.

24 The substance of the Memorial submitted by Geraldino to the Directors of the South Sea Company on May 11,1735, was divided into ten heads (Simancas, P. de E., Ing. leg. 7009):

1. 2 per cent on the profits of the *flota* and galleons was to be given in exchange for the negro trade and the Annual Ship.

2. This was to be raised on the *flota* or galleons in the same way as His Catholic Majesty's *indulto*.

3. The consent of the West Indian merchants of Cadiz to the scheme was to be obtained.

4. The sum was to be punctually paid to a person named by the Company, and might be shipped to England without paying any *indulto*.

5. The South Sea Company should have eighteen months in which to withdraw their effects from the Indies, and wind up their trade.

6. If any effects should remain, these might be shipped back to Europe in the *flota* or galleons, or Register Ships duty free.

7. In case of rupture within eighteen months (which God forbid) neither the effects in the Indies nor the ships sent to recover them should be embargoed.

8. His Catholic Majesty will not grant the Asiento to any other nation during the rest of the thirty years, for which the English Asiento was supposed to run.

9. During this period, negroes were to be supplied to the Spanish Indies by English and Spanish subjects.

10. English merchants might enter into agreements with His Catholic Majesty to supply negroes to places where the South Sea Company has at present no factory.

25 A Letter to the South Sea Shareholders—in the *Daily Post*, 1736, July 21/Aug. 1. Seville, A. G. de Ind., Indif. Gen. leg. 2793.

26 An official note on Geraldino's offer of May 11, 1735, was that this was less than the profits of the *Royal Caroline*. Seville, A. G. de Ind., Indif. Gen. leg. 2791.

27 1735, May 2/13: Sir Thomas Geraldino is the only person who has made an offer for the trade. The Directors are to lay his offer before His Britannic Majesty, and beg his permission to licence the trade. Brit. Mus. Add. MSS. 25,545, Gen. Court Minutes.

28 Keene to the South Sea Company Directors, 1735, May 3. Brit. Mus. Add. MSS. 32,787, f. 152.

29 Humble Address of the South Sea Company to His Britannic Majesty, 1735, Dec. 12: "...begging His Britannic Majesty's interposition in relation to a new grievance....Don Thomas Geraldino objected that only English goods were to be sent which was a restriction would have made it impossible to provide a proper cargo for the Annual Ship." Simancas, P. de E., Ing. leg. 7006.

30 Geraldino to Patiño, 1735, May 19. Seville, A. G. de Ind., Indif. Gen. leg. 2791.

31 Geraldino to Patiño, 1736, Aug. 2. Seville, A. G. de Ind., Indif. Gen. leg. 2793.

32 Geraldino to Patiño, 1736, Feb. 16: "Horace Walpole said that he was acting purely *motu proprio* but that he would like to see the South Sea Company's disputes with His Catholic Majesty ended. He asked me for my Proposal of May 11, 1735." Seville, A. G. de Ind., Indif. Gen. leg. 2792.

Geraldino to Torrenueva, 1737, April 4: "...I have convinced Sir Robert Walpole of the justice of His Catholic Majesty's demands, it is only lack of authority that prevents him from compelling the South Sea Company to give satisfaction. The Directors find themselves without the Ministerial support on which they reckoned." Seville, A. G. de Ind., Indif. Gen. leg. 2793.

33 The Plan of 1737, June 30/July 11, sent to Spain enclosed in Geraldino to Torrenueva, 1737, July 11. Seville, A. G. de Ind., Indif. Gen. leg. 2793.

34 1732, April 20/May 1: "Nine members having demanded a General Court, proposed a division of the Capital into ¾ Annuities and ¼ trading stock." April 25/May 6: This scheme was passed in the affirmative. Brit. Mus. Add. MSS. 25,544, Gen. Court Records.

Geraldino to Patiño, 1734, Nov. 11: "I must tell you that these ministers consider the representations of the Company with great indifference now that only a quarter of the capital is directed to trade." Simancas, Hacienda, leg. 973.

35 *A Defence of Observations on the Asiento Trade* (1728), p. 56.

36 For references to the illicit trade from the British colonies see the Shel. Photostats, *passim*. The Dutch illicit trade was enormous. The Guipuzcoan Company was continually taking Dutch prizes, as is shown by the Correspondence of Lardizabal, Governor of Caracas, with the authorities of Old Spain, as for example Lardizabal to His Catholic Majesty, 1734, June 5. Seville, A. G. de Ind., Aud. S. Dom. leg. 492.

Horcasitas (Cuba) to Torrenueva, 1737, June 25: "The Dutch especially carry on a great deal of illicit trade. This is their only reason for keeping their colony at Curacoa." Seville, A. G. de Ind., Aud. S. Dom. leg. 2167.

Manning and Merewether (Jamaica) to Burrell, 1736, Jan. 6: "The Dutch who carry on a great deal of illicit trade...meet with no interruption from the Company's servants." Brit. Mus. Shel. Photostats, II, iv, ff. 867–8.

37 Merewether to Burrell, 1736, Sept. 6: "It is these cargoes which are not fit for the honourable Company or this island that give cause to the illicit trade ...what is called the private trade of this island is the clandestine trade carried on with the French & Spaniards, & it has been on the decline for some years past, & is now at a very low ebb...when I see a person entering largely into it I think him to be in no good way." Brit. Mus. Shel. Photostats, II, iv, f. 875.

38 Shortage of coin was one of the reasons given for the number of bad debts owing to the South Sea Company. See for a long list of these debts Brit. Mus. Shel. Photostats, I, ii, ff. 291–9.

39 Merewether to Burrell, 1736, Jan. 25: "Portobello seems the only factory where it is possible to get a penny." Brit. Mus. Shel. Photostats, II, iv, f. 862.

40 The Accounts of the Cartagena factory are in Seville, A. G. de Ind., Indif. Gen. legs. 2793, 2851.

41 Findlay (London) to Burrell, 1736, May: "Though the negro trade of Vera Cruz is of less importance to the Company than that of any other of their factories from the small demand there is for slaves, yet the advantages that would accrue from the regular dispatch of an annual ship made it a settlement of the greatest consequence." Brit. Mus. Shel. Photostats, II, ii, f. 280.

42 Butcher (Caracas) to Burrell, 1738, June 9: "The Guipuzcoan Company absorbs all the money of this place." Brit. Mus. Shel. Photostats, II, iii, f. 620.

43 De la Rocha (Santo Domingo) to His Catholic Majesty, 1730, Dec. 29: Suggested that the Governor of Sta Marta was once over eager to condemn prizes: Seville, A. G. de Ind., Indif. Gen. leg. 1597.

Don Josef de Audia (Sta Marta) to His Catholic Majesty, 1729, Nov. 15: "The proceeds of three prizes brought about 18,000 dollars into the Royal Treasury. This will pay the garrison for five months, and is very useful as supplies from Quito and Santa Fé are uncertain." Seville, A. G. de Ind., Aud. Santa Fé, leg. 1243.

44 Butcher (from St Kitts) to Burrell, 1738, Jan. 13: Brit. Mus. Shel. Photostats, II, iii, f. 629.

45 1729, Feb. 7/18: "The factory at St Iago de Cuba is to be discontinued." 1736, July 2/13: "In Cuba there is to be only one factory—those of St Iago de Cuba and Havana are to be united." Brit. Mus. Add. MSS. 25,503 and 25,508, Directors' Court Minutes.

46 *The South Sea Company's trade with Buenos Ayres.* Faure (Buenos Ayres) to Burrell, 1738, March 12: "Whilst the colonial trade was open ours was much prejudiced by their introductions, which could not be remedied on so wide a coast as this; and since the war began our supplies have been irregular." Brit. Mus. Shel. Photostats, II, ii, f. 366.

47 1729, Jan. 17/28: It was debated whether it were better to supply Buenos Ayres with negroes from Madagascar or Angola; Feb. 7/18: It was decided to supply half the negroes from Angola and half from Madagascar. Brit. Mus. Add. MSS. 25,503, Directors' Court Minutes.

48 *A Defence of Observations on the Asiento Trade,* p. 54.

49 1717, Nov. 27/Dec. 8: Two ships hired to go to Guinea and then Barbadoes. Brit. Mus. Add. MSS. 25,497, Directors' Court Minutes.

50 Accounts of the Barbadoes agency are in Seville, A. G. de Ind., Indif.

Gen. leg. 2847. See also "Some observations on the Agency of Barbadoes", Brit. Mus. Shel. Photostats, I, i, f. 141.

51 1721, Oct. 26/Nov. 6: It was decided to allow the factors at Vera Cruz credit that they might buy negroes at Jamaica; Nov. 2/13: Certificates for the Company's sloops that were to carry negroes from Jamaica were sealed; Nov. 23/Dec. 4: It was decided to advertise for private traders to supply negroes; 1722, March 1/12: The Jamaica agents were to supply negroes to the factories at Vera Cruz, Cartagena, Panama and Havana as the factors write for them. Brit. Mus. Add. MSS. 25,500, Directors' Court Minutes.

52 1723, Nov. 28/Dec. 9: The Royal African Company agrees to supply six or seven hundred negroes. Two ships are to be taken up to carry these to Jamaica. Brit. Mus. Add. MSS. 25,501, Directors' Court Minutes.

53 1724, Feb. 11/22: *Don Luis, King of Spain* to be built; Feb. 27/March 9: New sloops were built for the Jamaican trade—the *Queen of Spain*. Brit. Mus. Add. MSS. 25,502, Directors' Court Minutes.

54 1724, April 16/27: The Committee of Shipping was instructed to take up ships to go to Widah and the Gold Coast and then to Jamaica. Brit. Mus. Add. MSS. 25,502, Directors' Court Minutes.

55 1729, Dec. 19/30: The method of supplying negroes considered, and, as a result, the South Sea Company decided to advertise in the *Gazette* and other papers "that they intend for the future to purchase of them (merchants trading to Guinea & Jamaica) or their agents in that island, what negroes they shall want for supply of the Asiento, in exception of their importing sufficient numbers, & that they shall continue in that method if it be not attended with any unforeseen inconvenience". Brit. Mus. Add. MSS. 25,503, Directors' Court Minutes.

56 1732, Sept. 15/26: The Committee of Shipping report a need for economy. Ships are to be hired instead of built. Brit. Mus. Add. MSS. 25,505, Directors' Court Minutes.

57 For a study of the right of "internation" see Keene to La Paz, 1730, May 6, P.R.O., S.P.F., Sp. 103.

58 On the question of the right of the Company to have a factory at Panama see Keene to La Paz, 1728, Nov. 21, and La Paz to Keene, 1728, Dec. 5, P.R.O., S.P.F., Sp. 99.

59 See South Sea Company Accounts, Brit. Mus. Shel. Photostats, I, i, ff. 4–5.

60 Geraldino to Patiño, 1735, April 14: "The Sub-Governor laid great stress on the value of the new administrative reforms, though it cost me enormous trouble to get them to agree to the change originally." Seville, A. G. de Ind., Indif. Gen. leg. 2791.

61 For the accounts of the Annual Ships, see Brit. Mus. Shel. Photostats, I, i, f. 11.

62 Merewether and Manning (Jamaica) to Burrell, 1736, Jan. 6: "The Minister at Madrid may give what orders he pleases, and the commerce at Seville may take their own measures, but still a people who want goods will find out ways for a supply, and the advantage of the trade is now enjoyed by the Spanish buyers who have a profit adequate to the risk they run." Brit. Mus. Shel. Photostats, II, iv, f. 867.

63 "As some must be had to answer the present want, the people are forced in such exigencies to...supply themselves...with those of other nations which, though of different specie, & neither so intrinsically good, nor so much liked,

are thus first of all taken through necessity, and afterwards worn till they are preferred & the other by degrees laid aside and forgot agreeable to a received principle of commerce, that where the supply of a commodity is uncertain the consumption of it will be so too." Brit. Mus. Add. MSS. 32,819, ff. 189–90.

64 Between 1713 and 1739 twelve *flotas* sailed for New Spain, and six fleets of galleons for Portobello. On four occasions *azogues* sailed for New Spain instead of a *flota*. See Chap. 1, note 71.

65 *An Address to the Proprietors of the South Sea Capital* (1732), p. 12: "After all these risks run, give me leave to ask, what profits we have to boast of? & where is our mighty advantage? The outset & amount of the cargo of the said ship (the *Prince William*) was nigh £222,000 & the return about... £280,000 the difference & gains thereof is £60,000 but when a Present is deducted... expenses... and many other charges, there will little if any profit appear. And must not this give us some strong apprehension of villainy somewhere carried on, for the Spanish merchants make profits." See also pp. 13, 15.

66 Spanish complaint made 1732, April 17, mentioned among other grievances the illicit trade of the *Royal George*, and the *Prince Frederick*: enclosed in Keene to Newcastle, 1738, Sept. 22. P.R.O., S.P.F., Sp. 131.

67 As late as April 1739, in a statement prepared by the accountant of the South Sea Company, the sum of £27,896 odd was entered as being still owing to His Catholic Majesty for his share in the *Royal Caroline*. Simancas, P. de E., Ing. leg. 7006.

68 For an illuminating study of the policy of Carvajal, based on an analysis of his Testament, 1745, and Pensamientos, 1753, see Manuel Ferrandis Torres, "El equilibrio europeo de Don Josef de Carvajal y Lancaster", published in *Revista Histórica*, Organo de la Facultad de Historia de Valladolid, Oct.–Dec. 1924, *passim*.

69 These terms were discussed by Macanaz at Breda in 1746: see Olbes Fernandez, "*La Paz de Aquisgran*" (tesis doctoral), *Contribución al estudio del reinado de Fernando VI* (Pontevedra, 1926), *passim*. They were also discussed by Wall in his secret mission to London in 1747. His correspondence with Carvajal, Huescar the Spanish ambassador in Paris, and Sotomayor the Spanish plenipotentiary at Aix-la-Chapelle is in Madrid, A.H.N., Estado, Ing. legs. 4264, 4277.

70 For the negotiations at Lisbon see Sir Richard Lodge's introduction to *The Private Correspondence of Sir Benjamin Keene, K.B.* (1933), pp. xiii–xv.

71 Carvajal to Wall, 1747, Nov. 15: "Even if we cannot obtain Gibraltar we have conquered so much that, unless God changes the whole course of the war, we ought to have enough to secure an establishment." Madrid, A.H.N., Estado, Ing. leg. 4277.

72 The Preliminaries executed on April 30, 1748: "Article 4. The Duchies of Parma and Guastalla, and the town of Placentia, to be assigned to Don Philip...." Wm. Coxe, *Memoirs of the Administration of the Rt. Hon. Henry Pelham* (1829), vol. 1, p. 417.

73 Carvajal to Wall, 1748, May 14: "The Preliminaries are not bad, except for the clause which allows the prolongation of the Asiento and the years of the Annual Ship, if this is removed we shall rest satisfied although offended at the method of concluding the agreement...." Madrid, A.H.N., Estado, Ing. leg. 4277.

74 Masones, Duque de Sotomayor, to Wall, 1748, May 14. Madrid, A.H.N., Estado, Ing. leg. 4264.

75 Masones to Wall, 1748, June 2. Madrid, A.H.N., Estado, Ing. leg. 4264.

76 Masones to Wall, 1748, June 18: "The Duque de Huescar has given His Most Christian Majesty a letter from the King our Master saying that I have orders to sign; so I can delay no longer." Madrid, A.H.N., Estado, Ing. leg. 4264.

77 Masones to Wall, 1748, June 26. Madrid, A.H.N., Estado, Ing. leg. 4264.

78 Masones to Wall, 1748, Oct. 20: To the effect that, "The Definitive Treaty was signed on October 18 by the representatives of France, England & Holland. All the articles that interest us are arranged as we wished. I acceded today." Madrid, A.H.N., Estado, Ing. leg. 4264.

"The Definitive Treaty of Peace & Friendship...concluded at Aix-la-Chapelle the 18th Day of October, N.S. 1748." C. Jenkinson, *A Collection of all the Treaties of Peace, Alliance and Commerce between Great Britain and other Powers from...1648 to...1783* (1785), vol. II, pp. 384-5.

79 Masones to Wall, 1748, Aug. 8: "France promises to do all in her power to have it explained in the Definitive Treaty that the Asiento is to be renewed for only 4 years"; Masones to Wall, 1748, Aug. 29: "Mons. St. Severin has supported us thus far with constancy...the French Project for a Definitive Treaty arranges our disputes very satisfactorily"; Masones to Wall, 1748, Oct. 1: "On September 27, Mons. St. Severin gave the English plenipotentiaries his project for a Definitive Treaty...articles 4 and 10 are reasonable and just." Madrid, A.H.N., Estado, Ing. leg. 4264.

80 Maria Theresa had refused to guarantee the Barrier Fortresses or to cede the territories demanded by Spain and Sardinia in Italy. See W. Coxe, *Pelham*, vol. I, chap. 17; vol. II, chaps. 18-20.

81 Masones to Wall, 1748, Aug. 23. Madrid, A.H.N., Estado, Ing. leg. 4264.

82 Masones to Wall, 1748, Oct. 1. Madrid, A.H.N., Estado, Ing. leg. 4264.

83 Wall to Carvajal, 1749, May 19: "Lord Sandwich is a great friend of the Duke of Bedford, but is disliked by the Pelhams for they blame him for the omission of the Peace Treaty." Simancas, P. de E., Ing. leg. 6914.

84 Extract from a letter from Port St Mary to Sir Daniel Lambert & Co., 1748, Dec. 23, enclosed in Bedford to Keene, 1749, Jan. 12. P.R.O., S.P.F., Sp. 135.

85 Extract from a letter from Cadiz to Mr J. Mannock, 1748, Dec. 31, enclosed in Bedford to Keene, 1749, Jan. 12. P.R.O., S.P.F., Sp. 135.

86 Wall to Carvajal, 1749, Dec. 4. Simancas, P. de E., Ing. leg. 6914.

87 Bedford to Keene, 1748, Dec. 4, with Credentials and Instructions. Brit. Mus. Add. MSS., Keene Papers.

88 Keene to Bedford, 1749, Oct. 13: "...the omission of the Treaty of '15 has made us lose our hold upon this Court. I have supported our right to it in spite of omissions, and have never met with a reasonable answer. All I am told is, dryly, that a treaty omitted is a treaty *deshecho*..." Quoted in Sir Richard Lodge, *The Private Correspondence of Sir Benjamin Keene, K.B.*, p. 176.

89 Keene to Bedford, 1749, June 26. P.R.O., S.P.F., Sp. 135.

90 Keene to Newcastle, 1750, Oct. 8. P.R.O., S.P.F., Sp. 138.

91 Keene to Bedford, 1749, June 8. P.R.O., S.P.F., Sp. 135.

92 Wall to Carvajal, 1749, March 27: "The South Sea Company is such a large financial concern that the Ministry treat it with consideration. They also want to save their face over this negotiation, although they know that if the Company is to supply Spanish America with slaves there must be friction between this Court and Spain because of contraband." Simancas, P. de E., Ing. leg. 6914.

93 Wall to Carvajal, 1749, April 24: "I said that it was odd that Mr Keene should ask for *cedulas* (to renew the Annual Ships and Asiento trade) without even mentioning the agreement concluded at Aix-la-Chapelle to treat for an Equivalent. The Duke of Bedford replied that he knew nothing of this, and I believe him, but he seems ready to cede the Asiento." Simancas, P. de E., Ing. leg. 6914.

94 Carvajal to Wall, 1749, June 14: "I am very surprised to hear from you ...that the Duke of Newcastle said that Lord Sandwich made a mistake in not annulling the agreement to treat for an Equivalent when the number of years of nonjouissance was fixed." Simancas, P. de E., Ing. leg. 6914.

95 Wall to Carvajal, 1749, June 8. Simancas, P. de E., Ing. leg. 6914.

96 Wall to Carvajal, 1749, Aug. 11: "I asked if the Ministers had yet met the Director of the South Sea Company to discuss the equivalent, but they had not. Mr Pelham is the person with whom I have most discussed this point.... They will not treat without the renewal of the Treaty of 1715, or at least the lowering of the duties. If things are left in the air the old troubles in America will begin again. There will be much contraband from the English Colonies; rich register ships and *azogues* will be captured; and what are a few merchantmen taken by our Guarda Costas in comparison with one register? If we concede a Commercial Treaty they may give up their claims to the Asiento. When the time approaches for the opening of Parliament they may become more explicit." Simancas, P. de E., Ing. leg. 6914.

97 Wall to Carvajal, 1749, Aug. 11. Simancas, P. de E., Ing. leg. 6914.

98 Wall to Carvajal, 1749, Sept. 11. Simancas, P. de E., Ing. leg. 6914.

99 Wall to Carvajal, 1749, Oct. 13: "When your dispatch arrived I went at once to see the Duke of Newcastle, who asked me what was the news. I answered: 'Bad; we have no treaty of 1715 nor ever shall. But our expedient, sent on September 11th, has been accepted.' He read Mr Keene's letters, and embraced me." Simancas, P. de E., Ing. leg. 6914.

100 Wall to Carvajal, 1749, Oct. 14. Simancas, P. de E., Ing. leg. 6914.

101 Wall to Carvajal, 1749, Oct. 23. Simancas, P. de E., Ing. leg. 6914.

102 Wall to Carvajal, 1749, Nov. 6. Simancas, P. de E., Ing. leg. 6914.

103 Wall to Carvajal, 1750, Feb. 12: "At the Council meeting...some said that the claims should be ceded *quantum nobis est*. The Duke of Newcastle said...that they were not there to decide points of jurisprudence but that if they let slip this opportunity of settling their disputes with Spain, they would seem the most negligent and torpid ministry on earth." Simancas, P. de E., Ing. leg. 6917.

104 Wall to Carvajal, 1750, Feb. 5: "I also think that the Duke of Bedford, advised by Lord Sandwich—for particular ends—is making difficulties." Simancas, P. de E., Ing. leg. 6917.

105 Wall to Carvajal, 1750, Feb. 23: "When I went to see the Duke of Bedford he said that he had good news, from his point of view, and produced a Counter Project....There are now three methods of settling the South Sea Company's claims, one is to pass them over in silence, the second is to grant the Company the monopoly to import negroes to His Catholic Majesty's colonies for 20 years, the third is to pay the £200,000 suggested by England. You in your great wisdom will be best able to judge of the relative merits of these schemes, but my personal opinion is that the most advantageous course would obviously be to pay the money. Honestly I have lost all hope that our reasons or insistence can produce the least effect on this ministry." Simancas, P. de E., Ing. leg. 6917.

106 Wall to Carvajal, 1750, April 9: "Stand firm. We have much time before the Parliament opens, though war may break out in the north, or France may try to spoil our negotiations. If the English answer is not as you wish do not make any further suggestions. Seem to abandon the whole negotiation, talk of granting *cedulas*, and begin to work on the South Sea Company accounts." This is an excellent example of the way in which Wall advised Carvajal on matters of policy. Simancas, P. de E., Ing. leg. 6917.

107 Keene to Bedford, 1750, Feb. 16: "...Ensenada does not enter into any approbation or otherwise of Carvajal's Conduct on this occasion, but wishes we were to come to an adjustment, because, as he often repeats to me, he can take no solid measure with regard to His Department without having the Foundation and Security of Great Britain." P.R.O., S.P.F., Sp. 137.

108 Keene to Newcastle, 1750, Aug. 13, Private and particular: "...The money matter, though I have made so much stir about it, is not the most concerns me. For if I was authorised to conclude upon the Footing of yielding up seizures etc. which would have included almost All, I might fairly infer, that taking £100,000 was better than nothing—and it is not dishonourable for the Nation to receive a larger sum for a Reconciliation than that which gave occasion to a Rupture between the Two Crowns.

"The prompt payment, I think I could procure by touching Ensenada's vanity....

"...I take this Gentleman's (Mr Carvajal's) real System to be to live well with England, though at as cheap a Rate as he can; to be cautious in entering into Engagements, and as punctual in the Execution of them." P.R.O., S.P.F., Sp. 138.

109 Wall to Carvajal, 1749, Oct. 30: "...The Duke then went on to say that the debts claimed by the Company from His Catholic Majesty amounted to a considerable sum, almost £800,000...." Simancas, P. de E., Ing. leg. 6914.

110 Wall to Carvajal, 1749, Oct. 23: "The Duke of Bedford...says there are very great difficulties over the claims of the South Sea Company which he values at about £500,000." Simancas, P. de E., Ing. leg. 6914.

111 Wall to Carvajal, 1750, Feb. 22. Simancas, P. de E., Ing. leg. 6917.

112 Keene to Bedford, 1750, March 22, Secret: "...I found him (Ensenada) well informed of what had passed in England by Mr Wall *en Droiture* (for he seldom or ever talks with his Colleagues) and when I mentioned the sum of 300,000 Pounds, he smiled and told me, my Instructions would allow me to strike our Bargain for £200,000....

"As he has named most of the Ministers employed abroad and pays all of them, they have a direct correspondence with him, tho' not their Chief, which is another matter of complaint M. de Carvajal has against him, because with such a Partner, he is not master of the King's Secrets." P.R.O., S.P.F., Sp. 137.

113 Keene to Newcastle, 750, Aug. 3, Private and particular. P.R.O., S.P.F., Sp. 138.

114 For the test of the Commercial Treaty of Oct. 5, 1750, see C. Jenkinson, *Treaties*, vol. II, pp. 410–13.

115 Keene to Bedford, 1750, Jan. 9. P.R.O., S.P.F., Sp. 137.

116 See the *cedulas* of approbation for the British Consuls in the *Consultas* of the *Junta de Comercio*. Madrid, A.H.N., Estado, Ing. legs. 606, 613, 630, 639.

117 *Rights of foreign Consuls*: see also notes Chap. III, n. 84; Chap. IV, nn. 80, 89. *Consulta* of the *Junta de Comercio*, 1735, Oct. 22. To the effect that, "The

Governor of Malaga reported that...the previous Consul had had an Agent or Secretary but that this was a private innovation although the merchants had given him some salary because they found him useful." Madrid, A.H.N., Estado, Ing. leg. 639.

118 *Consulta* of the *Junta de Comercio*, 1749, July 29: "The Assistente of Seville Don Gines de Hermosa y Espejo sends the following information about Consul Pringle.

"When the last war broke out his goods were embargoed, but they were very few because he had been warned in advance. He seemed therefore to be a man of considerable cunning, and prudence, between fifty and sixty years of age. The Irish merchants resident in Seville have provided some further lights on his character. Originally he came to Spain because he had fled from England where he was said to have committed a murder. He arrived as poor as Job, but by his industry and great frugality he succeeded in accumulating more than three hundred thousand *pesos*.

"In the year 1719, when an expedition was attempted to restore King James to the throne of Great Britain, this fanatical Pringle was the first person to warn the English Court of this Spanish plan; he having given himself out to be a loyal Jacobite under which character he had been admitted to the meetings of the Irish merchants, and those English who were followers of King James....For this most valuable service he was given a Consular Patent, and he performed the duties and appropriated the pay of a Consul for three years although his appointment had never been approved by His Catholic Majesty. This was the reason why he was fined, and his goods sold publicly in San Lucar, but he did not suffer any great hurt because he was protected by the intervention of the English Court.

"He returns to his Consulship now with the single object of gathering together his valuables. This done he will return to his adored country to enjoy his estate which he will buy or inherit." Madrid, A.H.N., Estado, Ing. leg. 613.

119 *Consulta* of the *Junta de Comercio*, 1751, Jan. 16. To the effect that, "It does not appear that the English nation previously had either a Consul or Vice-Consul at Cartagena...as other nations have Consuls there the *Junta* advises His Catholic Majesty to allow the English to have one there." Madrid, A.H.N., Estado, Ing. leg. 616.

120 Consul Banks (Cartagena) to Lord Holderness, 1752, Feb. 2: P.R.O., S.P.F., Sp. 227.

121 *Colebrook and his dispute with the Cadiz factory.* Don Gines de Hermosa y Espejo to the *Junta de Comercio*, 1749, June 25: "The Consul is a notorious gentleman, essentially English by descent and sympathies...he owns a coach, and has a salary of three thousand *pesos*...he is sixty years of age, or perhaps a little more, very formal, and a man who has seen much of the world. He is honestly attached to Spain, and cordially detests France. He worked hard and with success to get England to extinguish the four remaining years of the Asiento for an Equivalent, because he knew the damage done by the Asiento to the trade to America, and he represented strongly to the chief Minister, to the Duke of Bedford, to the Parliament how useful it would be to both Crowns, if the English illicit trade in America could be suppressed." Madrid, A.H.N., Estado, Ing. leg. 613.

Colebrook to Bedford, 1750, July 14: "Upon the breaking out of the War in 1702 the English merchants were forced to retire from Spain, and left their concerns under the care of their Irish clerks who being of the religion of the place were permitted to stay behind.....In the year 1713, the fatal acquisition of Asiento ruined the Trade of England with Spain, so that few of the remaining English merchants thought fit to return to their once flourishing Houses and a new Factory sprung up consisting at first of such as had been brought up by the English. To these flocked numberless relations and dependants from the depths of Ireland, and the more considerable of the old people going off to the Spaniards, these newcomers by their numbers made up what was continued to be called the English Factory, and chose two Deputies annually to whom they gave power in express words to act with the Consul or separately." P.R.O., S.P.F., Sp. 227.

Colebrook to Bedford, 1750, July 14: "There having been great abuses in the collection and distribution of the moneys called the national contribution. But Parliament passed an Act for the better collecting and more equal paying that money, which Act is the cause of the present misunderstanding, as it deprives the greater number of the Gentlemen of disposing of that money as it used to be formerly.

"I am well informed that in the year 1726 a privateer was fitted out with that money to cruise upon the English, and that it has been frequently employed in sending popish Missionaries to England and Ireland. By the books of the Deputies there are many articles charged thus:

Paid to a Gentleman in distress...
    to a Country man or Country woman...
    to a person who desires not to be known...

upon enquiry who these persons might have been, it appears that the distressed Gentlemen were Irish officers in the Spanish service and some of the Ladies without any other merit than being agreeable to the Deputies." P.R.O., S.P.F., Sp. 227.

Consulta of the *Junta de Comercio*, 1751, May 25 (quoted a paper from an English merchant explaining the various duties). To the effect that, "The National Duty is one voluntarily imposed on themselves, by the merchants of any one nation, to pay various expenses. This duty was extended, as expenses grew, until it was demanded of all those who received goods in English ships. Other nations demanded the same duties from English merchants who had received goods in foreign ships." Madrid, A.H.N., Estado, Ing. leg. 616.

Colebrook to Aldworth, 1751, Jan. 19. Mentions the expenses chargeable on the National Duty fund as "the relief of sailors, annual presents & charities". P.R.O., S.P.F., Sp. 227.

Colebrook to Aldworth, 1751, Jan. 19: "...I can now aver that at the rate they have recovered this contribution to the utmost of what is allowed by the Act, viz: one rial plate per ducat of eleven rials upon the amount of freights and two rials per tun on tunage goods, they have not made good near £1000 Sterling per annum, when it ought to have produced from two to four thousand £ Sterling. I have been frequently solicited to comply with customs and let things go on in the old way, but finding that way contrary to justice and the needs of my country, I have drawn great dislike on myself by not joining in the collusion...." P.R.O., S.P.F., Sp. 227.

Colebrook to Aldworth, 1751, Jan. 19: "...When I came hither I found the Deputies had not only levied to the utmost limits of one rial per ducat upon the English subjects, but had extorted double so much from other nations without any authority. I represented how criminal it was to levy more than the parliament allowed, and caused the overplus to be returned, and finding that even one rial per ducat regularly and equally raised would be much more than sufficient for all the purposes directed by Parliament I proposed in the national Assembly to lower the contribution to one-half rial per ducat on the English shipping whilst the French took two rials per ducat, but this was opposed for obvious reasons." P.R.O., S.P.F., Sp. 227.

Colebrook to Bedford, 1750, June 30: "Upon my arrival here I had intimations given me, that the Factory had certain traditional customs that they could not be deprived of by the King's Commission, or an Act of Parliament; I endeavoured to convince them of the contrary without effect, and after declaring only at first that they should 'Esteem that I would confirm young Mr Archdekin in the post of Vice-Consul' they afterwards came to notify me in writing 'that they would assist and maintain the right of appointing a Vice-Consul, with an allowance of 50 rials per Ship out of the 150 it had been customary for all Ships to pay for Consulage'; and one of the Factory said at a National meeting that 'the King's Commission had been obtained clandestinely and collusively'.

"I have strenuously insisted upon my right by virtue of His Majesty's Commission, but though I had at first arrival proposed to divide the thirty-two rials plate that had been allowed by former Consuls to the Vice-Consuls between Mr Archdekin and Mr Taverner to prevent if possible any complaint on that account...." P.R.O., S.P.F., Sp. 227.

Colebrook to Aldworth, 1751, Jan. 19: "The relief of sailors, the annual presents, and charities, may be all defrayed within 6000 Dollars or £1000 a year, and as the contribution upon the present foot of one rial per ducat will produce at least £2000, I humbly propose that it be reduced to one-half per ducat. But if it be expedient to keep it at the present rate of one rial that the overplus which would always be above £1000 be remitted to England and invested in the public funds, in order to accumulate to such sum that the interest of it may be sufficient to answer the annual national disbursement and that this duty of contributions entirely cease to the great encouragement of the English navigation." P.R.O., S.P.F., Sp. 227.

An Act for more equal paying and better collecting certain small sums for relief of shipwrecked mariners and distressed persons, His Majesty's subjects, in the Ports of Cadiz and Port Saint Mary's in the Kingdom of Spain; and for other uses usually contributed to by the merchants to the said ports. Made law, 1736, May 5, Act 9 Geo. II, c. 25. *Statutes at large*, vol. VI, p. 222.

Consulta of the *Junta de Comercio*, 1751, May 25. Madrid, A.H.N., Estado, Ing. leg. 613.

Holderness to Colebrook, 1752, Feb. 20: "The King has commanded me to acquaint you, that he has thought proper, to put an End to your present Commission of Consul at Cadiz and St Mary; and that His Majesty has been pleased to appoint the Honourable Mr Edward Hay, to succeed you in that Employment...." P.R.O., S.P.F., Sp. 227.

122 Banks (Cartagena) to Holderness, 1751, Nov. 17. P.R.O., S.P.F., Sp. 227.

123 *Danish trade with Spain forbidden*. Keene to Holderness, 1753, July 15, Nov. 30. P.R.O., S.P.F., Sp. 144.

124 *Delay in executing Commercial Treaty of* 1750. Keene to Holderness, 1751, Nov. 24: P.R.O., S.P.F., Sp. 140; Keene to Holderness, 1752, March 21, Private and confidential: P.R.O., S.P.F., Sp. 141; Keene to Holderness, 1752, March 20: P.R.O., S.P.F., Sp. 141; Keene to Amyand, 1752, May 15: P.R.O., S.P.F., Sp. 141; Keene to Holderness, 1753, March 1: P.R.O., S.P.F., Sp. 143.

125 Keene to Holderness, 1753, March 1. P.R.O., S.P.F., Sp. 143.

126 Wall to Carvajal, 1748, March 1: "Higgs, the watchmaker whom you mentioned in your letter of January 24, is old, and does not want to leave England especially at this time." Madrid, A.H.N., Estado, Ing. leg. 4277.

127 *English workmen enticed to Spain.* Wall to Carvajal, 1749, Aug. 11: "Richard Metcalf has embarked about 20 people and some camels' hair in the *Dorothy and Magoire* (sic), which is now in the Downs and will sail in 8 or 10 days. He found the £234 sent by the Granada Company inadequate and was disconsolate, and said that he needed immediately the balance of the £2000, which had been promised him by the Company. I had already paid him the £234 and another £368 in letters of exchange...but, being convinced that he was in real danger of being arrested for debt, and in accordance with your instructions and those of the Granada Company I raised the remaining £1397 odd.

"On August 8 we heard that the ship had been stopped at Portsmouth on the pretext that she carried contraband. The people are now under arrest there. Richard says that whatever happens he is set on establishing in Spain a factory for making up silk and camels' hair to clothe priests, and that this can in no way injure the English woollen trade, but I fear that England may now put more difficulties in the way of the mechanics that you want." Simancas, P. de E., Ing. leg. 6914.

128 Wall to Carvajal, 1749, Aug. 25: "I had hoped that Richard...had escaped, but Alegre met him in the street. The other workmen are here. They will probably admit that Richard hired them to go to Spain, in which case the punishment is £100 fine or 3 months imprisonment. What I fear is that they will be imprisoned until it is too late for them to go to Spain. If Richard is really vitally necessary for the factory we shall have to get him out of here. One of the woollen manufacturers has given away, in his cups, that he has been engaged to go to Spain, and so has had to fly to France...." Simancas, P. de E., Ing. leg. 6914.

129 Wall to Carvajal, 1748, Sept. 17: "You asked me about the woollen manufacturers. They are Roman Catholics, married and quite ready to go to Spain with their families. The only delay will be because peace has not yet been concluded.

"I availed myself of the services of some missionaries educated in Spain. One of these, in particular, is very zealous but indiscreetly so. His ideas are good but incompatible with my public character.

"I enclose 5 yards of cloth as a sample. It is all made from Spanish wool." Madrid, A.H.N., Estado, Ing. leg. 4277.

130 Wall to Carvajal, 1749, Nov. 10: "The men that were with their principal in Calais have vanished. I think that they have returned home. The master workman begs me not to abandon him, and my servant Poyo dare not return for fear of being arrested; since if I were to reclaim him the whole affair would come to light. The two men had better travel to Spain together." Simancas, P. de E., Ing. leg. 6914.

Wall to Carvajal, 1750, Jan. 27: "I am glad to hear that Poyo and the textile worker have arrived safely." Simancas, P. de E., Ing. leg. 6917.

Wall to Carvajal, 1751, Jan. 21: "I am very glad that Beaven's son is going to join his father." Simancas, P. de E., Ing.leg. 6917.

Wall to Carvajal, 1751, July 22: "Lord Cartaret said to M. Abreu that the Spanish manufactures were progressing well, and that Spain was lucky to have secured the services of the best man in Europe—Beaven. He thinks that Beaven went to Spain of his own accord because of his debts." Simancas, P. de E., Ing. leg. 6917.

131 Jordan (Corunna) to Holderness, 1754, March 16: "Don Jorge...soon after he got Home, to Madrid, ventured from thence to England upon his own Scheme to Seduce our Shipbuilders and other useful Artificers to Leave their Country and to list themselves in His Catholic Majesty's Service...." P.R.O., S.P.F., Sp. 228.

132 Jordan (Corunna) to Holderness, 1754, March 16: "said Don Jorge is well known in London having had the honour (when a prisoner of war there) to be made a F.R.S." P.R.O., S.P.F., Sp. 228.

133 Wall to Carvajal, 1750, April 17. Simancas, P. de E., Ing. leg. 6917.

134 Abreu to Carvajal, 1750, May 14: "An Irishman I know, the one who helped Don Jorge Juan suborn workmen, and who after Don Jorge had left got the workmen's wives and families safely embarked for France, says he will find a faithful spy in Portsmouth, and another in the three arsenal ports in the Thames." Simancas, P. de E., Ing. leg. 6914.

135 Jordan (Corunna) to Bedford, 1750, May 1: "...since which time (i.e. March 30) I have had repeated intelligence of the arrival at Santiago of English men and women from London via Porto &c. and three Days ago had private advices that 8 or 9 of them were got to Ferrol one of whom is a Master Shipwright said to have been a foreman in one of His Majesty's Docks and is to be a master builder here and to have six hard Dollars per Day punctually paid which is equal to 27 shillings Sterling. He has his wife with him, another is a master Ropemaker, a third, master Sail Cloth weaver, a fourth a Sailmaker, the rest journeymen of the same trades to assist them and many more such are soon expected there who are all to be imployed in Building twelve Ships (of 60: 70: and 80 guns each)...and prodigious great works are projected, and some begun...." P.R.O., S.P.F., Sp. 227.

136 Jordan (Corunna) to Holderness, 1752, Jan. 19. P.R.O., S.P.F., Sp. 227.

137 Jordan to Holderness, 1752, May 24. P.R.O., S.P.F., Sp. 227.

138 Jordan to Holderness, 1753, March 8. P.R.O., S.P.F., Sp. 228.

139 Banks (Cartagena) to Holderness, 1752, Aug. 30: "...There has been here lately a ship called the *Tryton* Michael Brown Master with Timber and Plank for building Men of War here, this Ship has for owner Richard Rooth the Builder at Ferrol, and he is the owner of another large ship of which I do not yet know the Name, these two ships are employed in Transporting Timber and Plank for the King of Spain with English passes and English Colours and Bryant the Builder here, and Mullins the Builder at Cadiz has ordered four Ships to be bought for them, which are to be employed in the same manner...." P.R.O., S.P.F., Sp. 227.

140 Colebrook (Cadiz) to Bedford, 1749, Nov. 10: "One William Maguire of the *Dorothy and Mary*,...this is the ship and Master that were stopped at Portsmouth upon account of having artificers on board engaged for the fabrics of Granada. The people were taken out at Portsmouth but the frames, tools, etc. proceeded in the ship to the quantity of $3\frac{1}{2}$ tons, and are to be landed at Malaga. The ship is said to belong to one of the name of Macnamara of London." P.R.O., S.P.F., Sp. 227.

Abreu to Carvajal, 1752, Aug. 24: "Our Chaplain Shaw has embarked the dyer Keating for Spain in the ship *Andaluzia* belonging to Captain Macnamara, and bound for Cadiz." Simancas, P. de E., Ing. leg. 6917.

141 Banks (Cartagena) to Holderness, 1752, Sept. 27: "...There is one Steward a Master of a Ship who is a constant trader from London to Cadiz this man has been and is the Greatest Seducer of artificers in England, he has seduced and brought over a great many workers both in Cloth and Silk Manufactures, he also was the chief instrument in seducing John Laughtman the Assistant Builder at this place, and was the very person that agreed with him in London for two hundred pounds Sterling a year which he did by an order from the Marquis of Ensenada to the Intendant of Cadiz, he also brought him, the said Laughtman, over to Cadiz in his vessel and delivered him to the Intendant there.

"If the said Stuart be prosecuted it will be easy to prove that he has seduced several of His Majesty's Subjects, being artificers both of Cloth and Silk, and brought them to Spain within these 12 months, as well as the Said Laughtman, which is Humbly Submitted." P.R.O., S.P.F., Sp. 227.

Banks (Cartagena) to Holderness, 1752, Oct. 10: "...I hope this will reach your Lordship's hand before Stuart a Master of a Ship in London sails for Cadiz he is with the Assistance of some others to seduce and bring away fourteen Carpenters out of Deptford yard whose names he carried with him from Cadiz and a Certain Irish Merchant in London is to pay to each of them two hundred pounds sterling in London and give them security for two hundred pounds Sterling yearly each man during their lives in Spain." P.R.O., S.P.F., Sp. 227.

142 Jordan (Corunna) to Holderness, 1751, Nov. 13: "...the Ship *Tryton*, upward of Three hundred Tons burthen, laden with New Castle Coal for Account of His Catholic Majesty, Commanded by Michael Brown, an Irishman, whose wife is Rooth the builders Sister, and has been with him for some time past which I mention only to show that they are all of the same Clan. The Master Joyner's wife who went not long since to England to do mischief there, is Returned in said Ship, as is likewise, the Captain R. M. mentioned in my last, who has brought Several Sorts of Goods, Designing as I am informed to turn Merchant and to settle with his Family at Ferrol, Brown has brought from England an Experienced Boatswain who is to order the Rigging of their Ships etc....all after the English fashion, and Brown's Ship is to be imployed in the Timber Trade...." P.R.O., S.P.F., Sp. 227.

143 Banks (Cartagena) to Holderness, 1752, July 5: "On the 28th ultimo, arrived here a small Spanish vessel from Cadiz, who brought two English Men from thence for the King of Spain's Yard at this place, one of them is called John Loughlin a Ship Carpenter; and son to a Brewer of that Name in London who was engaged in to the Spanish Service about six months ago in London, by one Shaw an Irish priest Chaplain to Mr W—l, the S—h, E—r, he is come here to be Assistant to Bryant the Builder, his Salary is £200 Sterling a year.

"The other is Thomas Arm late a mate on board the *Rainbow* M: of W: who reports that he was Discharged in the Bay of Cadiz by Captain Rooney, and had his leave to enter into the Spanish Service. This man is to have Direction of Rigging M: of W: at this Port, but his Salary is not yet settled; the above Mentioned Shaw and his Brother are Engaging English Blockmakers and Sail Makers to come here to be emploi'd in this Yard." P.R.O., S.P.F., Sp. 227.

APPENDIX

1 For Patiño's career see *Patiño y Campillo, Reseña histórica-biográfica de estos dos ministros de Felipe V* (Madrid, 1882), by A. Rodriguez Villa, and the *Fragmentos históricos para la vida del excelentisimo Señor Josef Patiño*, edited by Sotomayor (1790), *passim*.

2 At Carraca, said to have been so called because a ship of war, or carrick, once went ashore there: *Fragmentos*, ed. Sotomayor, p. 37.

3 A. Mounier, *Les faits et la doctrine économiques en Espagne sous Philippe V*, p. 57.

4 Cayley to Newcastle, 1738, May 6. P.R.O., S.P.F., Sp. 222.

5 *Fragmentos*, ed. Sotomayor, pp. 73–4 and 94.

6 *Fragmentos*, ed. Sotomayor, p. 97.

7 Dennis (Cuba) to Burrell, 1731, Nov. 2. Brit. Mus. Shel. Photostats, II, ii, f. 345. Abadia (Porto Rico) to Patiño, 1735, June 6, reporting the aggressiveness of his foreign neighbours; Orcasitas (Cuba) to His Catholic Majesty, 1737, Aug. 23. Seville, A. G. de Ind., Aud. S. Dom. leg. 2513.

8 Cayley (Cadiz) to Newcastle, 1735, April 26. P.R.O., S.P.F., Sp. 221.

9 Cayley to Newcastle, 1728, Sept. 28. P.R.O., S.P.F., Sp. 218.

10 Cayley to Newcastle, 1729, Aug. 25. P.R.O., S.P.F., Sp. 219.

11 Cayley to Newcastle, 1730, Aug. 19. P.R.O., S.P.F., Sp. 219.

12 Cayley (Cadiz) to Newcastle, 1731, Jan. 16. P.R.O., S.P.F., Sp. 219.

13 Cayley to Newcastle, 1731, March 27. P.R.O., S.P.F., Sp. 219.

14 Cayley to Newcastle, 1731, April 10. P.R.O., S.P.F., Sp. 219.

15 Cayley to Newcastle, 1731, April 3. P.R.O., S.P.F., Sp. 219.

16 Cayley to Newcastle, 1731, June 26. P.R.O., S.P.F., Sp. 219.

17 Cayley to Newcastle, 1731, Dec. 11. P.R.O., S.P.F., Sp. 219.

18 Cayley to Newcastle, 1736, May 1. P.R.O., S.P.F., Sp. 221.

19 Cayley (Cadiz) to Newcastle, 1730, Dec. 26. P.R.O., S.P.F., Sp. 219.

20 Cayley (Cadiz) to Newcastle, 1731, May 29. P.R.O., S.P.F., Sp. 219.

21 Cayley (Cadiz) to Newcastle, 1735, Feb. 8. P.R.O., S.P.F., Sp. 221.

22 Cayley to Newcastle, 1736, March 20. P.R.O., S.P.F., Sp. 221.

23 For Uztariz's theories and their relation to the facts of the eighteenth century see A. Mounier, *Les faits et la doctrine économiques en Espagne sous Philippe V*, *passim*.

24 G. de Uztariz, *Teorica y Practica de Comercio y de Marina* (Madrid, 1742), book I, chap. xv, p. 63.

25 A. Mounier, *Les faits et la doctrine économiques en Espagne sous Philippe V*, p. 278.

26 Published in Canga Arguelles, *Diccionario de Hacienda*, vol. II, pp. 121–5.

27 Cayley (Cadiz) to Newcastle, 1734, Feb. 23. P.R.O., S.P.F., Sp. 220.

INDEX

149; need for peace, 100; policy of, 171 n. 1; reforms in trade, 151; reforms of, 12

Tinagero, rival of, 147

Peace, treaty of (Utrecht), 1713, *see* Treaty of Peace, Anglo-Spanish, 1713

Peace Conference, Utrecht, 1712, 61; commercial questions referred to, 52; France and, 48, 49; Great Britain and, 48, 49, plenipotentiaries, 56, 63; opening of, 48; preliminaries, signed at London, 48; Spanish exclusion from, 48; Spanish independence and, 48; trade to the Indies, Anglo-French discussions, 49

Peace negotiations: at Gertruydenberg, 1709, 47; 1711, 47–8

Peace of Aix-la-Chapelle, 1748, *see* Aix-la-Chapelle

Peace of Ryswick, 36–7

Peace preliminaries of 1727, 87

Pedro, captain of *Guarda Costa*, 188 n. 46

Pelham, Henry, British minister, b. 1696, d. 1754: negro trade: continuation of, desired by, 1749, 137, need of commercial treaty, 137; proposal for extinction of Asiento, 137

Permission ships: illicit trade in, 79; mismeasurement of, 79; Parliamentary interest in, 198 n. 121

Peru, trade to, 25, 128

Peso, Spanish coin, 115–16

Philip, Don, younger son of Philip V and Elizabeth Farnese, Duke of Parma, 1748–65: appointed Grand Admiral, 99; establishment in Italy, 134; French marriage of, 120

Philip II, King of Spain, 1556–98, trade killed by fanaticism of, 11

Philip III, King of Spain, 1598–1621, Moriscos expelled by, 11

Philip V, King of Spain, 1700–46, 49, 96 Accession, 35; accession of, acquiescence in, 32; British attitude towards accession of, 32; Dutch opinion on, 180 n. 10; effect on British trade, 33, 38, 39, 44; effect on French trade, 35; French advantages from, 37

British trade under, 31; characteristics of, 31, 68, 69, 100; claim to French throne, 33, 35; death of, influence on Carvajal's policy, 133; Dutch approval of, 32; Dutch recognise, 36; duties under, 55; Franco-Spanish relations, 171 n. 1; Great Britain and, cordiality between, 68; Great Britain menaced by, 33; industry

encouraged under, 153; military interests of, 68, 100; Patiño and, 146, 148, 149, 155; peace preliminaries, 1712, 48; policy of, 100; political ambitions of, 148; popularity in Spain, 47; public expenditure under, 148; resignation of la Paz, 148

Philippine Company: British fear of, 98, 193–4 n. 84; Dutch attitude to, 194 n. 84; French attitude to, 194 n. 84; Patiño and, 193–4 n. 84; project for, 193–4 n. 84

Pig iron, trade in, 3, 10

Pintado, Don Manuel, commander of galleons and *flota*, Admiral Stewart co-operates with, to suppress piracy, 90, 176–7 n. 71

Pipe staves, trade in, 172 n. 17

Pirates: British ships seized by, 103; Governor of Havana sent orders to check, 106; pose as *Guarda Costas*, 106; posing as privateers, 106; ships seized by, 102

Piritu, British demand to trade near, 51

Pitt, William, Earl of Chatham, b. 1708, d. 1778, prefers Guadeloupe to Canada, 3

Pizarro, Francisco, 11

Plague: in the Morea, 97; in Turkey, 97

Plate River Region: British demands to choose territory in, 49; Spanish concessions in, 49

Playing cards, British duty imposed on, 47

Plenipotentiaries, *see* Bedmar, Bristol, Bishop of, Bubb, Castres, Keene, Monteleon, Sandwich, St Severin *and* Sotomayor

Plowes, servant of South Sea Company, 186 n. 2

Poland, Carvajal refuses to consider alliance with, 133

Polish Succession, War of the, 96–7

Poor Jack, *see* Fish, trade in

Port, trade in, 17

Port Mahon: concessions demanded by Great Britain, 48; small ships from, and tobacco inspection, 98

Portobello, 50; annual fairs at, guaranteed, 73; annual Spanish fleets trading to, 65; bullion at, 86; South Sea Company factory at, 127, 203 n. 1

Porto Rico: British complaints of, 102; British ships restored by Governor of, 95; depredations at, 89, 92; focus for much Spanish colonial trade,

81
/3/
85
78